BEING WITH A/R/TOGRAPHY

James G. Henderson D67
1215 West 69th Street
Cleveland, OH 44102-2013

Being with A/r/tography

Edited by

Stephanie Springgay
Pennsylvania State University, USA

Rita L. Irwin
University of British Columbia, Canada

Carl Leggo
University of British Columbia, Canada

and

Peter Gouzouasis
University of British Columbia, Canada

SENSE PUBLISHERS
ROTTERDAM / TAIPEI

A C.I.P. record for this book is available from the Library of Congress.

ISBN 978-90-8790-262-9 (paperback)
ISBN 978-90-8790-263-6 (hardback)

Published by: Sense Publishers,
P.O. Box 21858, 3001 AW Rotterdam, The Netherlands
http://www.sensepublishers.com

Printed on acid-free paper

TABLE OF CONTENTS

PART III · ETHICS AND ACTIVISM

PART IV · FURTHER OPENINGS

IMAGES

RELATIONALITY IN WEB-BASED HYPERMEDIA
RESEARCH: A WORKING EXAMPLE IN TEACHER
EDUCATION

LEARNING TO LISTEN: TRACES OF LOSS, VULNERABILITY,
AND SUSCEPTIBILITY IN ART/TEACHING

THE RHIZOMATIC RELATIONS OF A/R/TOGRAPHY

AFTERWORD: CONTINUING CONVERSATIONS OUTSIDE THE CIRCLE

ACKNOWLEDGEMENTS

This book is indebted to our authors who have ruptured the stasis of research practices through artful living inquiry and the community of a/r/tographers who have inspired our journeys as artists, researchers, and teachers.

We would like to express our gratitude to the Social Sciences and Humanities Research Council of Canada for their support of our various a/r/tographical research projects and their commitment to research/creation.

We also extend our appreciation to Valerie Triggs and Natalie Jolly for their editorial assistance.

A/r/tographers call out to one another from many different locations in many different voices, all enthused with the possibilities of attending to other ways of creating, researching, and teaching in rhizomatic connections without end. We look forward to this community expanding in hopeful ways as more and more artists and researchers and teachers recognize themselves in the following poetic invitation by Carl Leggo, and in the many invitations offered in *Being with A/r/tography*:

A TANGLE OF LINES

we need a poetic line,

     not a prosaic line,

        a line that plays   with possibilities of
space,

  draws attention to itself,

            contravenes convention,

will not parade from left to right margins,

       back and forth,   as if there is
nowhere else

to explore,   knows instead lived experience

knows little of linearity

  knows the only linearity

    we know is the linearity

       of the sentence

which waddles across the page like lines of penguins, sentenced by the
sentence

to the lie

of linearity,

chimeric sense of order, born of rhetoric,

and so instead a/r/tographers weave their ways in tangled lines,

know wholeness

in holes and gaps, in fragments

that refract light with fractal abandon, and
savour

the possibilities of prepositions and conjunctions

LORRI NEILSEN

FOREWORD

We are the blood in all the languages that create us: sound, movement, word, image, colour, touch. Our season is short, but if we think for a moment that what we say and do goes unnoticed, we are mistaken. We are connected in infinite ways across time and space. When we hear of another roadside bomb on the other side of the planet, our tissues chill; another natural disaster, and we are alert to signs around us. Our capacity to imagine allows us to take pleasure in others' joy, to cringe at others' pain, to be present even when we are not. Our capacity to imagine gives shape and direction to how we, as a species, learn from one another and transform our experience. We are connected.

There is a net, it is said, over the palace of the Buddhist god Indra, and on each of the knots of the net is a jewel; each of the jewels reflects and extends the light in all the others. When we understand this resonance in terms of how we create, teach, and inquire alongside one another, we recognize the incalculable abundance of the one in the many and the many in the one and our collective capacity to effect change.

Basho says that change in the universe is the basis of art:

> Cherry blossoms whirl, leaves fall, and the wind flits them both along the ground. We cannot arrest with our eyes or our ears what lies in such things. Were we to gain mastery over them, we would find that the life of each thing would vanish without a trace. (cited in Hass, 1994, p.233)

We can extend Basho's thoughts to include research and teaching—the basis of each of these practices is change; to arrest these processes is to reject their *duende*, their spirit.

The insights gathered in this fine collection provide multi-faceted perspectives on the nature and aims of a/r/tography; as well, they open us to its profound possibilities for generating new connections and apprehending the depth, the shadows, and the responsibilities such new connections create. This is a fluid, generative, heuristic enterprise, this a/r/tography, in tune with truths that prevail, even as the contextual, political, and sociological dimensions of learning and inquiry realign them in new ways. And we know language always catches us—and itself—out; even the concept 'truth', waiting patiently with its bulging suitcases at the door, has learned to accept a place to rest for awhile, but to prepare for change.

About twenty years ago, after studying as an ethnographer and undertaking research in literacy—particularly in contexts where women worked and learned—I began to chafe at what research seemed to demand of me as an educator and artist. I was not alone in my unease: the language for the enterprise suggested a uniform and weapons would be necessary—capture, threat, validity, defence—although I was never certain who the enemy was except, perhaps, a quick-witted but hapless strategy, and contemptuous about ideas such as wisdom, generosity, silence, liminality, unknowing, love and faith (Neilsen, 2002). I was as certain then as I am now about the necessity of "a living inquiry....the work of the heart, the hands, our sensemaking body, our many-toned voices" (Neilsen, 1998, 207); a living inquiry welcomes movement and change, does not aim for mastery of cherry blossoms or ideas, is comfortable not only with the body resonant (Neilsen, 2004) but with the resonances, ruptures, emergences, and urgencies of bodies larger than our own: classrooms, societies, ecosystems. A living inquiry, the kind of research I am drawn to and began at that time to immerse myself in, was best undertaken outside the academy in community and personal settings where the false distinctions we create between the personal and the professional fall away: the academy of the kitchen table, as I referred to it then. It was, as well, the academies—or the bodies—of the boreal forest, the Atlantic coastline, urban street performance, a shelter, hospice centre, or skateboard park. All this inquiry asks is that we attend, that we listen (Neilsen, 2003), attune ourselves so that we may come to our senses (Neilsen, 1998).

The research many of us once apprenticed ourselves to has lost its authority, and for many reasons, not least of which is that we have lost faith—there's that word again—in the values it stood for, including the investment in epistemological hierarchies for understanding human behaviour and creativity. The impulses, insights, and corporeal understandings such as those revealed here in this collection make apparent instead what we have always known: that human inquiry is as complex, generative, curious, conflicted, nuanced, dark, particular, transitory, changeable, enduring, and hopeful as is a single human life—mine, yours, that of an Iranian child, an African grandmother, a Canadian adolescent. Human inquiry is what life is; it is that simple. The language we have learned so well to use for building frames and fences, theories and theologies, and—especially in education over the last sixty years—to create specious divisions and to play methodological games is a language we continue to question. We have so many languages available to us; a/r/tography's richness brings these to bear, and in doing so, deepens what it means to inquire. We know that to live with curiosity, compassion, integrity and mindfulness is to inquire; to know, as Heraclitus did, that we cannot step in the same river twice, is to inquire. To engage in a living inquiry is to learn to let go, to leave the spurious safety of Research—that crumbling roof over Education that often separated us from life and rarely protected us anyway—and to enter an open field, ears and wings bristling.

The world of inquiry in other disciplines is similarly restless: our conversations with colleagues across the spectrum of inquiry—art, aesthetics, philosophy, spirituality, ethics, poetics, among other threads—have created new and stimulating connections. Genres are regendering and this regeneration is giving us hope that the work we do might matter after all. After all—and for all, A/r/tography, as we see from the essays here, is invitational at its core.

And what again of those truths? As philosopher Emmanuel Levinas (cited in Hand, 1989) says, "the subject who speaks...is situated in relation to the Other.... By offering a word, the subject putting himself forward lays himself open and, in a sense, prays" (p.149). Simone Weil (2004) suggests that faith is a process of emptying out oneself, scouring out the self in order to be taken up, fully, giving oneself over to—in her case—her god. To open ourselves to work such as the inquiry we read here—work that by its nature is generous and generative and keeps the wilderness inside of us alive—will feed our faith in human possibility.

RITA L. IRWIN AND STEPHANIE SPRINGGAY

A/R/TOGRAPHY AS PRACTICE-BASED RESEARCH

Being With A/r/tography is a collection of essays that perform a/r/tographical research. Each author's explorations of a/r/tography embed the practice of living inquiry in and through the arts in diverse and divergent ways. The book is framed around three sections and concludes with a discussion chapter that continues to raise questions about the processes and challenges of doing a/r/tographical research. Each section opens with an essay by one of the editors and illuminates the complexities of a/r/tographical research. A/r/tography, we maintain, is concerned with self-study, being in community, relational and ethical inquiry, and as such the three sections are organized around these guiding principles. This, however, is not to suggest that each chapter is limited in its discussion of one single thematic understanding, but rather these sections are intended to allow for the imbrication of each into the other.

In this introductory chapter, we introduce the features of a/r/tography. We draw on scholarship from philosophy, phenomenology, educational action research, feminist theories, and contemporary art criticism to theorize the methodology of a/r/tography, with an attention to the *in-between* where meanings reside in the simultaneous use of language, images, materials, situations, space and time.

A/r/tography has grown out of a fluid and constantly evolving community, and the chapters in this collection are evidence of the various understandings and practices inherent in this methodology. The chapters are not meant to provide a linear nor rigid structure through which one could define a/r/tography. Rather, the chapters work in tension with each other, sometimes complementing and extending one another, while at other times becoming discordant. This tension, we argue, is important to the evolution of the methodology and to the substantive features of the inquiry itself. A/r/tographical research is not subject to standardized criteria, rather it remains dynamic, fluid, and in constant motion.

In what follows, we establish the theoretical features of doing a/r/tographical research and of becoming an a/r/tographer. The thematic sections further develop a/r/tographical concepts and provide examples of what it is like to be in the midst of a/r/tographical research.

We're waiting for the bus that travels South on Granville Street in Vancouver, British Columbia. For weeks we've been staring down the street from the bus stop at a storefront window that appears to function as a type of shelter for the public— sometimes seemingly random people stop and step inside only to emerge again and continue on their journey. It dawns on us one morning, when the coffee is extra the Canadian artist Germaine Koh at the Katriona Jeffries Gallery. *Shell* is one of Koh's recent explorations into the behaviours and situations that define and construct public and private space. Fashioned from aluminum, plexiglass and plywood, Koh has modified the glass-fronted private space of the gallery. An enclosure is built on the inside of the space, attached to the existing glass front of the gallery, but with a pane of glass removed in order to create free access to the structure from the street. In contrast to the gallery, the public has access to this space 24 hours a day. Resembling a bus shelter, and conjuring up metaphors of crustacean shells (Szewczyk, 2005), this in-between space is both and neither private or public. It exposes the vulnerability of private space, the fragility of safety, seclusion, and property (Koh, 2005). As Monica Szewczyk (2005) writes in the exhibition text, Koh's space accentuates both the contemplation of time, and the wasting or killing of time. Koh's architectural intervention is a transitory space, waiting to be filled and acted upon, inviting participation in the in-between. It is this openness, uncertainty, and exposure of meaning that situates this work and others like it as potential acts that allow us to inquire into and create new models for thinking and conducting research. Just as Koh's art presents a vulnerable space between private and public, how might we begin to think of research methodologies as relational situations that provoke meaning through contemplation, complication, and as alternative models of space and time?

A/r/tography is a research methodology that entangles and performs what Gilles Deleuze and Félix Guattari (1987) refer to as a rhizome. A rhizome is an assemblage that moves and flows in dynamic momentum. The rhizome operates by variation, perverse mutation, and flows of intensities that penetrate meaning, opening it to what Jacques Derrida (1978) calls the "as yet unnameable which begins to proclaim itself" (p.293). It is an interstitial space, open and vulnerable where meanings and understandings are interrogated and ruptured. Building on the concept of the rhizome, a/r/tography radically transforms the idea of theory as an abstract system distinct and separate from practice. In its place, theory is understood as a critical exchange that is reflective, responsive and relational, which is continuously in a state of reconstruction and becoming something else altogether. As such, theory *as* practice becomes an embodied, living space of inquiry (Meskimmon, 2003).

In turn, rhizomes activate the *in-between;* an invitation to explore the interstitial spaces of art making, researching, and teaching. According to Elizabeth Grosz (2001):

> The space of the in-between is the locus for social, cultural and natural transformations: it is not simply a convenient space for movements and realignments but in fact is the only place—the place around identities, between identities—where becoming, openness to futurity, outstrips the conservational impetus to retain cohesion and unity. (pp. 91-105)

Like Koh's *Shell*, the in-between disrupts dualisms (private and public or neither). Similarly, it is not merely a physical location or object but a *process*, a movement and displacement of meaning (Grosz, 2001). Contemporary art criticism argues that the relationship between artist and place is a complex discourse where place is re-imagined as "situation". Site moves from a fixed geographical category to a relational constitution of social, economic, cultural and political processes (Doherty, 2004; Kwon, 2002). Process becomes intertextually and multiply located in the context of discursive operations. It is a process of invention rather than interpretation, where concepts are marked by social engagements and encounters. Again we turn to Deleuze and Guattari (1994) and their arguments: "[c]oncepts are centres of vibrations, each in itself and every one in relation to all the others. This is why they all resonate rather than cohere or correspond with each other" (p.23). Meaning and understanding are no longer revealed or thought to emanate from a point of origin, rather they are *complicated* as relational, rhizomatic, and singular.[1]

A/r/tography as practice-based research is situated in the in-between, where theory-as-practice-as-process-as-complication intentionally unsettles perception and knowing through living inquiry. Our chapter will examine the constructs and conditions of a/r/tographical research: as practice-based research, as communities of practice, as relational aesthetics and through six renderings of engagement. The chapter further complicates the space of doing a/r/tographical research, unfolding a series of questions about the possibilities and challenges of practicing this form of qualitative research.

Practice-Based Theoretical Underpinnings

Our understandings of practice-based research are informed by feminist, post-structuralist, hermeneutic and other postmodern theories that understand the production of knowledge as difference thereby producing different ways of living in the world (St. Pierre, 2000). One way of understanding this is through theories of touch and intercorporeality (Springgay, 2003, 2004a, 2004b, 2005a, 2005b, 2006; Springgay & Freedman, 2007). Western thought has been primarily influenced by Cartesian rationalism which isolates the distinct and autonomous subject, whose "vision" of the world is separate and distanced from the object perceived. "I see" is commonly understood to mean "I know". Thus, distant, objective vision is a means by which to judge or examine phenomena. However, a phenomenological, feminist, and/or a/r/tographical approach to understanding through touch reconfigures the ways in which we perceive objects, providing access to depth and surface, inside and outside (Grosz, 1994; Merleau-Ponty, 1968). Touch expresses active involvement with the subject matter. Touch becomes a mode of knowing through proximity and relationality and poses different ways of making sense of the world, challenging the mechanisms of visual perception. Similarly, it draws attention to sensory experiences and knowledge that is interconnected with our bodies and with others.

In contrast to rationalist thought which imposes system and order, classifying and categorizing the world in dualistic terms (where individual consciousness is viewed as private, self-contained, and invisible), theories of touch propose that subjects are interconnected. According to Maurice Merleau-Ponty (1968), "to comprehend is to apprehend by coexistence" (p.188), and Jean Luc Nancy (2000) re-iterates this concept maintaining that meaning is constituted between beings. A/r/tography resides in this intercorporeal space, and attends to the forms and folds of living bodies. It is a thinking that reflects on inter-embodiment, on being(s)-in-relation, and communities of practice. Research becomes a process of exchange that is not separated from the body but emerges through an intertwining of mind and body, self and other, and through our interactions with the world.

What emerges from such considerations is an understanding of embodiment as "being in motion" (Ellsworth, 2005). Yet, this "being in motion" is not the act of a hand moving a paint brush, or a dancer's limbs being catapulted across the stage. Such understandings of the arts and embodiment are limiting and superficial, akin to Gardner's theories of multiple intelligences. While "movement" can be embodied, it isn't always. Likewise, a painter can sweep their arms across a canvas and it can be a disembodied action. Rather, embodiment is constituted through the self/body's movement, force, action, and transformation "in the making" (Ellsworth, 2005). Accordingly, Elizabeth Ellsworth (2005) contends: "embodiment puts us into a moving relation with forces, processes, and connections to other in ways that are unforeseen by consciousness and unconnected to identity" (p.121). This immediate, living, and unfolding body is enmeshed with an understanding of the cultural location and the specificity of the body.

> Embodiment is not about identity per se, a topic of earlier performative representations, but about subjectivity. As such, embodiment is not an immutable signifier of identity, but is a signifier of multiplicity existing within a complex web of cultural understandings and significations. (Garoian & Gaudelius, 2007, p.9)

Likewise, it is dangerous to suggest that the arts are more suited to embodied forms of learning and research. This continues to perpetuate a cognitive/bodied divide between the arts and other (the "serious" or "hard") disciplines. Rather, as Ellsworth (2005) argues, "some knowings cannot be conveyed through language" (p.156) and as such invite us to "acknowledge the existence of forms of knowing that escape the efforts of language to reference a 'consensual', 'literal', 'real' world" (p.156). This knowing, Ellsworth purports, moves us beyond "explanation" that can be commodified, captured, and in essence "taught", towards a way(s) of knowing that is rooted in embodiment as being in motion, relational, and singular. The arts, or a/r/tographical research, we argue, provide potential time-space intervals for the "coming of a knowing" (Ellsworth, 2005, p.158).

For instance, recent bodies of literature in the arts and education are exploring how practices inherent in the work of artists and educators are indeed forms of research. The intellectual, imaginative and insightful work created by artists and educators as practitioners is grounded in ongoing forms of recursive and reflexive inquiry engaged in theorizing for understanding. This perspective is in contrast to long standing traditions that have enveloped both the arts and education, where research is perceived as a means of gathering and interpreting data using traditions steeped in social science disciplines such as sociology, history and anthropology, or in natural science disciplines such as biology. Though these traditions and their research paradigms address questions of great interest to society, they have a particular orientation to knowledge that is quite different from inquiry steeped in the practices of many artists and educators. Whereas the disciplinary-based science traditions perceive research and theory as a means of explaining phenomena or revealing meaning, practitioner based research perceives research as a disposition for knowledge creation and understanding through acts of theorizing as complication. In the earlier instance, theory and research are used to find answers to questions. In practitioner-based research, theorizing through inquiry seeks understanding by way of an evolution of questions within the living inquiry processes of the practitioner. In other words, practitioners are interested in an ongoing quest for understanding, a questing if you will. This active stance to knowledge creation through questioning informs their practices, making their inquiries timely, emergent, generative and responsive to all those involved.

Many people see artists as practitioners (see Bird, 2000; Brown, 2000) and educators as practitioners (see Britzman, 2003). Graeme Sullivan (2005), an advocate of art practice as research, argues for practice-based research and states that theorizing for understanding through practice is "grounded in the praxis of human engagement and yield[s] outcomes that can be seen to be individually liberating and culturally enlightening" (p.74). He goes on to state: "If a measure of the utility of research is seen to be the capacity to create new knowledge that is individually and culturally transformative, then criteria need to move beyond probability and plausibility to *possibility*" (italics in original, p.72). These ideas resonate with the work of Terrance Carson and Dennis Sumara (1997) who talk about action research as a living practice. In educational circles, teacher research is a practitioner-based form of action research. Carson and Sumara talk about educators who, as action researchers, are deeply committed to meditative and contemplative practices: "lived experiences that permit an openness to the complexity of the relations among things and people" (p.xv). Although they suggest that a commitment to writing is required in living a life of awareness, they also acknowledge the potential of an artistic commitment to changing habits of expression. In this way, practices are not comfortable taken-for-granted ways of being but are rather the challenging practices of learning to perceive differently within our everyday practices. Carson and Sumara state: "As all artists know, the greatest challenge to producing works that interrupt normalized ways of perceiving and understanding is to learn to perceive freshly... Learning to perceive differently, then, requires that one engage in *practices* that, in some way, remove one from the comfortable habits of the familiar" (italics in original, p.xvii). When asked how one conducts a life committed to educational action research, they suggest:

> Who one *is* becomes completely caught up in what one knows and does. This effectively eliminates the tiresome *theory/practice* problem that continues to surface in discussions of educational action research, for it suggests that what is thought, what is represented, what is acted upon, are all intertwined aspects of lived experience and, as such, cannot be discussed or interpreted separately. (italics in original, p.xvii)

We would go a step further by saying that knowing (theoria), doing (praxis), and making (poesis) are three forms of thought important to a/r/tography (see Leggo,

2001; Sullivan, 2000). Relationships between and among these ways of understanding experience are integral to an intertextuality and intratextuality of ideas and form a foundation for a/r/tography (see Irwin, 2004). All three ways of understanding experience—theoria, praxis, and poesis—are folded together and form rhizomatic ways of experiencing the world. This is important as we come to appreciate how a/r/tography is conceived as research. Thus, "action research [and a/r/tography] practices are deeply hermeneutic and postmodern practices, for not only do they acknowledge the importance of self and collective interpretation, but they deeply understand that these interpretations are always in a state of becoming and can never be fixed into predetermined and static categories" (Carson & Sumara, 1997, p.xviii). Whereas many forms of research are concerned with reporting knowledge that already exists or finding knowledge that needs to be uncovered, action research and a/r/tography are concerned with *creating the circumstances* to produce knowledge and understanding through inquiry laden processes (see Irwin et. al, 2006).

Communities of Practice

Practitioner-based research is necessarily about self but it is also about communities of practice. Individuals committed to inquiry are situated in communities of practice. Deborah Britzman (2003) suggests that for teachers: "To theorize about one's experience means to engage one's reflective capacities in order to be an author of that experience...The sources of theory, then, are in practice; in the lived lives of teachers, in the values, beliefs, and deep conviction enacted in practice, in the social context that encloses such practice, and in the social relationships that enliven the teaching and learning encounter" (pp.64-65). Through a dialogical perspective teachers are able to engage in independent and socially transformative activities by theorizing practice.

Relations between and among teachers, students and society are important to this dialogical perspective. Yet, this is also true for artists, audiences, and institutions. Relations in artistic communities of practice are equally important. Artists do not create in a void. Their work is necessarily related to the work of others, and their theorizing happens within communities of affiliation. Whether as an artist, educator or researcher, a/r/tographers acknowledge the work of others in the documentation of their own work. For many this would mean attending exhibitions or performances or reading about artists and sharing this knowledge in one's a/r/tographic work. It would also mean reading about research in education and sharing the work of educational researchers. Citational practices are important for a community of practice-based researchers wanting to understand a body of literature and work in their fields while positioning their own work within those and potentially other fields. Furthermore, as a/r/tographers work with others, the potential exists for many individuals and groups to become a/r/tographers in a way that is appropriate for them. Thus, primary teachers can be a/r/tographers working with young children who may engage in age appropriate forms of a/r/tographic practice. Alternatively, community-based artists could be a/r/tographers working with community members who in turn become a/r/tographers as they rethink taken-for-granted ways of being in their communities. In essence, it is the intertextual situations that provoke a/r/tographical research, not necessarily academic intentions.

A/r/tography is steeped in the practices of artist-educators committed to ongoing living inquiry and it is this inquiry that draws forth the identity of a researcher. Artist/researcher/teacher identities contiguously exist in relationship to one another (see Springgay, Irwin, & Wilson Kind, 2005). In communities of a/r/tographers, it may be that separate communities of artists, educators, and researchers exist, yet it is more likely that hybrid communities of artists, educators, and researchers locate themselves in the space of the in-between to create self-sustaining interrelating identities that inform, enhance, evoke and/or provoke one another. It is here that a definition of artist and educator should be considered.

A/r/tography as living inquiry necessarily opens the way to describing and interpreting the complexity of experience among researchers, artists and educators, as well as the lives of the individuals within the communities they interact with. As a result, it also opens the topics, contexts and conditions of inquiry. Although a/r/tography privileges the identities of artist, researcher and teacher within its name, one needs to be thoughtful about how these identities might be conceptualized. For instance, educator may be a more inclusive title for the identity of the individual we are imagining. Many artists and educators have questioned the boundaries placed upon their identities and as such have interrupted the hegemony of schooling as a primary location for education (see Barone, 2001) as well as the hegemony of art world establishments as primary gatekeepers to art and art institutions. With this said, it is important to point out that education in the context of a/r/tography is broadly conceived to mean any contexts concerned with learning, understanding and interpretation. Therefore, educators who consider themselves a/r/tographers are those individuals who are committed to acts of learning, teaching, understanding and interpreting within communities of learners. Similarly, within a/r/tography, art is broadly conceived to mean sensory-oriented products understood, interpreted or questioned through ongoing engagements and encounters with the world. Artists are therefore committed to acts of creation, transformation, and resistance. Artists engaged in a/r/tography need not be earning a living through their art, but they need to be committed to artistic engagement through ongoing living inquiry. Educators engaged in a/r/tography need not be K-12 educators, nor educators within higher education, but they need to be committed to educational engagement that is rooted in learning and learning communities through ongoing living inquiry. In this way, both artists and educators can be found in many contexts employing a range of ideas and materials. Perhaps more importantly, the relationship between artists and educators becomes somewhat blurred using our definitions. Both artists and educators are concerned with learning, change, understanding, and interpretation. It is in this complex space of the in-between that the disposition of inquiry brings us to a researcher identity through an implicit and explicit commitment to ongoing living inquiry across the domains of art and education. Earlier, we stated that action research is concerned with creating the circumstances to produce and complicate knowledge and understanding through inquiry-laden processes. In effect, a/r/tographers are concerned with creating the circumstances that produce knowledge and understanding through *artistic and educational* inquiry-laden processes.

The Relational In-Between of Space and Time

A/r/tography is a process of unfolding art and text together (art in this sense could mean poetry, music or other forms of artistic inquiry). As a research methodology that intentionally unsettles perception and complicates understandings, how we come to know and live within space and time is subsequently altered. Since the 1960s, visual artists have engaged in what has commonly come to be understood as site-specific work. Miwon Kwon (2002) identifies various permutations of this form including site-determined, site-oriented, site-referenced, site-responsive, and site-related. All of these various terms are concerned with the relationship between the art work and its site; how the production, presentation, and reception of the work incorporated the physical conditions of a particular location (Kwon, 2002). However, as Kwon argues, the term "site" itself needs to be re-defined not through physical or local terms, but as a complex figure in the unstable relationship between location and identity. In other words, "sites" are not geographically bound, but informed by context, where "context [is] an impetus, hindrance, inspiration and research subject for the process of making art" (Doherty, 2004, p.8). Site is not a fixed category but constituted through social, economic, cultural and political processes, which Nicholas Bourriaud (2004, 2001, 2002) calls *relational aesthetics*. Like Kwon, Bourriaud contends that in "site-specific" art or "situations" (see Doherty, 2004) both process and outcome is marked by social engagements. These encounters break down the conventional relationships between artist, art work, and audience. The artists and art works that are the subjects of Kwon and Bourriaud's investigations create art as a socially useful activity: "The forms that [the artist] presents to the public [does] not constitute an artwork until they are actually used and occupied by people" (Bourriaud, 2004, p.46). In this instance the audience moves from beholder of art (interpretation) to interlocutor (analyser). In many instances audiences are actually called to a specific time and place where they become active participants in the art work and, thus argues Bourriaud (2004), alternative modes of sociality are created. *Shell* exemplifies this slippage between time and space, a condition of relational aesthetics. Meaning making within relational aesthetics is embodied in the intercorporeal negotiations between things.

Another theoretical way of understanding relationality of space and time is through complexity theory. According to Sumara and Carson (1997), complexity theory "suggests that the world is organized and patterned in ways that can be mathematically modelled but not in a predictive, linear, or deterministic manner" (p.xviii). Understandings emerge "from the associative relations among complex interactions" (p.xix). Therefore how we make meaning of images and texts is contingent upon the relations between artist (or in this case let us say a/r/tographer), art work, text, and audience and social, cultural, economic, and political contexts, and the ways these relations are altered by what Derrida (1978) calls the "as yet unnameable which begins to proclaim itself" (p.293)—that which is not readily apparent. Thus, relationality is more than just the contexts that are brought to bear on particular "sites" but the potentialities and the "other thans" (Springgay, 2004) that continuously evolve and provoke meaning. Merleau-Ponty (1968) writes of this intertwining between self and other, inside and outside, as a way of becoming folded together in a porous encounter that leads to openings between subjects. Each subject is created through encounters *with* others and it is this *with* that creates the contiguity and distinctiveness of aesthetic forms (see Nancy, 2000).

In western cultures, time is typically perceived as uniformly flowing without regard for individuals, events or contexts. Space is typically perceived as a container or even a vast emptiness (outer space). Yet artists, poets, performance artists, novelists and musicians perceive time and space differently. They often speak of time as pausing, enduring, changing, interrupting, and pacing, and speak of space as openness, fragmented, endless, confined and connected. Artists see time and space as conditions for living; conditions for engaging with the world through inquiry. After all, how we perceive time and space in the world affects how we engage with the world.

Educators also see time and space in particular ways. Complexity theories of learning (Davis, Sumara, & Luce-Kappler, 2000) describe learning as participatory and evolutionary. Learning therefore is never predictable and is understood to be a participation in the world, a kind of co-evolution of those learning together. Thus, learners would be interested in keeping pace with their changing yet evolving circumstances. One might call this relational learning in that contiguous entities such as mind/body, theory/practice, or artist/researcher/teacher are not separate or dichotomous but are "enfolded in and unfold[ed] from one another" (p.73) as learning becomes more sophisticated, flexible, and creative within acts of relationality. The notion of a fold (see Springgay, 2003; 2004) is important to a/r/tography as it suggests an infinite number of undulating entities unable to be separated into parts: in fact, through un/folding more folding may result. Understanding a/r/tography as un/folding the phenomena and/or identities being studied "can be simultaneously seen as a whole, a part of a whole, or as a complex compilation of smaller wholes" (Davis, Sumara, & Luce-Kappler, 2000, p.73). Therefore learning becomes concerned with critical concepts rather than isolated facts, and the interconnections between concepts—learning as rhizomatic.

Conceptual Practices: Renderings

The research conditions of a/r/tography reside in several notions of relationality: relational inquiry, relational aesthetics, and relational learning. Mieke Bal (2002) and Irit Rogoff (2001) have informed our work through their discussions of interdisciplinarity. Rogoff suggests that an emphasis upon process rather than method allows an active space for participation that lies between existing disciplines and their methodologies while resisting the formation of new methodological criteria. It is this process space that alludes to the conditions for research. Furthermore, we look to Bal for an understanding of how to engage with these relational aspects. She suggests that interdisciplinarity "must seek its heuristic and methodological basis in *concepts* rather than *methods*" (italics in original, 2002, p.5).

We interpret concepts to be flexible, intersubjective locations through which close analysis renders new understandings and meanings. These concepts or renderings, as we prefer to call them, guide our active participation in making meaning through artful, educational and creative inquiry. Renderings offer possibilities for engagement and do not exist alone but in relation to one another. Though it is tempting to suggest these renderings are criteria for a/r/tography, they are better perceived as rendered possibilities.

Renderings are embedded in the processes of artful inquiry (in any art form such as music, dance, drama, poetry and visual arts) and writing. To be engaged in a/r/tography means to inquire in the world through both processes, noting they are not separate or illustrative processes but interconnected processes. Relational inquiring through relational aesthetics and relational learning is constitutive rather than descriptive and may represent the work of a single a/r/tographer, a community of a/r/tographers and/or an audience member's process of meaning making. Each individual and group informs and shapes the living inquiry. Therefore, renderings are concepts that help a/r/tographers portray the conditions of their work for others. Elsewhere, we have interpreted each rendering in great detail (Springgay, Irwin, & Wilson Kind, 2005). For the purpose of this chapter, we would like to briefly describe each of the six renderings: contiguity, living inquiry, metaphor/metonymy, openings, reverberations, and excess.

Contiguity

Contiguity is a rendering that helps us understand those ideas within a/r/tography that lie adjacent to one another, touch one another, or exist in the presence of one another. This happens in several ways. First of all, contiguity is found with the artist, researcher and teacher identities existing simultaneously and alongside one another. The forward slash or fold portrays this act of contiguity. Secondly, contiguity is found in the relationship between art and graphy, that is, between the artform and writing with, in or about the phenomenon. And thirdly, contiguity is found in the act of double imaging between art as an activity or product and a/r/t as a symbolic representation of the three constituent identities. To live the life of an a/r/tographer is to live a contiguous life sensitive to each of these relationships and particularly to the spaces in-between. Being attentive to the in-between spaces opens opportunities for dynamic living inquiry. A/r/tographers may visualize these in-between spaces as parts of an endless fold, or folds within folds, or as concepts linked together. A/r/tographers may or may not choose to include text as part of their artforms but they will always include textual materials and writing in their ongoing inquiry processes (Richardson, 1994). This includes citing and engaging with the work of other artists, researchers and educators as a/r/tographers pursue their inquiries. These acts of contiguity ensure relational inquiry and learning amidst an attention toward relational aesthetics.

Living Inquiry

Living inquiry, another rendering, refers to the ongoing living practices of being an artist, researcher and educator. Elsewhere we have defined living inquiry as "an embodied encounter constituted through visual and textual understandings and experiences rather than mere visual and textual representations" (Springgay, Irwin, & Wilson Kind, 2005). Though this definition privileges the visual, any sensory form can be applied. Living inquiry is a life commitment to the arts and education through acts of inquiry. These acts are theoretical, practical and artful ways of creating meaning through recursive, reflective, responsive yet resistant forms of engagement. A/r/tography is a methodology of embodiment, of continuous engagement with the world: one that interrogates yet celebrates meaning. A/r/tography is a living practice, a life creating experience examining our personal, political and/or professional lives. It uses a fluid orientation within the contiguous relationships described earlier. Its rigour comes from its continuous reflective and reflexive stance to engagement, analysis and learning. This can include any qualitative form of data collection such as interviews, journal writing, field diaries, artifact collections, and photo documentation, yet it can also include any form of artistic inquiry such as painting, composing music, and writing poetry, and educational inquiry such as student journal writing, teacher diaries, narratives, and parent surveys. The reflexive and reflective stance to analysis will be ongoing and may include aspects from traditional ethnographic forms of inquiry such as constantly comparing themes that emerge from the data. What is important is the attention given to ongoing inquiry through an evolution of research questions and understandings. It is here that the difference between thesis and exegesis is important. Most research is designed to answer, address or create a proposition that is advanced through an argument. This is called a thesis. In a/r/tography and other arts-based or arts informed types of research, an exegesis is more suitable. An exegesis is a critical explanation of the meaning within a work. In the arts, an exegesis is often extended to include any documentation that contextualizes the work (see Sullivan, 2005) and helps to critique or give direction to theoretical ideas. Some theorists suggest that this documentation should not be considered research but rather the method by which ideas are conceived (see de Freitas, 2002). We prefer to see the process of living inquiry, as well as the understanding created through the inquiry, as comprising the full research enterprise. An exegesis provides opportunities to do just that.

From time to time, a/r/tographers may choose to share their inquiries with others and it is here that products are refined and shared. These living inquiry moments are not end results, but rather understandings of experiences along the way. Thus, a/r/tography needs to be pursued continuously over time while searching for ways to disseminate aspects of the work at particular moments in time. Artists may wish to display or perform their artistic works in particular venues while educators may wish to share their scholarly engagements in other venues. Though these endeavours are not separate, there are times when particular aspects may be highlighted for unique audiences.

Metaphor and Metonymy
A/r/tographers will naturally use the third rendering: metaphor and metonymy. Through metaphors and metonyms, we make sense of the world and we make relationships accessible to our senses (see Richardson, 2002). Both tropes open possibilities for meaning making: metaphor through its substitution of signifiers and metonym through its displacement of subject/object relations (see Aoki, Low & Palulis, 2001). Metaphors and metonyms exist as intertwined relationships in which meaning un/creates itself. There is at once a loss of meaning, a realization of meaning, or neither. Just as there is contiguous movement between other concepts, so too is there between metaphor and metonymy. This movement reverberates in and through each rendering as struggles in understanding emerge and shifts in awareness take place. It is in these struggles that openings are created.

Openings
One purpose of a/r/tography is to open up conversations and relationships instead of informing others about what has been learned. Another purpose of a/r/tography is to open up possibilities for a/r/tographers as they give their attention to what is seen and known and what is not seen and not known. Openings are not necessarily passive holes through which one can see easily. Openings are often like cuts, tears, ruptures or cracks that resist predictability, comfort and safety. It is here that knowledge is often created as contradictions and resistances are faced, even interfaced with other knowledge. Meanings are negotiated by, with, and among a/r/tographers as well as with their audiences. It is in these conversations that multiple exchanges co-exist and reverberate together.

Reverberations
Reverberation refers to a dynamic movement, dramatic or subtle, that forces a/r/tographers to shift their understandings of phenomena. Reverberations often take us deeper into meanings or they shift us toward a slippage of meaning. Pollock (1998) talks about nervous performative writing in a similar fashion, suggesting it "anxiously crosses various stories, theories, texts, intertexts, and spheres of practice, unable to settle into a clear, linear course, neither willing nor able to stop moving, restless, transient and transitive" (pp.99-91).

Excess
Research then becomes an evocation, a provocation, calling us to transformation. This transformation often happens with some attention to the final rendering of excess (see Bataille, 1985). Excess is that which is created when control and regulation disappear and we grapple with what lies outside the acceptable. Excess may deal with the monstrous, the wasteful, the leftover, and the unseen, as well as the magnificent and the sublime. It is also the "as yet unnameable" the "other than"—those aspects of our lives and experiences that are potentials and filled with possibility. Excess opens up opportunities for complexifying the simple and simplifying the complex by questioning how things come into being and the nature of their being.

Renderings, as the conceptual practices of a/r/tography, move into the boundaries between theory, practice and creative activity and allow each to impact one another. A rigorous attending to the renderings will result in deep interactions within the relational conditions of relational inquiry, relational aesthetics and relational learning. An assessment of any a/r/tographic work will depend upon its compelling ability to provide access to, and new insights about, a particular phenomenon.

Practicing A/r/tography: Contributions and Challenges

If encounters like the work of *Shell* embody an a/r/tographical position, how does one engage in a/r/tographical educational research? Without appearing pedantic in responding to this question, we firmly believe that a/r/tographical work entails living and inquiring in the in-between, of constantly questing, and complicating that which has yet to be named. The chapters included in this edited collection were selected because they embody the features of a/r/tography and are located in living inquiry. Moreover, the chapters themselves, or the spaces they investigate, intertwine various traditional and non-traditional art forms. As opposed to creating a book with an equal representation from poetry, visual art, narrative, music, drama, etc., we extend the interdisciplinarity of the arts through an understanding of intermedia (see Barbour, 2007). Intermedia, in this respect, moves away from labelling something as "visual art", "drama", or even "mixed media" towards an in-between where multiple art forms, aesthetic knowings, and technologies blur together to create something else altogether. Intermedia thus enables us to engage with theory as practice and with concepts that perform outside of disciplinary boundaries.

The transformative power of theory as practice changes our understandings of research methodologies beyond the bounds of specificity and objectivity towards an articulation of research as intercorporeality, relationality, and process. Residing in the in-between, a/r/tographers dwell in the space and time of contemplation insisting on the openness of everyday phenomena. Like *Shell*, a/r/tography is an interstitial process, where encounters between subjects, thoughts, and actions propose new assemblages and situations. Furthermore, a/r/tographical research calls for an inter-relation between texts, not a description of texts. Thus, for example, the construction of a/r/tographical research goes beyond the insertion of images into a research paper or dissertation, or transcribing one's "data" into a musical score. A/r/tography is a way of living, inquiring, and being that is relational.

This last point, however, enters us into other struggles, namely that of assessment and impact. How do we evaluate and judge an a/r/tographical work? How do we measure its impact? The concluding chapter is presented as a discussion that entertains and takes up these challenging and complex spaces. The chapter does not offer definitive answers, but rather provokes and proposes alternative possibilities and new questions to consider.

In closing this chapter, we tender our own thoughts on assessment and impact by turning once again to the work of Jean Luc Nancy (2000). In his essay *Human*

Excess, Nancy contends that the engagement with measurement is a matter of bringing a certain responsibility to light. Rather than an understanding of excess as a numerical equivalent (10, 400 or 2 million), we need to think of excess as elements of discourse in its totality. Measurement is not a degree of magnitude, but rather magnitude itself is the infinite totality of Being—the measurement of no other. Excess becomes an unheard of measure. In other words, measurement is not qualifying something against something else—the setting of criteria or an established norm. Rather, the conditions for measurement are contingent upon and exist within the structure itself—an absolute measure.

In this sense, an a/r/tographical act is its own possible measure. A/r/tographical research in every respect generates itself from within—the processes, the modes of inquiry, the methods by which one conducts research, the analysis, and even the assessment—is created in the act of being in the midst of a/r/tography. In other words, assessment and impact can't be something that exist outside of, or prior to, the a/r/tographical research that it is then measured against. Rather, how the research is assessed (both in terms of validity and impact) is generated during the a/r/tographical process and could be quite different for each a/r/tographical endeavour. Instead of thinking of our actions, encounters, and thoughts—our living inquiry—as substance that can be arranged in discrete moments, counted, and subjected to normative evaluations, we need to understand living inquiry as responsibility.

However, "to be responsible is not, primarily, being indebted to or accountable before some normative authority. It is to be engaged by its Being to the very end of this Being, in such a way that this engagement or *conatus* is the very essence of Being" (Nancy, 2000, p.183). We are not responsible *for* our own actions or the actions of others (a passive approach that separates and distances), but our very Being, our subjectivities, identities, and ways of living in the world are gestures and situations that struggle with, contest, challenge, provoke, and embody an ethics of understanding and a responsibility. Responsibility itself resides in the in-between. Stepping outside the glass-front of the gallery—our personal shell—turning a corner onto the city street, we may be hailed by other situations; unexpected gestures and invitations to all responsible persons.

NOTES

[1] Singularity in this usage is derived from Jean Luc Nancy's (2000) theories of "being-singular-plural". For Nancy (2000), to be a body is to be "with" other bodies, to touch, to encounter, and to be exposed. In other words, each individual body is brought into being through encounters with other bodies. It is the relationality between bodies that creates a particular understanding of shared existence. Relationality depends on singularity. A singular body, argues Nancy (2000), "is not individuality; it is, each time, the punctuality of a 'with' that establishes a certain origin of meaning and connects it to an infinity of other possible origins" (p.85). Peter Hallward (2001) substantiates this with: "The singular proceeds internally and is constituted in its own creation. The singular, in each case, is constituent of itself, expressive of itself, immediate to itself" (p.3). Criteria are not external but are determined through its actions. Nikki Sullivan (2003) provides us with a further explanation: "Each 'one' is singular (which isn't the same as saying each 'one' is individual) while

simultaneously being in-relation" (p.55). Singularity, as a theoretical construct, demands that self and other no longer hold opposing positions. Bodies/selves cannot exist without other bodies/selves, nor are the two reducible to one another.

PART I

SELF-STUDY AND AUTOBIOGRAPHY

CARL LEGGO

AUTOBIOGRAPHY: RESEARCHING OUR LIVES AND LIVING OUR RESEARCH

Why Do We Tell Stories?

I regularly attend to the stories of Angelina Jolie, Brad Pitt, Britney Spears, Mel Gibson, Jennifer Aniston, and George Clooney. I watch *Entertainment Tonight* and *Access Hollywood* and *Biography*; I read *People* and *Us* and the *National Enquirer*; I attend to the stories of hockey players and rock stars and Hollywood actors. In all this attending to stories—the narratives of success, scandal, grief, joy, loss, rehabilitation, foolishness, hope, and sorrow—lived by celebrities, even aspiring celebrities, around the earth, I need to ask myself frequently why I pay such eager, almost addicted, attention. And just as significantly, why do I tell my own stories in poetry and fiction and autobiography? I currently live in Steveston, a corner of suburban Richmond, British Columbia, held close in the arms of the Fraser River, huddled on the rim of the Pacific Ocean, faraway from Newfoundland on the North Atlantic coast of Canada, the place where I grew up. On this late autumn Saturday morning, I just ran along the dike, smiled at neighbours I will never know, marvelled at the stillness of a heron, discussed with my wife Lana my concerns about the conservative Christian perspective on same sex marriage, noted the new housing developments, including the one where Lana and I recently bought our first home, wondered about the seeming promise of rain, choked back a few tears with the burnt orange maple tree like a burst of blood.

This paper on autobiography begins with recollection, rumination, confession, and question. I am writing myself with the abiding hope that you will linger with my words. But for all my blathering on in a market where there are endless stories vying for attention, I need to continue to ask: Why is it important that I write and tell my stories as a poet, teacher, teacher educator, and social science researcher? Why is it important that others read and hear my stories? Why is it important that others write and tell their stories? Why is it important that I read and hear the stories of others?

As a teacher I am committed to supporting others so they can develop as writers, in both their desire for writing as well as their confidence in writing. I invite my students to write creatively, interrogatively, and expressively. I encourage them to take risks, to experiment with diverse discourses, to challenge conventions, and to seek truth. Ideally, in my writing and narrative inquiry classes, I want to nurture a vibrant community where our differences of opinions, beliefs, experiences, and personalities can be celebrated. We write and share our writing with one another. We tell stories of our lives, and we reveal ourselves in intimate ways, and we grow more confident in our conviction about the power of words for

S. Springgay et al. (eds.), Being with A/r/tography, 3–23.

writing our lived stories, and transforming our living stories, and creating possibilities for more life-enhancing stories.

When I was interviewed in March 1990 for a position in the Department of Language Education (now the Department of Language and Literacy Education) at the University of British Columbia, I explained that I was a poet, educator, and scholar with a keen interest in promoting poetry and creative writing, and especially ways to support educational research, theory, and practice by attending to issues of poetic discourse and poetic knowing. In my teaching, researching, and writing, I have continued to promote the significant value of attending to language from creative perspectives. I am committed to exploring the lively intersections between critical discourse and creative discourse. Too often in the academy, the creative arts are separated from the social science disciplines. My goal is to open up spaces for the creative arts to inform education research. For a long time I have known myself as a poet-educator-scholar. So, I have found in a/r/tography a research methodology that honours and supports my long commitment to autobiographical writing. As Rita L. Irwin and Stephanie Springgay explain in their introductory essay, *A/r/tography as Practice-based Research*, "a/r/tography radically transforms the idea of theory as an abstract system distinct and separate from practice. In its place, theory is understood as a critical exchange that is reflective, responsive and relational, which is continuously in a state of reconstruction and becoming something else altogether" (p.xiv).

Autobiography and the Intersection of the Personal and Public

Teaching is my life. No other vocation has come even close to compelling the kind of commitment of heart, imagination, passion, and energy that I have devoted to teaching, first in schools for nine years, and then in university classrooms for the past seventeen years. My research is devoted to understanding the processes of teaching, language and literacy education, curricular reform, and teacher education. Much of my research is focused on autobiographical writing in which I seek to know the experiences of being a teacher. In addition to writing autobiographically, I invite other educators to write their stories, too, and I seek to guide and support them in using the resources and strategies of autobiographical research for examining their practices and experiences. Because so much of my teaching, writing, and researching emerge from the intersections of the personal and the public, I contend that autobiographical writing is always both personal and public, and that we need to write autobiographically in order to connect with others.

Robert V. Bullough, Jr. and Stefinee Pinnegar (2001) note that "self-study points to a simple truth, that to study a practice is simultaneously to study self: a study of self-in-relation to other" (p.14). I readily agree with this perspective and emphasize that there can be no understanding of the self-in-relation without attending to the study of the self. They go together. But for all the support that Bullough and Pinnegar provide for this view, they still seem to hedge on acknowledging the integral role of the personal. They clearly intend to draw a sharp distinction between the value of autobiographical writing for personal development and for professional development, especially regarding what stories

4

deserve to be published. But in their essay, there is an intriguing deconstructive turn where they contend that "there is value in autobiography to the writer; autobiography is a means for *personal* development" (p.17); then, they note that "those engaged in self-study recognize this value", and, by way of support for this perspective, they cite two leading scholars in self-study research, Ardra Cole and Gary Knowles, who actually write: "'We engage in self-study work because we believe in its inherent value as a form of *professional* development'" (p.17, italics added). So, while Bullough and Pinnegar claim to draw a distinction between personal development and professional development in order to make the claim that publishable autobiographical writing needs to inform more than personal development, in fact, by using the quotation from Cole and Knowles, Bullough and Pinnegar actually conflate the distinction in their essay. And I think that this distinction needs conflating. There is no need to separate the personal from the professional any more than we can separate the dancer from the dance. The personal and the professional always work together, in tandem, in union, in the way of complementary angles. Only together do the two complementary angles compose the right angle. I agree with Bullough and Pinnegar's conviction that "the autobiographical self-study researcher has an ineluctable obligation to seek to improve the learning situation not only for the self but for the other" (p.17). All my autobiographical research is devoted to my own professional development and the professional development of other educators. But for me to grow professionally, I also need to grow personally. Autobiographical writing is both transcendent and immanent, both inside and outside, both internal and external, both personal and public.

Writing about personal experiences is not only egoism, solipsism, unseemly confession, boring prattling, and salacious revelation. We need to write personally because we live personally, and our personal living is always braided with our other ways of living—professional, academic, administrative, artistic, social, and political. Therefore, in the creative practice of a/r/tography which acknowledges and researches the rhizomatic connections and interstitial spaces and contiguous relationships that shape and compose our ongoing living inquiry, I next present a few autobiographical poems and ruminations that I hope will evoke and provoke a lively conversation about themes of autobiographical research including: memory and agency; performance and voice; revelation and representation; identity and subjectivity; fragments and possibilities.

Memory and Agency

CHERRY

I'm sitting in the lounge of the Regal Oriental Hotel

with a view of Hong Kong like a fireplace full of embers

after flying all day across the international date line

(left Vancouver yesterday to arrive today, lost a day

somewhere over the Pacific, and like most losses, will

5

likely forget to look for it on the way back) and Cherry

begins to sing, and you asked me how often I have fallen

in love, and I said, Once, I am always falling, and I didn't

want to sound facetious, flippant, frivolous, flatulent,

flirtatious (f-words everywhere, the poet's curse pokes

me like a hoe), since all I really wanted was to explain

how falling in love is like breathing, knowing lightly I am

alive, and Cherry says, What would you like me to play?

and I think, Cherry, play me, but of course I don't say that,

since I don't want to sound like a lecherous buffoon

or a lascivious bassoon with a base note like a drunk crazed

barroom bore with no more sense than a lottery machine

where the cherries never line up, and I recall the cherry on top

of the sundae I ate in Disneyland in July, sitting on Main Street,

bought with Tigger dollars in the Gibson Girl Ice Cream Parlor,

waiting for a parade while the cherry sank through cream

and ice cream and I didn't have the heart to eat the cherry

like a dollop of congealed blood and hope, the stem still intact,

and Twin Peaks Sherilyn Fenn's Audrey Horne once tied

a cherry stem in a reef knot with her tongue and teeth, and

that's how Cherry makes me feel, and I say in my best Bogart

impersonation, Play *Yesterday*, and Cherry's songbook is thicker

than *Gray's Anatomy* like all the songs in the world have been

gathered in one place, and I know all of them or none of them,

and Cherry sings, and I drink a glass of red wine, and Cherry's hair

is no longer Filipino black, but auburn, like hers, now faraway,

and I probably first fell in love with her hair, the way it flowed

like a river in autumn, full of fallen leaves, a red brick road

to another world, red ribbons tied in the air to show me the way

back, but when I turn, heart like a butane flame in a block of ice,

I can't see her, but know she is there, no erasure, only écriture, scratches in a palimpsest that holds close all origins and traces

without end, sure only our story possesses me still since Cherry

in the lounge of the Regal Oriental Hotel in Kowloon City reminds

me of her, as if everything I write now propels me forward to a place

I left long ago, never left, can't return, can't remember, won't forget

Much of my autobiographical writing is about remembering the past. I have published many poems and stories about the past. At fifty-three years of age, I feel that I have a lot of past to remember. Like Patrick Lane (2004), "I am crowded by stories too many to put down" (p.60). I do not recount the past simply for the sake of recounting the past. As Lane writes, "without the past I can't learn to live in the unfolding present" (p.117). When I recount a story, I seek to hold it in the present in order to understand how better to live now and tomorrow. Jill Ker Conway (1998) asks the pertinent question, "what exactly is the process of questioning the past?" (p.177). She recommends that "cultivation of that voice—the power of speaking for oneself—is a prerequisite for maturity, because until we've found our own voices we can't settle down to ask ourselves and others probing questions about life in the present" (p.180). And this is my biggest challenge in writing autobiographically. In a writing class many years ago, Rudy Wiebe, one of Canada's finest writers, commented that I wrote fiction as if I was aware of an audience looking over my shoulder, an audience that I assumed was conservative and censorious. I still remember that comment, and I don't think I have escaped the sense that my writing must always be censored or it will offend somebody. I am always concerned about offending others. I grew up at a time and in schools and family and community contexts where I frequently heard advice about not spreading gossip or intimate tales or criticism. I still do not like to be critical. But I also know that I need to be critical in order to make sense of the past. Robert Fulford (1999) understands that "by imitating our own life experience, narrative gives us a way to absorb past events on an emotional as well as an intellectual level" (p.38). This is what I seek to do, to imitate experience in narratives, so I can make sense of them. Like Helen M. Buss (2005), I am seeking in my autobiographical writing "a greater conscious agency in the lived life" (p.19).

Therefore, in my writing I am not trying to record the historical accuracy of events and experiences and emotions (as if any such historical accuracy is really possible). I am instead trying to hold the past in a certain light in order to interpret it. I am not hoping to exhaust the meaningfulness of the past, to claim a clear understanding, to consume the past and spit out a kernel. Instead I am seeking to know enough of the past to get on with living now. But in order to address the past, I need to write in my own voices, to try on voices, to write stories that might offend some people some of the time. I will not set out to be offensive, but I will almost certainly sometimes be offensive. And in the process of remembering, and writing, and saying what compels the saying, I will also learn to forget the past, to let the past go. And this is ultimately a pedagogical engagement—leaning on the past in order to leave the past.

CARL LEGGO

IF I BUMP INTO YOU IN WAL-MART
when the longing is a long error,
how can one still long for so long?

If I bump into you in Wal-Mart,
I will say, Hi, how are you?
I guess. What else could I say?

Should I rehearse as I would rehearse
for any urgent contingency?
In case of fire, pull alarm.
    For an emergency, call 911.
        In the event of an earthquake,
            stand in a door jamb.
                If a drowning person panics
                    and clings to you, kick him
                        in the groin.

Or perhaps I will run away (you know I can),
just turn and run as fast as my middle-aged
Ben Johnson legs will propel me, faster
than a horse or a train or a speeding bullet.

Or perhaps I will be fixed like a mosquito mired
in mucilage, Maxwell Smart stuck in instant cement
(with no shoe phone for help), a guppy in Epson salts,
transfixed like a zombie in *Night of the Living Dead*.

Or perhaps I will be somebody else, and contort

my face like Jim Carrey or yank it off like Tom Cruise

or imitate an accent or whistle Dolly Parton tunes

or respond to a name like Dickie or Jim or Bob or Dave.

Or perhaps I will be stricken with catalepsy or epilepsy

or narcolepsy or amnesia or consumption or glossolalia

or soap opera afflictions that render me unfamiliar

or heatstroke or cardiac arrest or at least heart-burn.

Or perhaps I will say, What are you doing here,

with the conviction of muddleheaded epiphany, like

I don't know you returned years ago, stayed, now

live down the road in a whole story, evermore.

All of my autobiographical writing is really a kind of performance. I try on different voices like I try on different styles of clothes at the Gap and Banana Republic. I am exploring different possibilities in my writing. Like Fulford (1999) says, "sometimes people improvise on the facts of their lives, like a jazz musician improvising on a composer's melody" (p.17). I am always improvising in creative ways, never satisfied that what I know is all there is to know, never convinced that I understand all there is to understand. So, I engage in an ongoing performance in my writing, a performance that informs me, on the one hand, and then transforms me, on the other. Ultimately I am always committed to transformation. Essentially, pedagogy is all about transformation. I never want to be the same person two days in a row. I always want to be changing and experimenting and embracing new challenges.

Carolyn G. Heilbrun (1999) notes that "in the old days, one wrote an autobiography or memoir only if one was famous; one related how that accomplishment had been achieved. Now, the most significant memoirs are being written by hitherto unknown authors, and the memoirs themselves confer fame; Maxine Hong Kingston and Maya Angelou are two who became famous through and after publishing their memoirs; there are many other examples" (p.46). While I don't disagree entirely with Heilbrun's observation, I think that there are many ways of writing an autobiography or memoir, and I think that historically many people have written them, especially in diaries and journals and poetry. I just don't think many of these autobiographical writers were read or heard. Everybody lives autobiographically, all the time. We make sense of our lives in stories. Nevertheless, there are many people who are not closely connected to their stories.

CARL LEGGO

Fulford (1999) notes: "There's poignancy in the idea of an individual thwarted by the lack of a good story. We have no term for it: we might call it narrative deprivation, or we might say the person is story-poor" (p.20). Is a person who is story-poor really a person without a voice? Can we live without stories? I don't think so, but many of us do live without the privilege of telling our stories, or the privilege of being heard.

And this is a pressing problem for teachers because autobiographical writing is always about performance, self-definition, self-representation, and self-exploration. We grow as people as we engage in literate practices of writing, speaking, and representing our stories. Our autobiographies are really fictions, stories that are made up, and the most informative and transformative autobiographies are steeped in the dynamics of language—well-written, engaging, expansive, imaginative, and critical. Autobiographical writing is about claiming and gaining and nurturing a sense of voice(s).

Revelation and Representation

ETCH-A-SKETCH

(*York Harbour, 2004*)

on a late January blustery day we snow-shoed

from our side door over the fence and through

the backyard of a neighbour who long ago

moved to Fort MacMurray, then wrote a trail

through the woods to the beach where

we followed the traces of snowmobiles

along the jagged edge of the frozen sea

where we could see the houses of York Harbour

and cottages on Wood's Island and a hint

of the Gulf of St. Lawrence and Wee Ball

and other islands whose names we are still learning

while gulls hung in the air like they hoped

we had food or perhaps were food, and Lana said,

when you left me, did you miss me? and I answered,

yes, obviously, I came back, didn't I? with only

an iota of feigned tenderness or imagination,

because I wished she wouldn't spoil walks

in beach snow with questions twisted in the past

because I want only to ignore her question, occupied

with the way snow erases like an Etch-a-Sketch

which can be turned upside down and shaken

to obliterate all the lines and permutations

of past images, but she persists, why did you return?

and I want to tell her I returned because even if

I can't or won't remember, I still couldn't forget her,

the stories that have composed us for thirty years,

but I can't find words for explaining how I am

rooted in the past, especially as I seek to forget,

and suspended on snowshoes, I seem to defy

the laws of physics and walk across the plain

of snow like Jesus walked on the sea of Galilee,

the muck and marsh below our feet, almost

forgotten, focused only on the lightness of snow

walking in a world draped for a wedding feast,

held firm and secure in the becoming moment when

only a little makes sense, still even beyond words

All my autobiographical writing is akin to seeking shapes amidst the stars. In all my living and teaching and writing, I am engaged in a constitutive activity that involves seeking the lines of possibility among the points of light in the night sky. I am not trying to see only the shapes that others have named. Instead I am seeking the shapes that have not been named. All my life, I have been named by others in various configurations. Now I seek other constellations, and in the process of knowing creative combinations, I find that there are revelatory possibilities for living each day.

I agree with Martin Amis (2000) who observes that "writers write far more penetratingly than they live" (p.215). According to Amis, in their writing, writers are "stretched until they twang" (p.215). I know that in my writing I can express a wisdom that is not necessarily the wisdom I am living successfully at all. But at least I am writing with hope, especially with the hope that I can learn to live well. And again, this is the pedagogical imperative, to learn to journey well in the world by learning to journey well in words. Heilbrun (1999) notes that "one no longer looks back for a pattern, but writes, and looks both backward and forward in the hope of perceiving a possible pattern in advance of its having been lived" (p.46). And in this process of seeking patterns, we are engaged in the activity of creating ourselves in constitutive processes that include choice, hope, intention, and flexibility—all parts of an ongoing process of lifelong engagement with language and discourse.

I grew up in a working-class home in a working-class neighbourhood in a working-class town, and in these familiar contexts I imbibed many attitudes and views about class structure and privilege, and especially my role in relation to others. I never wrote about personal experiences when I was in school. Indeed, only in my thirties did I begin to write in the voices of autobiographical poetry and stories. And even now, after almost two decades of writing, I still question the value of my writing; I still fear that the voices in my writing are too homely, too unsophisticated, too earthy to be valuable. And ultimately, I have to remind myself (almost daily) that I write my autobiographical narratives, first, for myself, not in some kind of egocentric, narcissistic self-obsession, but out of a conviction that by writing about myself in process, with all the hopes and joys, as well as the struggles and disappointments, I can enter into a dialogic conversation with others, including students and colleagues. As Conway (1998) suggests, the "magical opportunity of entering another life is what really sets us thinking about our own" (p.18). In a similar way, I am suggesting that by thinking about my own life I can enter into the lived experiences of others, all of us engaging in conversations that contribute to the constitution of understanding and connection.

Identity and Subjectivity

TRUE ROMANCE

on Lynch's Lane I had many heroes

daily watched John Wayne Matt

Dillon the Lone Ranger Tonto Roy

Rogers Trigger Huckleberry Hound

the Cartwrights Fred MacMurray

Hogan's Heroes Maxwell Smart Tarzan

Walt Disney Rin Tin Tin Lucy Ed

Sullivan Jed Clampett Quickdraw

McGraw Number 99 Batman Gordon
Pinsent the Cleavers Bugs Bunny
right a wrong world

and I needed heroes with the mad
Mercers out the living room kitchen
bedroom windows Mercers watching
everywhere round us like sharks
after old man Mercer divided
his strip from Harbour to Heights
divided it in parcels big parcels
for the sons little parcels
for the daughters and went away
to shoot a moose and never came back

leaving Billy Mercer sitting
in the dark watching black and white
television through sunglasses
afraid of ultraviolet rays

and Lil Mercer who hid in her house
all winter but danced naked
in her front yard under the full May moon
and spent summer on the fifth floor
of the Western Memorial Regional Hospital

and Sam Mercer on his verandah
drinking rum watching the world go by
wondering where the world was going
since he'd never gone further
than he could see from his verandah

CARL LEGGO

and Sal Mercer who talked without end
and never said a word I can remember
using words to fend off the darkness
the terrible darkness around her

and Dougie Mercer who survived polio
tuberculosis diabetic comas cancer
for more than eight decades with words
like talismans you don't have to worry
about me I won't be here much longer

and Sylvie Mercer who spent
her widow's pension on gifts
for the neighbours a steady stream
of Avon and Pot of Gold chocolates
like a Kwakiutl or Doukhobor
protesting no earth-licking fondness
for possessions going even one better
than Jesus by giving away her only coat

and I grew up reading *True Romance*
left in the bathroom by Carrie
who spun romance out of movies
and magazines from Tom's Store
while baking bread and jam jams
and pushing wet laundry through
the finger-crushing wringer
and listening to the stories of her
neighbours like a radio hotline host
and serving french fries to sons
who thought her kitchen was a take-out

and I grew up waiting for Skipper
who always woke early with dark
still filling the windows
and walked alone to the mill
through the warm hot cool cold seasons
and all day inhaled the heat and noise
of the world's biggest paper mill
his laughter still heard
over the endless pulse of machines
and at day's end burst into the kitchen
chased by the dark his face a grin

and I grew up with Carrie and Skipper
at the centre of Mercer madness
listening to Sal while Billy
watched television and visiting
Dougie and Lil in the hospital
and sitting on the verandah
with Sam and delivering
Sylvie's gifts to the neighbours

and often I asked Carrie and Skipper
why do you put up with them
their only reply they're family
and on television I saw Neil Armstrong
walk on the moon and I know it is true
even though Billy Mercer still claims
it was all a hoax

All my autobiographical research is about the construction of identity, especially in the spaces between self and subjectivity. As Susan Griffin (1995) observes, "the self does not exist in isolation" (p.50). Instead, "to know the self is to enter a social process. One does not know oneself except by being mirrored" (p.51). I find this a very powerful notion for understanding issues of self-identity, especially the ways that we are often mirrored and represented, and hence shaped, in the discursive practices of the dominant culture. I agree with Griffin's comment about "a desire that is at the core of human imaginings, the desire to locate ourselves in community" (p.146). The challenge that we constantly face is the challenge to fit into the community but not be swallowed up by the community, to live communally while also developing our individual talents and personalities. All of this is accomplished in telling stories, as Griffin understands, "for each of us, as for every community, village, tribe, nation, the story we tell ourselves is crucial to who we are, who we are becoming" (p.152).

In my autobiographical writing I examine the differences between the metaphysical and phenomenological emphasis on self and the postmodern understanding of subjectivity. There are ways in which self and subject identities overlap or resonate with one another, but notions of subjectivity acknowledge multiple identities and the ways that these identities are constructed and shaped in language and culture and ideology. As Ursula A. Kelly (1997) explains: "A notion of auto/biography as readings of selves positioned within a larger textuality insists that this larger textuality be interrogated for ways in which we read and are (culturally) read to, for the ways in which we have learned to look and the ways in which we are looked at" (pp.65-66). According to Kelly, "the allure of auto/biography is…the illusion of the seamless web of experience, at the centre of which is the (modernist) self coming into fuller rationality" (pp.51-52). In my writing and living, I do not rescind the sense of selfhood; instead, I seek diverse possibilities for identity. Like Linda Warley (2005) who writes that "human subjectivity is a constant process of fashioning and refashioning the self" (p.31), I am never simply named and categorized. In fact, I seek a creative vitality for living in fiction. I am always writing myself in new ways, and always re-writing the ways that others write me, and always revisiting the ways that I have written myself and been written by others. In my autobiobiographical writing, I am committed to emancipatory projects of learning and teaching in language that extend far beyond boundaries and borders and limits. I am constantly exploring, contesting, and negotiating the possibilities of identity.

In the process of autobiographical writing, I find that I often experiment with the range of voices that I use, too. I am not interested in developing a single voice, and living with that voice as if it is the primary or only voice available to me. Instead, I experiment with diverse textual styles, and I often challenge the structures of the typical expository essay, in order to try on different voices. Regarding women's autobiographical writing, Conway (1998) claims that "memoirs full of abrupt transitions and shifting narrative styles are sure signs that their authors are struggling to overcome the cultural taboos that define these women as witnesses rather than actors in life's events" (p.88). Conway then argues that "whenever someone tells her story straight and in an authoritative voice, we know she has developed her own sense of agency and can sustain it despite nagging cultural doubts" (p.88). I find this observation problematic, especially because I think that Conway is laying claim to a notion of essentialized selfhood that is not sufficient for understanding the complexities of identity formation. Instead, I argue for a perspective that is the opposite of Conway's view. The authoritative voice hides the processes of subject positions by presenting an apparently seamless façade. Instead, we need to write autobiographically in creative and courageous ways that acknowledge how each of us is composed in the intersections of multiple processes of identity shaping and re-shaping.

Fragments and Possibilities

SWALLOW LIGHT

In September trapped sun, for the first time,

Carrie and I sat on her back porch, and talked

about growing old and holding fast to life.

My mother said, *Learn to be happy.*

I almost asked,

What is the curriculum of joy?,

but I didn't want to sound like Mr. Rogers.

Recalling childhood is like swallows

flying light in a blackberry bramble.

For our mother's birthday, my brother and I once bought

a beer mug from Woolworth's, a wild woman's image,

wide grin, flared nostrils, like the monstrous other that scares

Abbott and Costello in *Africa Screams*, and my brother and I

carried our amazing find to Carrie who aped our glow, even

though we then knew she'd never win an Oscar.

She still has the mug.

Remember Maxine Porter?

In middle age, she said, I have wasted much of my life.

I don't want to waste any more. I hope I have the heart for life.

She told me about Canada Day, how she went
to Margaret Bowater Park and amidst the crowds
celebrating, saw no one she knew.
One time, I knew everybody in Corner Brook.

She knows the peril of a long healthy life,
the memory seared in longing.

Carrie said, *Stuart Stuckless joined the circus, hurt his back,*
got a settlement, everything taken into account, he did well.

On Wednesdays when Carrie baked bread she wore
faded blue mauve pink panties on her head to prevent
stray hairs falling into the dough, and the kitchen window
always steamed up, the world condensed, hidden.

You can never have enough life
to do all the things you want to do.

Carrie told me stories about other mothers
like she was seeking the ingredients for a stone soup
we might enjoy together in late lean winter days.

When Daisy Parsons got Alzheimer's,
her sons Fred and Ted cared for her
like two nurses on Dr. Kildare.
They couldn't put her in a home
because they needed her old age pension.

Memory is a winter window, stained frost, light etched lines.

Every Sunday Francis Dove's mother went to church.
Francis parked his car at the bottom of Lynch's Lane,
and slid his mother down the hill on a piece of linoleum,
and the neighbours always said, Like a saint, nothing stops her.

I grew up on winter weekends eating moose meat stewed
long and tender, and my mother's homemade bread
spread with Good Luck margarine and Demerara molasses,
mouthfuls of sticky soft sweet steam.

Did you know if you eat a lot of beets you will pee red
and scare yourself half to death with fears of death?

Like the pond skater knows shadows, fissures, vibrations,
the resonant text read hypertextually, poised between
sun and night, I no longer know the way back, but
Carrie's wisdom like fridge magnets might guide me still:

always remember to forget
        what you don't know won't hurt you
always remember somebody nice
        kindness somehow stays with you
be open to new ideas
        we're getting older like everybody else
be nice to want nothing
        everything is good

As a boy Carrie always bought me McGregor Happy Foot socks.
The other day I bought a pair. I might even take up dancing.

CARL LEGGO

I regard all my autobiographical writing as a tantalizing search for wholeness by dwelling with the fragments. I write fragments of narrative out of the fragments of memory I cherish, and the fragments of stories others, especially family, offer me, and the fragments represented in photographs. The autobiographer is akin to a person putting a jigsaw puzzle together with most of the pieces to the puzzle, long lost and no longer recoverable. I know this, but I am still fascinated by the fragments and the possibilities of story-making even with the holes and gaps. Perhaps we dwell too long on what is not there, and attend too little to what is there. Perhaps our autobiographical writing is numerous fragments that, like fractals, hold the possibilities of the wholes. In my autobiographical writing I am hoping to catch hints of the whole story in the glimpses offered by the fragments.

Conway (1998) acknowledges that "we all practice the craft of autobiography in our inner conversations with ourselves about the meaning of our experience" (p.178). Nevertheless, as Conway also notes, though we are all autobiographers since we are always writing and representing our living experiences, "few of us give close attention to the forms and tropes of the culture through which we report ourselves to ourselves" (p.178). Conway points out that cultural forms and tropes for composing autobiographies might "capture universals in human existence" but are still "not necessarily the perfect expressions of our experience in our unique passages through time" (p.178). She, therefore, cautions against being trapped in "inherited modes of expression" (p.178). I not only appreciate Conway's caution, but I recommend that in our autobiographical writing, we need to begin from the location of the unique and individual and personal experience. In other words, we need to begin in our own backyards. Then, we can seek to understand how our idiosyncratic stories relate to the larger stories that, like fractals, unfold all around us.

A Lingering Note

For most of my life, I have been caught up in cultural roles for living. Most of my life has been devoted to trying to imitate the cultural expectations of being a man, a father, a husband, and the list of subject positions extends throughout the alphabet. I have had an abiding difficulty in navigating these culturally inscribed roles, but I am beginning to realize finally that I do not need to follow slavishly any roles. I can begin with who I am in the specific geographical, ideological, political, spiritual, physical, social, chronological, psychological, emotional, intellectual, psychoanalytic, economic locations where I dwell, and from these local locations, I can seek to understand my relationships to others in their locations. In other words, I am simply refusing the authority of grand or universal narratives to write me in given positions. Instead, I will write my stories as fragments of diffuse and diverse narratives that are unfolding constantly throughout the earth.

And I will be guided in my story-making by a commitment to exploring writing that is alive with rhythm and heart and imagination, writing that acknowledges how the personal and the professional are never any more separate than the chambers of the heart. I write autobiographically because, as a teacher, I am engaged in an ongoing process of studying myself so I can grow in knowledge and wisdom, especially so I will have knowledge and wisdom to offer others. And, so, I draw these speculations to a temporary close with one more poem, convinced that the creative energy of autobiography is really only known in the practice of autobiographical writing. I do not focus my writing on theoretical, philosophical, and scholarly arguments to defend and explain autobiography. I am not trying to convince readers about the efficacy of autobiographical research for research and pedagogy. Instead I invite a conversation. I seek to engage readers with a performance in words. My concern is ultimately an ethical conviction. Simply, I think we live with too many lies, and, therefore, with little sense of who we are and who we can be. We need to tell our stories more. And we need to tell more stories. In the end, the stories we write and tell about our living experiences will teach us how to live with more creativity, confidence, flexibility, coherence, imagination, and truthfulness.

SCRIBBLED SUBJECTS

in the verdant Azores,

a volcanic archipelago

anchored in the Atlantic Ocean,

an impertinent eruption

from the centre of the earth,

I heard a philosopher

who was rather beautiful

(especially for a philosopher

with blond hair and long legs

in a meticulously cut black suit

and lavender ice blouse

like few scholars favour,

no drab, dowdy bookworms,

at least my keen preference)

with enough lava in her eyes

to shrivel your heart, spewed

her words with a TV evangelical

preacher's scary conviction

CARL LEGGO

the philosopher said,
stories are not meant
to pull us out of the world,
but to reconcile us to the world

and I wanted to ask,
where is the world?

the philosopher said,
the danger of story-telling
is the failure to look
at the horrors of the world

and I wanted to ask,
how can a story hide horror?

the philosopher said,
stories are a search for revelry,
the reprehensible narcissism
of poetry lost in an evil world

and I wanted to ask,
why is revelry unworldly?

and the philosopher cited
Arendt, Benjamin, Camus,
worked her way through the alphabet
with a Pentecostal pastor's passion
for railing against revelry

but told no stories, not even

an anecdote, knowing how

the wild revelry of stories

always refutes containment

in the linguistic contortions

of philosophers with words:

bloodless, blonde, bland

and I asked,

do you ever laugh?

I guess my question wasn't

sufficiently philosophical,

since the Azorean sun was suddenly

tepid in her glare like a ray gun

and I'm still dabbing Ozonol ointment

on the burning circles of my skin

Unlike the philosopher in the poem "Scribbled Subjects," each of the authors in this section on self-study and autobiography celebrates the efficacious and energetic effectiveness of story-making for research and pedagogy, for understanding how our multiple roles of artists, researchers, and teachers are inextricably interwoven, both individually and collaboratively. Above all, Anniina Suominen Guyas, Renee Norman, Pauline Sameshima, Erika Hasebe-Ludt, Cynthia Chambers, and Antoinette Oberg all acknowledge how we are always located in an intricate network of relationships that shapes our stories and identities, our desires and hopes, our ecological connections to one another throughout the earth, always breathing with the heart's rhythms.

ANNIINA SUOMINEN GUYAS

WATER: MOVING STILLNESS

How we live, interact with others and our various environments, engage in art, teach, and research is intertwined and inseparable from our identity. These active engagements serve a larger ontological and epistemological inquiry and form a holistic way of being—a living inquiry (Irwin & de Cosson, 2004). My quest for knowledge is directed by my desire to teach, learn, and conduct research in ways that are open to the visual and verbal language of possibility (Giroux, 1995). I imagine a "language", unbound from predetermined and pre-accepted classifications and categories of identity. A communication, understanding, knowledge that reaches beyond the limitations of "what has been", meaning(s) more complex than what can be achieved through functioning within or by stretching boundaries.

hooks' "engaged pedagogy" (1994) strives for the well-being of students and teachers and reminds us that "teachers must be actively committed to a process of self-actualization that promotes their own well-being if they are to teach in a manner that empowers students" (p.15). Practicing engaged and holistic pedagogy, or what I refer to as a pedagogy of constant and endless search, my research and art question "what narratives of identity and difference shape [my] authority, and how can [I] use the authority conferred to [me] to challenge and expose [my and my students'] narratives?" (Hesford, 1999, p.xxx). It is my goal to guide my students toward critical awareness of identity construction that is not limited to given and pre-accepted categories and classifications. To do so, I consider it my responsibility to first study my self and expose my contextual understanding of my identity to critical inquiry. This is achieved through my intensive artistic work with moving water to gain new understandings of self.

Knowledge is relational, dependent on contexts and philosophy, and cannot be separated from an understanding of the self and its multiple embedded identities. I base my understanding of art and artistic knowledge construction on relational aesthetics (Bourriaud, 2002) and view self through relationality (Eakin, 1999) and performed identities (Smith, 1998). In acknowledging that awareness is based on relational inter-trans-subjective and interstitial temporalities, I assert that new understandings are negotiated in the encounters with previously unattached and disconnected/separate realities. What guides my research in the form(ation)s of relational understandings is a complex web of bodily, visual, artistic, and tacit knowledge, as well as a critical consciousness. New formations of understanding or critical awareness are negotiated through my relational encounters with nature in particular and in the interactions of the different modes of being aware of and constructing knowledge. Based on these encounters, understandings are presented, albeit partially, in the visual and verbal artistic and research presentations created.

S. Springgay et al. (eds.), Being with A/r/tography, 25–32.

What is performed in this chapter is an example of a complex state of artistic activity during which inter-subjectivity and interstitiality b(l)end to form a holistic awareness. Like Bourriaud (2002) states, "the image is a moment" (p.80) that plays with the complexity of past, present, and future, negotiating new potentialities. A/r/tography (Irwin & de Cosson, 2004) and artistic inquiry methods have guided me to new concepts of study that help me define new intersubjective and relational formations and subjectivities.

The complexity of my living situation also guides the development of my interpretations of a/r/tography. I define and understand the obscurity of my life through travel, nomad(ism) (Pryer, 2004), strangeness and an inability to settle into a context, physically, mentally, or metaphorically (Kristeva, 1991). In my artistic inquiry I search for moments of complex aesthetic and artistic engagement. More specifically, my work grows out of an active meditative stillness in which the senses direct cognition and understandings toward a metaphorical or literal formation of "concepts." Theory, practice, philosophy, and my life merge into new awareness. This happens not only around and in-between, but also through (ir)relevant and (un)bounded (per)formed contextual identities. It is always flexible enough to move in and within interpersonal understandings.

In the following, I attempt to unfold the process of rhizomatic and relational work toward new renderings. Although presented here in an order that might appear linear, the process is hardly organized and systematic. I attempt to analyse the creative inquiry process by breaking it into parts to demonstrate how multiple modes of being form the holistic inquiry process.

Filling Lined Pages

Placing passion aside, my autobiographical notes fill the pages of my pre-lined public and private metaphorical journals. Most of my researcher-teacher-artist-wife-mother life is less than glorious. Often felt as such, I lack the courage and knowledge to change predetermined patterns and I perform my duties. I find challenge and pleasure in my daily tasks, in the lines I read, and in the everyday of my teaching, but I struggle with time—minutes, hours and weeks do not naturally align with the need to reflect and understand. My life, while hardly more exciting than the filling of the pre-lined pages, forms the necessary basis and, surprisingly, the inspiration for moments of altered awareness of space and time (Bourriaud, 2002). As if cooking on the lowest setting of an electric crock-pot, ideas simmer; theory, practice, research, art, and teaching slowly fold and unfold (Springgay, 2003). I prepare for the anticipated moments of holistic understanding by reading, writing, and analysing my work and the work of others. I live surrounded by my images, the evidence of previous stages of inquiry. Mostly, I strive to be attentive to the details of everyday. And I wait.

Anticipation

The artistic or cognitive thinking processes never begin with the urge to act; however, the sudden anticipation of what-is-soon-to-happen is often so immediate and strong that it forefronts my awareness. My understanding of time and space changes when intuition, bodily reactions, and aesthetic sensibility and tendencies begin to code my awareness. If I am at home writing when I begin to feel the anticipation, I might have to dance to a song to ease the anxiety. I always need to move. I begin repeated snacking, both my body and mind working in overdrive. My conscious thoughts race and spin, theories flash and re-flash and begin to make new connections. I quickly plan, re-plan, connect and re-connect, distanced from logic; then slowly and in stillness, I begin to consider my words again. I move into a slower time, a sensual time, reality marked by the humming of my computer; the first loud spring song of the birds keeping me connected to the space. I am with the light beyond the window and with the fresh air slowly streaming through the door crack. I form words and sentences and consider connections to texts and the experiences of others.

Active Stillness

Sometimes I cannot sit still but need to photograph and be physically and aesthetically active when the sense of anticipation arises. The artistic activity then functions as the discharge of an overcharged battery, a direct relief for the hyped mind and body. Most often, however, seemingly less happens during the moments of visual artistic creation. Oddly refined active stillness, a calmness-within, levels the hyperactivity of anticipation. I am serene, almost earthy, mundane. While I "work my camera", I distance myself from my surroundings and focus on the aesthetics of presence. And yet, I am simultaneously present and can pause and be attentive to others or my surroundings if needed. I often work surrounded by others and no traces of a stereotypical grand, artistic, creative persona are visible to them; instead perhaps a calmness and a grounded sense of happiness can be observed. Connected to my vision, to my camera, to the materiality surrounding me, I follow the flow of water. I focus on patterns, movements, colours, smells, masses and changes in rhythm. Water bubbles my presence, brown, green and other colours evoke a need to touch through vision. The movement of water moves and floats me, re-dis-connecting me to/from the materiality through capture and the closeness of presence. Holistic awareness frames my philosophy, teaching me about myself, about ontology and about epistemology.

Hardly a bodily climax, this is when most of the "stuff" that I can never describe in words happens. I frame my awareness with my camera, supposedly freezing the rhizome with (around, surrounded physically and metaphorically) and within (myself) into the frozen, cropped, and limited frame of my capture. However, to me the capture of the materiality of my surroundings "hints at the potential for a radically different conception of time altogether. Indeed, instead of pointing to the limitations of the single picture for narrative, it illustrates its possibilities" (Irvine, 2006, n.p.). My images have a "duration component" (Irvine, 2006), a suggested continuity of time through the extended exposure of the image, and thus lack clear focus. They also indicate a far more complex time—*flexibility*—a sense of permission to visit and return, a layered presence of the past, present and future, a manuscript for loss, mourning, desire, and fantasy.

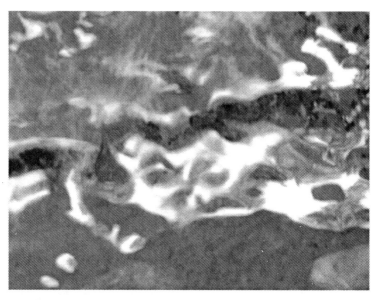

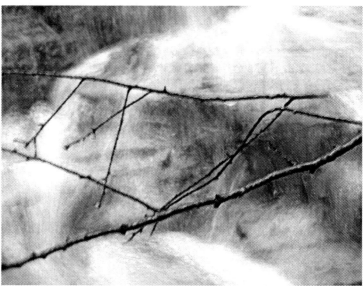

Water Series. 2005-2007. Anniina Suominen. Digital colour photographs.
Courtesy of the artist.

A Slow Process and Tracking Back Relational Autobiography

After stillness it is time to meditate, to let the images marinate and work their way into my cognitive thinking. What happens next is what hooks calls a "magical space" (1995, p.25). Meditative writing, or creative "photo-writing" (Suominen, 2003) is a process of "outing" some of the rhizomatic understandings created during my process of reading and preparing and then photographing water. Slowly, some of the photographs find their ways into my academic texts, onto gallery walls, into public parks, into my home and others. They continue to facilitate creativity and serve as a site of developing fantasies and stored memory. These photographs may be reworked over and over again, performing a "memory work" (Kuhn, 1995). At other times I need them for a specific purpose, such as when performing "photo therapy" (Spence, 1995; 1991; 1988); sometimes they aid in representing complex or emerging understandings. They always perform autobiographies through new representations of self.

Through writing the following brief photographic narration entitled "Water", I attempted to organize my thoughts about returning to photograph water as an artistic inquiry.

I return to the site and sound of water for comfort, wisdom, and guidance.
Water, my old friend and mentor, heals my sores and revitalizes my spirit.
I float, feel, observe and analyse the feeling—I find no answers, instead I find
a slowly moving stillness, and active pause, that helps me to think beyond
cognition.

It would be naïve to assume that what I experience in nature is something "pure", irrelevant to the sociopolitical and theoretical framework of my inquiry and life. Dean and Millar (2005) frame this succinctly: "Nature is a cultural construct, a place that feeds the urban imagination as much as the urban belly. It is here that we are said to find ourselves, our 'true nature'" (p.47). The impact of landscape, environment, and their representations is known to have a deep effect on how people perceive themselves, culture, and especially "nationness". I began my dissertation work (Suominen, 2003), a study of identity construction and an immigration narrative, with three assumed identity categories: cultural, gendered, and professional. During the arts-based inquiry process that involved photographing my life, photographs of nature surfaced even when I was not discussing my relationship to nature, geographic-cultural contexts, or my cultural heritage. I came to realize that not only did my relationship to the Finnish landscape (and later Ohioan), but also its representations in art and visual communication, had a profound impact even on the closest human relationships in my life. During the research process, when discussing gendered identity, generational legacies, and social roles within family, I struggled to find the needed understanding and support for the performed sensitive and personal memory work. It was in the nature setting I used in the photographic portrait of my mother that I was able to locate consolation. When analysing my relationship with my mother and the past generations of women in the family, I drew my focus to the landscape used as a background in the photograph, and was able to find words for the evolving understandings of these inter-subjective relations.

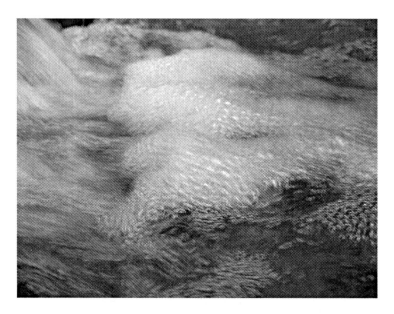

Water Series. 2005-2007. Anniina Suominen. Digital colour photographs. Courtesy of the artist.

I find the meaning, purpose, and justification of my artistic inquiry in the previously described realization. My photographic work with water plays with all of my subject positionings and with all relationalities of my understanding, those articulated as well as those beyond cognition. As Bourriaud (2002) states, "The goal of art is to reduce the mechanical share in us. Its aim is to destroy any *a priori* agreement about what is perceived" (p.80, author's emphasis). Being with water, photographing water, meditating with my photographic representations of water, presenting this artwork, and writing about it allows me to combine immediacy, intuition, and bodily reaction with systematic inquiry and cognitive idea development. This artistic interaction seeps into the interstices of my understanding and aids in concept development, allowing new renderings to develop. Water as a concept of study is not new to my inquiry or to art. I grew up on an island in a landscape of combined suburbia and preserved wilderness. The sea and its winds are present in my memory and its representations. Later, when I immigrated to Ohio, the lack of water's majestic presence confused me and made me question why anyone would live far from masses of water. Ironically, I soon found solace for my sense of dislocation from indoor water aerobics classes. Two elements of these exercise classes soothed my uneasiness in spite of the chlorine-smelling water: the presence of elderly members of the community and the comforting feeling of warm water surrounding my body. I believe that these kinds of deeply internalized connections and autobiographical life-tracks are what aid us in creating meaningful connections and artistic representations. These internalized realities are also inherently relational and neither the artistic "birth" nor the creations of representations can be analysed separately from shared and relational perceptions of realities. Thus, I would argue that while solely personal meaning does not exist independently from the shared and communal, a critical attention to what is perceived as personally significant is needed to study larger sociopolitical issues in a meaningful way through one's art.

Reflecting back on the arts-based research projects I have conducted and the processes I am currently involved in, I assert that our individual goals and purposes are always inherently personal and private as well as sociopolitical, philosophical, pedagogical, and public. The ability to accept and account for the benefits gained from this type of personal inquiry makes for holistic and healthy artistic research. While the goals for my work and the purpose of making it public are necessarily educational and aimed to benefit others, I also work toward a developed understanding of self. I recognize this aspect in my work with water. My work continues an unfinished process from childhood, one that is partially driven by an inability to let go of the "family romance" (Treacher, 2000). In other words, to accept the brutality and mental violence of imperfection, I repeatedly return to the physical elements of my environment. To do so forms a complex understanding through artistic encounters with the materiality of my living context. Interestingly and unexpectedly, I might find in this co-inter-inner-experience a sense of perfect momentary fantasy, a childish fantasy of directness and innocence. This connection to the materiality has therapeutic elements because it further helps me accept yet another layer of the brutality and violence of imperfect relational contextuality.

ANNIINA SUOMINEN GUYAS

Meaning of Photographic Work

My intercultural, transcultural, and transmigrant experiences continue to direct all my scholarly work (Mirón, Darder & Inda 2005). On the other hand, my artistic, constant, reactionary relationship with my physical environment and surroundings helps me question the discourse of my understanding and enables me to create new dis-un-contextual identities. As I previously described, the temporary perceived understanding of my surroundings and my self are formed in imaginary unsubstantial interactions between artistic creation, cognition, and sociocultural interaction. I continue to use my photography to create surfaces for understanding. At prior stages of my artistic inquiry these photos marked my existence, narrated my life, and created a memory line. Now they have become more precise tools for finding meaning. In the living inquiry, I find calmness and incorporeal space to question myself, and freedom and methods to critically evaluate everything else. I am more often content without words than I was previously. In my artistic practice, I find the necessary break for survival personally and professionally, a space in which shifting meaning, incoherence, and resonance replace coherence, permanency, and reaction. I focus on the complex layers and contextual manifestation of institutional and cultural citizenship, assimilation, and belonging beyond territories of geographic locations and nation-state borders. Importantly, however, I am not only looking to further my understanding of relationality of self and knowledge through a process of holistic inquiry, but also to learn to accept the importance of cherishing the strangeness within, that which cannot be fully understood.

RENEE NORMAN

THE ART OF POETRY AND NARRATIVE WITH AND BETWEEN LIVED CURRICULUM: AUTOBIOGRAPHICAL A/R/TOGRAPHY

I am hanging framed photographs of various drama performances from the last three years in the drama room, although performative work is only really a small part of our process-based Fine Arts program. But it's easier to capture the performances on film, the drama room work more fleeting, constantly in-progress and in-motion, more difficult to stop and freeze-frame, especially as I am so often immersed in it myself. As teacher-in-role, I can be busy in some jungle, kingdom, village, city, or other story world.

The children love gazing at these photographs, evidence of events meaningful to all of us, a cataloguing of our participation in arts-based work in the schools. Here a mask, there a green-painted face, here a fireplace made out of cardboard boxes, there the pink of costumes backlit by the hue of red-green-blue bulbs...

I hang the photographs right where the children exit the drama room, so they (children and photos) can absorb the many minutes we have been exploring, moving, emoting, wondering, creating, playing...All that is involved in making meaning of our lives and others in the context of so many worlds, so many images.

I have been teaching here for four years now, since the inception of the Fine Arts program, the memory of the sheer excitement and busy bustle of that first year still sharp. I'd walk down the hall and eager parents would hand me donated hats, an old silver wine goblet for a prop, old dresses and suit jackets, and whatever else we all thought could be useful for the drama program. So by the time I reached my room I could hardly hold everything, much less remember who I'd need to thank.

When I came to the program, it was with a damaged hip, and the children, my colleagues, and the parents supported me through painful limping, the emergence of a cane (later decorated by one of my daughters with a forest of flowers and ribbon), and finally, a hip replacement.

Why do you carry that stick, the Grade 1's would ask? Then later: Where's your stick?

TRANSFORMATION

1, 2, 3,

the doctor chants

as he removes the 30 staples in my hip

S. Springgay et al. (eds.), Being with A/r/tography, 33–44.

RENEE NORMAN

an old bulletin board display

flesh instead of paper

i am being changed

less Frankenstein

more wounded veteran

i lean on my crutches

the pinpricks of pain

only 1 on the 10 scale

that's my world these days

pain translated to numbers

28, 29, 30,

once the corner-curled artwork

is returned to owner or tossed away

(bent staples removed)

what possibility there seems

in the empty background

only a gash to mar the smooth surface

the dim rhythm of ordinals

"I decided not to teach in the Fine Arts program," a colleague at the school confided in me. "I'm near the end of my career." As I am, but that didn't stop me! Neither did my Ph.D. or a three year stint at the university as a poorly paid sessional lecturer. I remember so clearly that moment when I knew with crystal clarity that I could not be a sessional lecturer anymore. I was loaded down with a heavy backpack full of textbooks and handouts for courses I was teaching, and limping badly. I didn't really feel part of the academic community, and the pain I was experiencing from my hip was a burden I was bearing mostly by myself. Tenure track requests counted high above health concerns when it came to scheduling and the distance between office desks and classrooms on a large campus. Such considerations loom larger when dealing with a disability.

ARTHRITIC DREAMS I

"you're really limping"

this pronouncement

coming so often

from so many

i've perfected the non-reply

i wonder

why people feel they need to comment

on your gait

it's not as if

they make remarks

on snotty noses

dandruff

or hair loss

but your walk

is open season

and just when i'm feeling stronger

more measured

even

able to cope with the pain

someone i barely know

blurts it out

and then i wonder

just how long

i've been fooling myself

ARTHRITIC DREAMS II

first to go

the neighbourhood walk

down to a brief turn

of several blocks

woosh

then driving the youngest

on a field trip

poof

baseball in the park

gone

doing the dishes

(no real loss there)

if you don't mind the crumbs

no one but me ever sees

i could catalogue

the changes

bed rest Epsom salts

by the gallon

ice packs

sitting down to peel potatoes

the most difficult to bear

a disappointed look

in the eyes

when i have to say no

i can't

it's too hard

poof

So I returned to the public school system, but in a new way. I have always valued and taught the arts. I have a drama and music background, and (more recently) writing experience, which are part of who I am as a person and a teacher. A new Fine Arts program endorsed the arts, and our waiting lists attest to the support and interest such a program garners. By teaching in such a program, I would also have the opportunity to further promote arts curricula, just as I had earlier championed the power and importance of drama (Norman 1984, 2002, 2004). I would be returning to my teaching roots, too, full circle, ironically enough, after successfully completing a Ph.D. (Norman, 2001). My new job entailed enrolling a primary class as a classroom teacher, and teaching drama and some music across the grades, both primary and intermediate levels. I would be doing (praxis) in addition to knowing (theoria) and making (poesis), three forms important to a/r/tography (Leggo 2001).

One day early on in this new context, I was putting paper away in the cupboard. I was exhausted from setting up a very poorly stocked classroom, and overwhelmed by all the demands of parents eager to be in on the ground floor of a new program that meant so much to them, and an administration whose enthusiasm often extended to night meetings. I had some doubts that I was in the right place. Then the next day I drove into the parking lot, unlocked my classroom, and felt a deep sense of belonging compounded by the wonderful colleagues with whom I was working.

THE CALL OF TEACHING

a calling

some think this describes teaching

OK

calling children

to walk, not run

work neatly, not rush

clean up after themselves

pick up the scraps

or is it calling ourselves

to get up when it's still dark

to take one thing at a time

to jump off the gerbil's wheel

spinning ever faster

we call when we want something

need attention

forget

remember

want to catch up

so what is it

that calls us to teaching?

the voice that shouts

see you tomorrow

across the parking lot in the downpour

as you

exhausted

get into your car

ready to make your escape

mind already planning the next day

The drama room, which was my responsibility to organize, was beginning to feel like a haven, too. I'd walk in and we'd fill the space with our words. The children were so committed to the make believe that it was as if we were all living in the world we created in that room. We felt that world so profoundly that I'm certain emotions permeated the walls, were recorded there. Every time I opened the door and entered, I felt that emotion, heard the whispers of old dramas, could imagine how much more would grow in that room...

DANCING A POEM

i danced with children

on a carpeted classroom

the pain set aside for once

thoughts about imminent war

and stiff hips

trampled by playful steps

a winding changing throng

of circles

colleagues

and musicians

mothers

and lovers

this is education

at its finest

not foundation skills assessment

or political posturing

or meeting expectations for grade level

but joy

in its pure form

and passion

that fuels paintings and heartfelt words

dreams and poems

My daughters have been a part of my teaching life, helping me set up, donating their old toys and hats and purses, and coming to school to draw with children or play musical instruments for them. My daughters are all artistic and musical. One works with film and writing, another is in a university School of Music, and the youngest is a clever cartoonist and artist. During their younger years, they swirled around me as I completed my Ph.D., as I wrote the autobiographical poetry and stories that became so much a part of my being and becoming.

HOUSE LANGUAGES

the house quiet

all other mortal occupants

elsewhere

i listen for a reed

the lost language of marshes

but the language of my back yard intrudes

Stanley and Maple

(persistent tree squirrels

my daughters have named as ours)

if only i could summon the marsh of words

as easily as i spread peanut butter

over a giant pine cone

RENEE NORMAN

food for squirrels

and thought

(the fat nut taste of meaning)

instead i sink within house and noises

beyond wild yard and creatures

and hope: the whistle of wet grasses

Ruminating upon those years, I realize how much the arts constructed and re-constructed all of us, how much we absorbed from one another, how arts education begins in those places where we are literally and figuratively at home. But the places in which we nurture and are nurtured are not immune to growth and change. As I continue to story worlds with the children I teach, the stories of my world are changing in significant ways, ways that cause gaps, upheavals, absences in the fabric of our artistic and domestic world...

Confessions of a Music Mom

I was a music mom. That's like a soccer or hockey mom, except you go to concerts instead of games, and drive your child to lessons and rehearsals rather than rink or field practices. My husband Don was a music mom, too (by my definition). It started with piano lessons. Then our middle daughter begged to learn the alto saxophone, the bassoon, the flute, the bari sax, and then the piccolo, in that order. I balked when the cello was mentioned, pleading there was no more room in the house. Don kept looking at the marks on the newly painted doors.

We calculate that we spent $5000 per year on lessons, youth orchestra and ensemble fees, not even including instrument purchases (a modest bassoon costs $6500) or rentals, accompanists, reeds and repairs, or the cost of gas. $5000 is the cost of a year's university tuition, which is where our musical daughter is now studying and residing, playing her heart out as she pursues a music degree (along with a science one). We spent oh, so much more than money, though. We spent time.

I walk by her empty room, straining to hear the echoes of a bassoon solo or a flute trill, missing that ornate music and the young woman who could feel it so deeply.

I miss phoning to rearrange lessons like a juggler tossing the pieces of a calendar into the air, because she was always so busy. I miss finding new teachers, chatting with the old ones. I miss all the concerts. Six years of high school band and orchestra concerts, which also meant buying the fundraising chocolates or CD's or carwashes. Clapping for solos and duets and quartets and ensembles. Cheering for the pit band at the musical. I miss craning my neck to look for the 5'11" girl with the long hair and the big bassoon at the back of the orchestra.

Those times were hectic, too, and we often felt as if we were on a musical ride that would never end. Now I miss listening teary-eyed to a flute melody wafting from my daughter's room, or the high pitch of a piccolo piercing my eardrum. The jazzy sounds of saxophones once played outside my bedroom as if it were a New Orleans street or a French cafe.

I even miss the sheet music in the front hall, the reed making tools all over the floor, her instruments stuffed into the back of our Suzuki jeep, and oh, yeah, can we give Cindy and her cello a ride, too? I miss the broken reeds in the planters, the instrument cases strewn by the front door like barricades, the music stand in the living room between the couch and the love seat. I miss a partner for our piano duets.

Most of all, I miss Rebecca and all that is involved day-to-day with a child who is passionate about music. The silence is as poignant as a Beethoven sonata. The walls reverberate with the remembered notes of etudes, and the first or second parts of fullblown symphonies. Air in the hallway passes through the wind of silver/gold/wood and whispers to me of what is precious and past, of notes alternately sharp or flat or sustained.

I was a music mom, and every dollar of that $5000 per year slipping through nimble fingers was worth it, because you have to follow passion the way you follow a contrapuntal Bach melody: listening for the recurrence of themes, the suggestion of brilliance. With the quality of lasting love weaving in and out...

EMPTYING THE NEST

(Eldest Daughter Moves Out, 2 to Go)

i won't miss the 5 pairs of shoes in the front hall

the clothes drying in the laundry room

all week long until i finally remove them

the eyes rolling as she turns

thinking i don't see that because

i'm so old, so stupid, so--everything!

i won't miss her clutter spread out all over her bedroom floor

and radiating into the rest of the house

the extra charges on the credit card

waiting half-asleep for the front door

to open at 2 am

the unwiped cupboards, the dishes left for me

long after supper has been cleared away

you weren't so great yourself,

my mother reminds me

and i'm beginning to understand why

my mother gave all the photos back

refuses to accept plants as presents

she doesn't want to nurture so much as a leaf anymore

but i will miss that tall body lying beside me in bed

while we watch a video at night

or discuss her latest failed love interest

and how the hell will i ever learn to burn a CD

or install anti-virus

and no matter how much time is now returned to me

how much i love to hear myself think in the much neater quiet

traded for a vibrant young woman's noise

i'll keep wondering if i hugged her enough

if i savoured every passing stage

if i'll recognize myself in her poems

And all too suddenly, the swirling stops. The noise stops. I can hear my thoughts again, and they reverberate against the calm and the quiet. They are loud, my thoughts, loud and strong and sometimes sad. At school the parent group asks me to read at their Book Salon. They are supportive of my writing. At the Book Salon, I read poetry and other pieces, including the following one about noise, which has never seemed more prescient than now.

Noisy, Noiseless Noise

NOISE! Three children talk all at once: can-I-have-more-apple-juice-please-tell-me-another-story-about-when-you-were-a-little-girl-Mommy-look-at-the-elephant-I-made--in-the-centre-of-my-cheese   and   I   answer: once-when-I-was-a-little-girl-here's-your-apple-juice-please-don't-spread-that-cheese-around-any-more-I-stole-one-doll-shoe-from-my-friend...One husband filling my other ear full of penetrating chitchat on the state of the economy and the recent election and his motorcycle maintenance hobby, all delivered into this other ear while the first ear is being filled with the sweet and busy babble of childhood needs and joys.

NOISE! The television or a video blare behind me as I sit at the kitchen table or upstairs at the computer. I hate that television, I am always going around and turning it off. My children don't answer me when it's on and have glazed, unfocused stares when I look at them. Oh, how I am beginning to hate that family on Full House. My family likes the TV on while I talk to them; their eyes wander away from mine to the screen unless I turn that television off, an abrupt and unloving gesture of frustration.

NOISE! The whisper of the whisper-quiet dishwasher, the hum of the frost-free fridge defrosting, the whir of the dryer spinning a week's worth of musty towels or juice-stained children's clothes, the silent noise of our plants begging for water, the muffled snuffles of our dog pleading for food and water, the visual noise of a whole house full of toys which have steadily been overturned and rotated and circulated in ever-widening circles of clutter and disarray.

NOISE! Trapped with three children sick with the flu for two weeks and now they are fighting almost constantly between videos, and sometimes during the videos, and increasingly before the videos they choose to watch even begin, so that I am actually looking forward to going to the dentist by the time the babysitter comes. The call for honeynut cheerios for one, wice cwispies for another a half-hour later, and finally, when the all-day mess of the kitchen is finally tidied up and put away, the third one wants something to eat, too.

NOISE! A five-year-old adolescent learning to exert her independence wailing incessantly in my ears for a half hour, interspersing this siren of sound with I-hate-you's, and dummies, and you-are-so-mean's. And the noise of another child sneaking out to the hall just outside our bedroom, packing up her bed roll and twenty toys and settling down for the night closer to us because she feels someone sitting on her back and watching her at night. The noise of yet another child turning on our bathroom light, peeing, never flushing, and climbing up upon our bed between us, elbowing my ear, hitting my nose, and complaining because she doesn't have a pillow.

The most bittersweet, echoing noise of all, the knowledge that one day all too soon many of these clamorous sounds will be gone, I can talk to myself all I want, and I will miss each and every moment of this raucous, cacophonous symphony of sound just as badly as I now crave the silence.

In my calmer, quieter world, another labour of love is born. My poetry manuscript is accepted by Inanna Publications, and my book of poems, *True Confessions*, is published (Norman, 2005) and then receives the Canadian Jewish Book Award. Inanna is the Sumerian goddess of fertility, love, and war, and it was her duty to light fires and put them out, to cause tears and joy. This mythical goddess seems the perfect hostess for my poems, indicative not only of the birth of my book, but the fierceness it took to keep sending manuscripts out into the atmosphere, despite the hopelessness of rejection. I look up my records and discover it has taken ten years to get this manuscript published! Ten years! A decade! I share the manuscript with a colleague at school, also a writer, and he tells me the disturbing thing about my poems is that it took ten years for them to be published in a book!

By my desk at home, I have a shelf where I toss every writing rejection I have ever received. It is enough to wallpaper at least one room of our house, and that doesn't even include the advent of emailed rejections. It takes stamina to withstand such a barrage of negativity, and there were many times when I wavered, when the encouragement of friends and fellow poets like Carl Leggo was not enough. Carl sat beside me at someone else's poetry launch, listening to the poet's women-centred words, and declared to me, both soothsayer and mentor: You will have a book of poetry published.

This is part of a/r/tography, too, the dark underside of all that knowing, doing, and making. We are pummelled by forces that undermine our art, that make us in our darkest moments question the very purpose of why we engage in such art making. Still I write in the dark, soft language that Margaret Atwood mourns: "Mothertongue Mothertongue Mothertongue/falling one by one back into the moon" (Atwood, 1995, p.54). I pull my selves and the selves of the others with whom I am in relationship back out of the moon, and attempt to un/cover and complicate the relationships we form, hold and lose in the lived curriculum of our worlds: home, school, academy, earth.

And as I pull back out of the moon, I am pulled back out of my reminiscing, into my drama room once again. A new story begins. The children are in-role as detectives unravelling a deep mystery, and Imelda, so quiet, muses aloud with a complexity she rarely displays: Why would so many people be telling the same story? Her simple but profound question takes us into the heart of our drama, into artful inquiry that gives us permission to live, however briefly, other lives, in the powerful and transformative ways of drama. David Booth (2005) writes about this kind of drama and how it moves into areas of significance. Temporarily, significantly, we are carried away on the wind that arts education and a/r/tography blow.

PAULINE SAMESHIMA

AUTOETHNOGRAPHIC RELATIONALITY THROUGH PARADOX, PARALLAX, AND METAPHOR

All you need now is to stand at the window and let your rhythmical sense open and shut, open, and shut, boldly and freely, until one thing melts in another, until the taxis are dancing with the daffodils, until a whole has been made from all these separate fragments... That perhaps is your task—to find the relation between things that seem incompatible yet have a mysterious affinity, to absorb every experience so that your poem is a whole, not a fragment; to rethink human life into poetry. (Virginia Woolf, 1932, p.22)

I like to bake and make things with my hands. Special moments with my children are memories of working together in the kitchen, filling the house with smells of home; going out together and then coming back to the smell of cinnamon buns and apple or pumpkin pie. The aroma holds us; we cannot hold it, only imagine—a drawing together of fragments and memories that make love real. This is the same way I feel about my tile mosaic art practice. I pull together shards from other lives and make something new. The pieces lay down paths to new places. This metaphor further extends to the way I research as an a/r/tographer. I think about connections and situations from multiple frames. I like to dream, to imagine, to write fiction.

PARADOX IN APPLE PIE

the knife easily slides through the white meat

of the tart granny smiths

the peels fall zealously into the sink

coloured happiness haphazardly strewn

discarded shells

shiny and waxed

impenetrable in the natural world

but not immune to me

the knife is sharp

I close my eyes

and blot the dark away

S. Springgay et al. (eds.), Being with A/r/tography, 45–56.

I have to finish before the next song
Jade is getting ready for the recital
she can't remember the notes
she can't see the pattern
how it repeats, only with a tempo change
the speed and rhythm masks
what she has already memorized
what she already knows
I chop faster, throw in the flour, sugar, and cinnamon
never with a recipe
stir it fast
my body knows
I can smell if it's right
no, I need more *zing*

Jade is ready
she's played all the other songs
it's *Winnie the Pooh* that needs my help
I tell her to play it with the sheet music
"don't try to memorize it yet
just keep looking at the notes
and your fingers will begin to remember"
is that true? is that proprioception?
or is it only my body that remembers?
your skin, your touch, your lips
I try to stall her
"play it again
it needs to be perfect, with no mistakes
before you can play it off by heart"
by heart?

I roll out the crust
rich elastic dough, heavy
the edges begin to separate
I patch them but the scars are visible
it fits so perfectly into the pie plate

white Pyrex with a fluted edge
a wedding present
four hundred beautiful smiling faces
happy for the perfect couple
everyone proud
I am alone
Luke silently beside me
always warm and safe
everyone looking on
crystal figurines on a cake
too shiny to touch

I feel the touching now
words baked in the a/r/tographer's heart
cannot hide under skin
bare vulnerability
glistening white peeled exposure
strangers connected through naked texts
heavy wax on my apple skin, against my flesh
I want to wash myself clean, just to breathe
want to be alone

I turn the apples into the shell
they tumble and rest
I dot them with strawberries
they form a mountain over the base

PAULINE SAMESHIMA

I roll out the top crust

it fits like a mask

hiding the flavour of the pie

I flute the edges to further confine the insides

decorating the mask

sharp knife savagely cuts paths for escape

for the pie to exhale

to breathe

put it in the preheated oven

all preplanned

and I sit down with Jade

the *Enchanted Neighbourhood*

is filled with friends

Kanga and Eeyore, Rabbit and Roo

who also don't understand each other

another story

can't see through the crust

can't remember in their bodies

how to harmonize the right notes

how to play the song of love

we only taste

the warm overflowing joy

in apple pie

Writing stories of teaching and living as a researcher in creative and scholastic forms artifices reality, identity, and cultural histories. "Paradox in Apple Pie" illustrates the integrative aspects and unfolding poetic process of relationality through paradox while living as a reflexive researcher. The poem weaves together an embodied aesthetic of living and learning. My own understandings often come through my hands in motion—creating art forms or writing narratives which represent knowing or help me to come to understandings. When my body is in motion, I come to realizations: while gliding on the ice in the warm up of an ice-hockey game, going through deep concentration at the barre in my dance shoes, or even methodically kneading bread dough, my body and mind seek relational connection. I learn in my head what my body already recognizes (see Sameshima, 2006). The act of motion, touch, and manipulation produces a movement toward acknowledgement of the unexpressed known in both physical and metaphoric ways.

The relational act is the discovery of intersections of recognition, and acknowledges a creative site of learning which rests between the various roles, actions, and activities lived through and in by a/r/tographers. Learning becomes the act of knitting experiences together, webbing the various degrees of separation and using the experiences themselves as discourse. Relationality-as-learning is connecting with the other by distinguishing reflection in the other. Relationality-as-teaching is providing a broad mirror in which the other is reflected. By articulating the recognition, living in the transactional divide with an embodied aesthetic, and courageously and continually traversing liminal spaces, emotional and provocative connections can be made. Through emotion, the body is evoked and deep learning and synergistic possibilities arise. Learning becomes the act of the personal becoming public, and locating situatedness within a perceived whole.

Jacques Daignault, a poststructural curriculum theorist, says: "we can write something about teaching, the teacher, and education entitled 'Teaching' without saying a word about these" (quoted in Hwu, 1993, p.166). Teaching and learning occur everywhere, not only in the classroom. Learning occurs in the in-between spaces of liminality, between the lines of this poem, between the ideas and in the connections holding home and school, between the identities of mother and researcher, between fiction and non-fiction, between past and present. Daignault believes pedagogy and curriculum exist between theory and practice. Curriculum is thus the liminal space.

Learning is the movement of travelling along the fringe—navigating between the poetic spaces, not seeking a merging but being sensitized to difference and travelling the contoured, fractaling edges of living. Daignault believes the "gap" between perceived dichotomies is the curriculum and that "thinking is the incarnation of curriculum as composition" (quoted in Hwu, 1993, p.172). Curriculum understood as composition allows "a participation" in "continuing creation". The *in-between* (Ellsworth, 1997; Irwin, 2004; Minh-ha, 1999), the *third space of enunci*ation (Bhabha, 1994), and the *silence* (Ulmer, 1983) become curriculum once encountered and articulated (see Sameshima, in press; Sameshima & Irwin, 2006). Through attentive motion within relational spaces, embodied epistemologies can be realized.

A/r/tography is a pedagogy for artistry—the art of researching, teaching, and learning in the creative, relational, generative spaces of intra/inter-personal multiplicity. Living a/r/tographic inquiry is situating and accepting self as a continuous burgeoning being. This chapter provides examples of my conception of a/r/tography as autoethnoGRAPHIC relationality through connected spaces of paradox, parallax, and metaphor.

PAULINE SAMESHIMA

AutoethnoGRAHIC Relationality

The adjective *graphic* is concerned with vivid detail in written and visual representation. The phrase *AutoethonoGRAPHIC Relationality* is thus writing and rendering autobiography and ethnography in vivid detail braiding all aspects of living, learning, researching, and teaching in context. Carl Leggo (2005) explains:

> I write autobiographically as a way to know myself and others in words and in the world. The writing is part of living, a way to understand, a way to stand in the world, a way to wisdom even...My poems are journeys or performances in language. The person is always only a location where language works to reveal awareness and embodiment and identity. (p.116)

Laurel Richardson and Elizabeth St. Pierre describe the writing act as a method of inquiry. Richardson (2005) suggests that:

> Language is a constitutive force, creating a particular view of reality and of the self... Social scientific writing, like all other forms of writing, is sociohistorical construction and therefore is mutable...Language is how social organization and power are defined and contested and the place where one's sense of self—one's subjectivity—is constructed. Understanding language as competing discourses—competing ways of giving meaning and of organizing the world—makes language a site of exploration and struggle. (pp.960-961)

Richardson (2000, 2005) names ethnographic narrative genres Creative Analytical Processes (CAP) which describe many different reflexive narrative forms. These forms include, for instance: poetry, performance autoethnography, short stories, conversations, fiction, personal narrative, creative nonfiction, photographic essays, personal essays, fragmented or layered texts, and more (see Denzin, 2005, p.946). Critical personal narratives, performance texts, stories, and accounts which disrupt and disturb discourse by exposing the complexities and paradoxes that exist under official history are a central genre of contemporary decolonizing writing (Matua & Swadener, 2004). As creative analytic practice, these personal counternarratives are used to critique "prevailing structures and relationships of power and inequity in a relational context" (p.16).

Norman Denzin (2005) claims that the "utopian counternarrative offers hope, showing others how to engage in actions that decolonize, heal, and transform" (p. 947). He explains how poetry can embrace the critical democratic storytelling imagination. The storytelling imagination opens up the hopeful notions of peaceful and nonviolent change, which understands hope, like freedom, as "an ontological need" (Freire, 1992/1999, p.8). Denzin (2005) in his writing of emancipatory discourse argues:

> The critical democratic storytelling imagination is pedagogical. As a form of instruction, it helps persons think critically, historically, and sociologically. It exposes the pedagogies of oppression that produce injustice (see Freire, 2001, p.54). It contributes to reflective ethical self-consciousness. It gives

people a language and set of pedagogical practices that turn oppression into freedom, despair into hope, hatred into love, doubt into trust. (p.948)

Richardson and St. Pierre maintain that "CAP ethnographies are not alternative or experimental: they are, in and of themselves, valid and desirable representations of the social". They go on to say that "in the foreseeable future, these ethnographies may indeed be the most desirable representations because they invite people in and open spaces for thinking about the social that elude us now" (2005, p.961). Pedagogic relationality and the transformative potential of research rest in the quality of evocative GRAPHIC renderings of research—that is to say that research must be presented in provocative forms in order to move the reader/viewer.

William Ayers (1988) believes educators hold a particular responsibility for self-awareness, clarity, and integrity because they are in powerful positions to witness, influence, and shepherd the choices of others. Ardra Cole and Gary Knowles (2000) suggest that making sense of experiences and understanding personal-professional connections is the essence of professional development. These researchers purport that through personal life-history exploration, teachers make known implicit theories, values, and beliefs that underpin teaching and being a teacher. Connections between experiences, subsequent assumptions, and how these assumptions play out consciously or unconsciously, inform and influence pedagogic practice.

A/r/tographers are continuously in processes of artful crafting, creative researching, and attentive teaching, through ongoing narrative stories of living. Knowles (2004) believes that "by honouring the metaphorical and geographical places where we each dwell, work, and recreate, greater understandings of self in relation to a complex world can be had" (p.1). Through creative constructions which enable and acknowledge experiences as "encounters" of significance and mindful awareness of self "steeping" in context, every instance of living becomes a pedagogic possibility as relational understandings are revealed and expressed.

Relationality through Parallax

Our depth is the thickness of our body, our all touching itself. Where top and bottom, inside and outside, in front and behind, above and below are not separated, remote, out of touch. Our all intermingled. Without breaks or gaps. (Irigaray, 1985, p.213)

Parallax comes from the Greek work *parallagé* which means "alteration" and from *parallassein* which means "to change". Parallax is the apparent shift of an object against a background due to a change in observer position or perspective shift. When seen or experienced from one viewpoint an object may appear to be in front of a particular background. When the standpoint of the viewer is changed to another perspective, the same object very likely will appear in context within a different background. Depending on the angle of view, the object thus appears situated in front of different backgrounds or even embedded within different contexts. Translated to pedagogy, the concept of parallax encourages teachers and researchers to acknowledge the power of their own shifting subjectivities and situatedness, as well as to value and acknowledge learners' perspectives and experiences which directly influence the constructs conceptualized in learning. There is never one truth. The articulation of truths and meanings in teaching and the presentation of research is story telling, thus the more stories told, the greater our fullness of understanding.

The following poem, "Mixed Contexts", provides an example of parallax. The stories which unravel in my eyes are from my perspective; they are not the stories of these people—I develop my own truth. This concept, taken to the classroom—to value, assume, and be open to multiple stand points—suggests a re-evaluation of all assessment procedures based on confining single story lines and predetermined perspectives of truth.

MIXED CONTEXTS

The top's down, hot sun on my thighs, lip gloss smooth, life surreal

Wind gently sliding around my neck, Luke dashing in shades, children laughing

After outdoor swimming lessons, on our way home

Tomorrow is hat day in the pool, Savannah tells Jade to wear her bike helmet

A middle-aged overweight woman is cutting her grass, not lawn, long high

Yellow, over-dry and going to seed, an untended overgrown wildness like her

Or simply natural in another location

No way the electric lawnmower will cut through all the years they haven't kissed

She's trapped, stuck and alone in the tall tall grass leaning into her

What happened to the man she loved on her wedding night?

Down the road

A thin hunchbacked sun-parched man in a white undershirt

Contemplates the contents of his recycling bin close to the curb of the busy street

His driveway is decorated with lonely dry grass and effervescent weeds

Forcing their way through the cracks

His slippers worn, his cigarette his hollow pleasure

Where is she, the young girl with the moist lips he laughed with so long ago?

Another man rides his bicycle, upright, no helmet, loose short sleeves button shirt

Dress pants, leather sandals, oblivious to the traffic

In the world on Al Jareau's CD cover, he's on a hard packed dirt road, dust in his toes

Summer stillness, silent droughted grass on the side of the path, straight to his love

Displaced locations, strangeness, wrong places and wrong times

Turning 360 degrees alone and still not seeing

Never finding home, never feeling completely home

all the stories sink with our indebtedness into earth

to reach our belonging, to fade the surreal sharpness

and soothe the colour of context, of what is real, truth, important

Relationality through Metaphor

Whenever a poet employs a figure or story previously accepted and defined by a culture, the poet is using myth, and the potential is always present that the use will be revisionist: that is, the figure or tale will be appropriated for altered ends, the old vessel filled with new wine, initially satisfying the thirst of the individual poet but ultimately making cultural change possible. (Ostriker, 1985, p.42)

The following letter is an excerpt from my epistolary novel, *Seeing Red: A Pedagogy of Parallax* (Sameshima, 2006). The letters in this novel are written from a student to the professor with whom she is in love. The letter shares relationality through metaphor as a form of living inquiry practice. Joseph Campbell (1972), in *Myths to Live By,* claims that myths actually extend human potential. Knowles (1994) has looked extensively at metaphors for understanding the complexity of teaching and working in classrooms. He cites the research by Hunt (1987), Miller and Fredericks (1988), Munby and Russell (1989), and Woodlinger (1989) on metaphors as productive means to understanding teaching; and the work by Cole (1990a; 1990b) and Bullough, Knowles, and Crow (1991) on looking at metaphors to provide insight into conceptions of teacher identities. More recently, the work by Gail Matthews (2005) provides insight into the arts as a metaphor for learning about the teaching self. Lakoff and Johnson (1980) suggest that metaphors not only make our thoughts more vivid and interesting but that they actually structure our perceptions and understanding. Furthermore, they tout that "no metaphor can ever be comprehended or even adequately represented independently of its experiential basis" (p.19) pointing to the fact that metaphors both presented by the user and interpreted by the reader always present ambiguity and thus provide openings for learning. This letter and tile mosaic titled "Golem's Seduction" follow Campbell's vein of thought—that ancient legends and universal tales continue to influence our daily lives.

Dear Red,

I am most intrigued about sense of place, belonging, location and what you said about desire being rooted in location. David Wisniewski's (1996) *Golem,* winner of the 1997 Caldecott Award, is a beautiful picture book I read to my Grade 3/4 class today. The artwork is all cut paper. In the book jacket, Wisniewski writes about historian Jay Gonen who observed in his book, *Psychohistory of Zionism* that, like the Golem, Israel was created to protect the physical safety of Jews. I've been thinking that a sense of belonging is feeling that we fill a space: the teacher as the healer, filling the wounds (pedagogically unhealthy); or nations fighting for land. Finding a place to fill for some reason presents a sense of power. Seeking place and space is connected to the ephemeral feeling of belonging too. Maybe belonging is really recognizing responsibility and obligation to the other. I'm confused about how you feel about me. Why do I so desperately want to belong to you? I know you love me, but you don't make me feel like I belong. Is it because I am a student; I can't be responsible *for* you, only *to* you? We are so separated by role. You say you adore me so why do I doubt you? What part of the body is the "feeling" heart in?

Golem's Seduction. 2005. Pauline Sameshima. tile mosaic, 51"x 35". Courtesy of the artist.

This mosaic is "Golem's Seduction." It's finally done and I'm exhausted without any sense of accomplishment. This one had to be made. The art speaks for itself and I know you won't like it because we both can't face the truth of it. Originally, I was intrigued by the 16th century myth of Golem. There are many versions of this story. The most popular version is the Golem, who was made of clay from the River Moldau, as a servant and protector of the Jews by Rabbi Loew of Prague. Golem was much like an android under the control of his maker but he began to yearn for more, seeking independence. There are other versions of Golem. Adam is the most ancient—also created from the earth. Then there's Frankenstein and Gepetto's wooden son, Pinocchio. Others refer to the romantic analogy of Golem as the novel and the rabbi as the novelist. Michael Chabon writes, "Golem-making is dangerous; like all major creation it endangers the life of the creator—the source of danger, however, is not the Golem…but the man himself" (2000, p.1). In this metaphor, I am the Golem and also the Golem-maker. You see, Golem was brought to life by enchantment. Enchantment is incantation, spell-making, which has to do with language, writing. Is that how I fell in love with you? Did we construct our love through the words we've written to each other?

In some stories of Golem, the name of God is inscribed on Golem's forehead or shoulder, or written on a tablet and tucked under the Golem's tongue (I've hidden a red tile under the grout on the shoulder of the Golem). The Jewish Golem is mute and follows written directions placed in the mouth. If you look carefully at the mosaic, you'll see that the eyes are made from the same tile as the message in the mouth. My Golem can only see the world through the words and eyes of her maker.

I struggled with this piece. I saw an image similar to this by artist Barbara McDermott, but I didn't like it completely because her Golem was very ugly. I wanted to make the Golem story a metaphor for us. I wanted to evoke the love and care of the advisor for a fragile mentee but the materials, both my hands and the tile, would not allow that face to emerge. I liked McDermott's maker—eyes in shadow, like the blinded professor; hands too small to hold the protégé—loving cradle and good intentions all gone awry as the student becomes simultaneously dependent baby with a soother, fragile Madonna, and frightful despair, her mouth open revealing the words of her advisor and reflected in her unseeing eyes. There is a haunting pain and unrest in this piece. I cannot look at the baby. Why? Is it because I do not want to see myself?

We are like this, Red. I know you love me. I know you care about me. Look at the red tiles. They are a lot thinner so the hands look like they are depressing the swaddled Golem; it looks like the advisor is applying too much pressure on the student. I am confined in your hold and by your words. I want to see with my own eyes. I want to love you without needing you. I don't think we can "fix" anything. I just need to finish the dissertation like you've been saying all along. I need to graduate and change my role.

I wonder if the struggle in my art is about truth. I had to rework the student's face several times and always, the monster came out, so I let it rest like that. Maybe that's what the truth is for me. This piece also makes me think of Savannah. When I love her too tightly, she cries out in rebellion; how do I hold her so she knows my love but also feels her independence? How do I teach my students—trying to walk between challenging and provoking but not frustrating and discouraging?

Here's something also by Chabon (2000). He's talking about the Golem in terms of writing. He's talking about the fear I have about us, the story I'm writing of you as my dissertation, how I feel our story is growing out of control, constructing my own truths that can't possibly be true, truths you can't see or even imagine. How can I love you the way I do?

> If the writer submits his work to an internal censor long before anyone else can get their hands on it, the result is pallid, inanimate, a lump of earth. The adept handles the rich material, the rank river clay, and diligently intones his alphabetical spells, knowing full well the history of golems: how they break free of their creators, grow to unmanageable size and power, refuse to be controlled. In the same way, the writer shapes his story, flecked like river clay with the grit of experience and rank with the smell of human life, heedless of the danger to himself, eager to show his powers, to celebrate his mastery, to bring into being a little world that, like God's, is at once terribly imperfect and filled with astonishing life. (p.2)

I don't know how to be with you, Red. Tell me, professor. Teach me how to be.
Love Julia

Paradox, parallax, and metaphor provide insight into the relationality of living in the borderlands as an artful researcher teacher. Rita Irwin (in press) says that the arts offer practices that are inherently liminal because they highlight taken-for-granted experiences or conversely, make strange experiences seem familiar. They open up possibilities for different insights and thus expand notions of scholarly inquiry. Paradox, parallax, and metaphor encourage and enable new perspectives and insights for analysing and representing research in "a polyphony of lines of movement that grow in the abundance of middles, the "betweens" and "AND"; which resounds in aparallel polyphony that refuses closure—lines that refuse synthesis into a symphonic unity;" and which is a "textured landscape always in flux, a landscape of multiple possibilities in a shifting web of nomadic lines of movement" (Aoki, 1992, in Pinar & Irwin, 2005, p.271). Paradox, parallax, and metaphor portray the complexities of the human condition through relationality with "words plump and dripping with life juice, compelling and evocative images, [and] representations that [draw] readers and viewers in to experience the research 'text'" (Cole, 2004, p.16).

ERIKA HASEBE-LUDT, CYNTHIA CHAMBERS,
ANTOINETTE OBERG AND CARL LEGGO

EMBRACING THE WORLD,
WITH ALL OUR RELATIONS:
MÉTISSAGE AS AN ARTFUL BRAIDING

INTRODUCTION

What is métissage? The word comes from the Latin *mixtus* meaning *mixed*, like a cloth of different fibres. The Greek homonym is *metis* who, in Greek mythology, was a figure of skill and craft, as well as wisdom and intelligence (Harper, 2001). Metis was the wife of Zeus, and she was gifted with powers of transformation. So, the original Latin meaning of *mixtus* gives métissage the property of mixing, and its Greek correlate suggests the power to transform. Thus, as an idea and a practice, métissage opposes the easy transparency and clarity of concepts; some would say that, like the wife of Zeus, métissage has the power to undo logic.

Métissage is not only a theory but also a praxis (Lionnet, 1989; Zuss, 1997). It is a thoughtful *political* practice that resists "heterophobia" (Memmi cited in Lionnet, 1989), or the fear of mixing, and the desire for a pure untainted space, language, or form of research. What does *métissage* look like in practice? In our chapter, we focus on mixing oral renditions of text—(autobiographical) fragments that arise from our own lived experiences.

In this chapter, we perform our ongoing collaborative and individual inquiry about our relationships with/in the world. Through this inquiry, we ask questions about notions of difference in the local and global surroundings we inhabit and how these differences affect our kinship with others—students, teachers, family members, animate and inanimate forms—and with discourses and curricula of (in)difference. To these ends, we weave together our autobiographical texts, creating a *métissage* that simultaneously locates points of affinity while also remaining mindful of differences in context, history, and memory. Our performance illustrates *métissage* as a research praxis and illuminates issues and challenges that *métissage* offers educational research.

S. Springgay et al. (eds.), Being with A/r/tography, 57–68.

We mix binaries such as colonized with colonizer, local with global, East with West, North with South, particular with universal, feminine with masculine, vernacular with literate, and theory with practice. We braid strands of place and space, memory and history, ancestry and (mixed) race, language and literacy, familiar and strange, with strands of tradition, ambiguity, becoming, (re)creation, and renewal into a *métissage*.

Métissage offers a rapprochement between alternative and mainstream curriculum discourses and seeks a genuine exchange among the writers, and between the writers and their various audiences. Our aim is to go out into the world, to embrace it and love it fiercely (Arendt, 1958; Galeano, 1991), always returning home with the gifts of new knowledge, new hope that it is possible to live well in a particular place, at this time, with ourselves and with all our relations (King, 1990).

Working collaboratively with the concept of *métissage*, we mix our texts with the intention of creating dialogues between and across different educational sites and discourses. As scholars and writers located in Canada, we come together from blends of differing cultures, including Dene, Canadian, American, German, and Cree, and we work in differing genres, including narrative and poetic. In keeping with the aesthetic nature of our writing, our intention is to weave our texts together artfully to produce a *métissage* of autobiographical research writing. But our aim is not only aesthetic. Like Hannah Arendt, we believe "it is not generality but the multiplicity of particularity that accounts for the possibility of critical understanding" (Disch, 1996, p.160). We mix and braid issues and topics that arise out of our individual and collaborative interests and praxis.

FIRST BRAID

Carl: The Grasshopper Jumps

Last summer while visiting family in Newfoundland, I wrote a poem titled "Alex Faulkner". My wife Lana and I had recently received the dreadful news that Lana's father had been rushed to the hospital, and would not likely live through the night. Family rushed from Richmond and Vancouver on the Pacific Ocean to be with Lana's father in Newfoundland on the coast of the North Atlantic. Lana's father survived, and now as I write this, he and my mother-in-law are visiting us in Richmond for Christmas. Life is full of wonders, mysterious, always in process, indecipherable. I write poetry in order to acknowledge that I will never know much, that autobiographical agnosticism is steeped in humility, an earthy confession of dependence and vulnerability. In all my writing I locate scraps and fragments like flotsam floating in the currents of the oceans, finding from time to time, all the time, unpredicted, even unpredictable, connections—a dizzying proliferation of ecological connections. Because writing is always both a personal and a social act, autobiographical writing is especially connected to lively relationships of family and kin and community and culture. Writing about our lives, our personal and emotional experiences, inevitably generates lines of connection that hold us fast in the heart's rhythms.

the grasshopper

jumps, bumps

into my leg, tumbles

head over heels, somersaults

like a Cirque du Soleil artist,

perhaps just for the fun of it

ALEX FAULKNER

the first Newfoundlander to play in the NHL

was Alex Faulkner, and one time I stood in line,

a long time, outside the CBC in Corner Brook,

for his autograph, sure the Detroit Red Wings were

the greatest hockey team that ever played,

and when I told Aaron and Nicholas how great

Faulkner was, they nodded politely at

the tattered memory of my imagination

and last summer while bussing across Newfoundland

from one coast to another, Nicholas read

The Central Newfoundland Tourist & Shoppers Guide

and learned what happens to hockey greats after hockey,

slipped me a folded scrap of paper, like a secret,

an advert for the Beothuck Family & RV Park:

A Great Quite Family oriented Park to Relax

Owned and Operated by Alex Faulkner

The First Newfoundland NHL Player

6 foot water slide RV Dumping Station

(no punctuation between slide and RV Dumping, only

the image of sliding 6 feet into what RV's dumped)

and while I flinched with another stab of sadness for

Beothuck families who will never stay in Alex Faulkner's park,

my first thought was the predictable punctilious response

of an old English teacher: Alex needs a better editor

Erika: Berlin Myths

Berlin was the first place I moved to after I left home—West Berlin, that is, when it was still divided by the Wall. I went there to study and moved in with my fiancé. Four years later, I left Berlin with a degree, a scholarship to Canada, and without a fiancé.

After I had moved a continent away I was homesick for Berlin. I missed that city more than my home town—the western part, that is—its cosmopolitan flair mixed with monuments of Prussian Empire and Saxony history and culture. I longed to be back in Berlin's wide-open plazas, in *Charlottenburg* and its chateau; I missed the neighbourhood streets and the abundance of water. I remembered the destruction too, the ruins of churches and homes over two world wars. I had lived next to the Berlin Wall, but I was filled with an idealistic belief in the victory of democracy in the face of socialism gone wrong. I believed in a future of forgiveness, restoration and reunification, and my memory was all about that.

I made a new life in Canada, but I left my heart in Berlin, seduced by its global glamour and local charm and the city's place in the grand narrative of European history. It could have been me humming that popular tune by Marlene Dietrich, "Ich hab' noch einen Koffer in Berlin" (Dietrich, 2003). I still *had* a suitcase in Berlin, and my story slipped smoothly into Marlene's song about how everyone who leaves Berlin always yearns to return. Except that I didn't have Marlene Dietrich's voice. I didn't even have my own voice.

Cynthia: The North Star

There was this white guy sitting in his 1956 Buick. He pulled into the asphalt driveway beside his two-storey Tudor home in Shaunghnessy, an old swanky neighbourhood in Vancouver. His eldest daughter sat beside him, the plastic seat covers sticking to the back of her bare legs. That girl was from his first marriage, visiting him while his new family was on holiday in England. Usually that white girl lived up north with her mother.

Now that girl sat on the front seat of that 1956 Buick as still as a dog who senses danger just beyond the range of possibly of doing anything about it. And just like that dog knows better than to chase after trouble, that girl knew it wasn't time to open the car door and run.

That white guy started to yell at his eldest daughter, "What kind of girl lies out on the front lawn in a bathing suit?" Up north, sun tanning was what Annette Funicello and Frankie Avalon did at the Saturday matinee, when they weren't playing Beach Blanket Bingo. Now up north, mosquitoes and black flies made lounging in a bikini suicide. So when that white girl got to Vancouver she couldn't wait to sunbathe on a manicured lawn, with no bugs, just like Annette Funicello.

That girl kept her body real still. Like that dog who feels danger within striking range. And like that dog, that girl knew that instead of a stranger, sometimes it's the hand of the master you fear.

Now that 1956 Buick was parked in the dark. Glancing to the left, without turning her head, that white girl caught the fluorescent glow of a streetlamp reflected off the side of that white guy's face. Finally, he looked right at her and said:

"If you ever marry a Jew or a nigger, I'll kill you."

That white girl she waited until she felt safe to move and heaved the door open. She looked up into the wet night sky and that white girl she wanted to rise up and float over the house and the streetlamps, ride those city lights like the Chute-de-Chute water ride at the exhibition, and fly up over the mountains. Buoyed by the sea-salty air, she imagined herself floating through the clouds to the North Star. Once she found that star, then she knew she could find her way home. Instead, that white girl, she dropped her head and carefully picked her way across the wet asphalt to the still dark house. Waiting.

Antoinette: The Story I Tell

"What made you decide to leave the university? You're too young to retire." Once again I launch into the story I have refined through many tellings. "I met with a financial advisor...He asked me when I planned to retire...I said I hadn't thought about it...He said it was feasible any time...I felt an enticing unknown open up in front of me and I decided to walk into it."

SECOND BRAID

Carl: The Grasshopper Bumps

the grasshopper

jumps, bumps

into my leg, tumbles

head over heels, somersaults

like a Cirque du Soleil artist,

perhaps just for the fun of it

now we have all gathered in the hospital where Pop

is on a ventilator, propped up in bed, in forest green

pyjamas with a maroon trim like Hugh Hefner wears,

glad he is still alive, surprising himself and all of us

Sterling just dropped in, and Pop begins to tell

him a story about Jack Gullage who was in the bed

in the opposite corner, and was released this morning,

but we are now ten huddled around the bed, and nobody

can hear anybody, even if we've run out of things to say

and when Cliff asks Pop how he is, Pop holds

up the oxygen line, *I'm tied on too short*

and the nurses and assistants and doctors,

everybody with clipboards, come and go

like they are rehearsing for guest spots on *ER*

and none of us knows anything, so we make up

explanations and scenarios, more TV fictions

Erika: History Lessons

Recently, I read about the bombing of Berlin, its people's suffering during Hitler's Third Reich, and the building of the Wall during the Cold War (Bullock, 1952/1990; Hargittay, 2004). In *A Chorus of Stones* (1992), Susan Griffin writes about the psychological effects of war on her own and others' families, and the horrors of pre-meditated acts of destruction.

It has been over 25 years since I lived in Berlin. Reading these accounts and rereading my own writing after leaving Germany, I came to see Berlin and myself differently. I learned about my own ignorance of much of European history and began to see "the void at the heart of twentieth-century Europe" (Sebald, 2001).

Moving to Canada, I found the voices of others whose histories were not part of my limited Eurocentric education. Among them are writers and poets like Thomas King and Thomson Highway, Leonard Cohen, Margaret Laurence, and Margaret Atwood. They tell personal stories within the grand narrative of colonization and speak with wisdom about the importance of memory and myth. They write about the inconsolable sorrow of history and the sadness of geography, about the significance of attending to relations.

All these relations have taught me about how borders, like the Berlin Wall, always contain within themselves a trace of the other that constitutes the difference within. The stories of the separated families created an ambiguous territory on either side of the Berlin Wall and made it impossible "to think about identity as a homogenous and self-enclosed totality" (Borradori, 2003, p.147)—whether it be the lives of individuals or the lives of nations. These stories made it possible, after all, for the Wall to come down.

Cynthia: The Wedding

Now that white girl, she found her way back home but she never forgot what that white guy in the 1956 Buick said. She lived in Yellowknife, Northwest Territories and there she fell in love with a Métis boy—not much older than herself. And she was only seventeen. So that white girl and that Métis boy, they got married in the Catholic Church and that white girl she had to wear a girdle so the baby coming didn't show so much. And she didn't even think to invite that white guy in the 1956 Buick to the wedding.

And there was a big Catholic wedding and everyone ate bannock and roasted caribou meat at the Legion Hall. And that white girl, her mother was real worried about the new Indian relatives and how they might all be drunk and raise hell at the reception. But she didn't have to worry because at the reception it was that white girl's grandmother who got into the rye and ginger and then she was up on the dance floor jigging and jiving with anyone who'd have her. And that white girl's mother didn't say another word about the new Indian relatives.

Now...even though that guy was Métis; he was a Treaty Indian, too. So he was Métis and Indian. Craziest thing. Ever since those treaties and that Indian Act, this business of who's an Indian—and who's not—is very complicated. So when that white girl married that Métis boy, she became an Indian and she got herself a Treaty card. And when that white girl and that Métis boy had babies, they were Indians too and they had treaty cards; blue-eyed, mind you, and they didn't speak a word of anything but English, and their nicknames were kw'et'izha, little white boys.

So these two families were kind of mixed up. And that Métis boy, he loved his mother something fierce. "My mother is a saint", he used to tell his new wife.

And then his mother, the saint, and his new wife, they became best friends and they loved each other more than anything—more than their own husbands, if the truth were to be told. And that Métis woman she taught that young white girl how to sew and make bannock and dry meat. She told that young girl stories about how the world was made and what happened a long time ago when the world was new, when the people got their language and their laws, and when they could still talk to the animals. And she taught that white girl to speak a new language. And then when she put her arm around that young girl's shoulders, frozen with eighteen years of hard living, she taught that young white girl about love, about letting others carry your burdens for awhile, and about faith. That woman taught that white girl to believe that no matter what, spring thaw comes every year to the land and to our hearts.

Antoinette: The Untold Story

As I reflect on this story of being enticed by unknown possibility, I am compelled to question its truth. Is the lure of the unknown so strong that I would choose it over the comfort of the status, income, and fulfilment that I have had as a university professor? When I ask that question, I have to admit there is another untold story running parallel to the one I have been telling. This other story is very similar to one told by Canadian Women's Studies professor, Kathleen Rockhill. (1986) Her story is a passionate analysis of the existential splitting she suffered between her "sense of self and what she saw as demanded…in an academic world that prided itself on its intellectual excellence" (p.12).

Rockhill's words resonate for me. I too have lived a split—between the manner of inquiring that I practice and teach, and the mode of inquiry that is dominant in my corner of the academy. My manner of carrying forward understanding in both research and teaching has been to act first and reflect second. Reflecting occurs through a practice of emergent writing, which is writing in a place of non-judgment from the midst of unknowing without a predictable outcome. This sort of reflective writing becomes a means whereby awareness is extended. Affiliating with discourses of emergence, unpredictability, not knowing, and non-judgment has put me in opposition to the normative teleological discourses of research in the university that dictate that theory shall precede practice. Professors usually shun emergent writing, considering it at best preparatory to legitimate academic writing and at worst narcissistic.

I have never dared to write about this split, to write, as Rockhill says, "from my heart, from my body as well as my mind, from the life that I know best, the one I have lived" (p.12). I have never dared to admit, as Rockhill does, how "all that passion dries up, gets blocked, locked in my back, constricted in my throat, as I face this blank page" (p.12). Now, emboldened by her courage, I am ready to admit, along with her, that there is something "that is not said which… must be said, if we are to understand how our subjectivities are framed and constricted, and even, for some, like me, deadened by academic forms" (p.12). I make this move neither to defend nor to try to safeguard the manner of inquiring that I practice, but rather with the aim of telling a different story, one in which opposition is transformed into an alternative that is not a compromise, but something altogether different.

EMBRACING THE WORLD WITH ALL OUR RELATIONS

THIRD BRAID

Carl: The Grasshopper Tumbles

the grasshopper
jumps, bumps
into my leg, tumbles
head over heels, somersaults
like a Cirque du Soleil artist,
perhaps just for the fun of it

Michael Crummey's new novel *The Wreckage*
lies on the window ledge

as I watch people in the parking lot, far below,
I ask Nicholas, *Do you think this is what God sees*
when he looks down at us scurrying here and there

but Nicholas growls, *Don't make me come down there,*
and I like that line, a lot, and according to Pablo Picasso cited
on a stamp in my moleskin journal like Hemingway wrote in
(according to the sign in the Nikaido shop in Steveston),
There's nothing more difficult than a line

and I determine I will commit whatever life I might have left
to body-building and joy and writing zigzags
in the sharp brokenness all around me like shards of glass
holding fast the light from inside the moon

Erika: Vancouver Stories

Vancouver, Canada, with its mixed races and cultures, has been called "the face of the future of Canada, of the world" (Wong, 2004). My family lives here—the one I married into, Canadian Japanese *sansei* (3rd generation) husband, Canadian Japanese German *hapa* (mixed Eurasian) daughter. My other family—the one I was born into, still lives in my birth place of Saarbrücken. Ever since I left home, I have been writing about notions of belonging in relation to the métissage of stories in these places.

A recent CBC (Canadian Broadcasting Corporation) documentary presented a collage of the mixed stories that Vancouver is writing. This city is setting the trend, the pitch for the stories goes, for a new reality of cultural and racial diversity in Canada, a new discourse that constitutes a way through the dogma and dilemmas that still reside in many classrooms and communities.

In the documentary, Ron Yamauchi (2005) talks about the difference between his own growing up in a Vancouver defined by racism and the new reality of his children and their peers, for whom being *hapa* is hopeful and heartful. Could it be that this city, coming out of a troubled history, is learning the lessons that matter? Could it be that a new generation, with its fluid identities and fused narratives—of bangra dance blended with hip hop, of sushi infused with West Coast cuisine, of *Gung Haggis Fat Choy*, the Asian Scottish Canadian Robbie Burns Chinese New Year celebration, of the highest national percentage of mixed race marriages—*is* making a difference? Could it be that students and teachers in schools, through their determination to address contentious issues of racial and other discrimination, are changing Vancouver from a city of solitudes into a city of courageous children?

A call for transformation always originates from specific geographic locations and their unique narratives. But these stories reach out to a larger cosmos through their power to question dominant discourses (Davidson, Walton, & Andrews, 2003, p.28). They critique ideologies of indifference and homogeneity and confirm the "ethical value of heterogeneity and difference" (Borradori, 2003). We need more narratives like the one Vancouver is beginning to tell. This new ethos of mixed narratives holds the promise of freedom, equity, and humanity.

The Métis Cherokee-Greek Canadian writer Thomas King (2003) challenges us: "If we change the stories we live by, quite possibly we change our lives…The truth about stories is that there are no truths… only stories" (p.154; p.326). These new stories, like my students' and my daughter's, fill me with hope. The truth is that they are changing me and they are changing the face of Vancouver, of Canada, of the world.

Cynthia: The Rosary

Years later, that white girl and that Métis boy they couldn't keep all that trouble that comes from mixing everything up. And years after that, after those blue-eyed Métis boys and their brown-eyed *apitaw* (half-Cree; half-European) sister were all grown up and having kids of their own, that old Métis woman sent for that white girl; asked her to come and visit one last time.

So when that old Métis lady phoned, that white woman flew the two thousand miles back home to Yellowknife, and she took a cab straight to the hospital. Late that night, when all the visitors were gone, and the fear of dying crept in, that old lady called her friend, "Secha", which means "daughter-in-law" and "granddaughter". She asked, "Secha, say the rosary with me." And that white woman said, "Okay, setsi" which means "Mother-in-law or grandmother". So those two women picked up the beads, and that old Métis lady said, "You lead because I don't know the words in English". And Secha picked up the beads and she started the rosary as best she could, not being Catholic and all. And when they were done, that white woman helped that old lady to the toilet. And right there on the toilet, that old lady looked at her friend and said, "Secha, I have always loved you. No one can ever take that away from us."

And then that white woman knew that when she followed that North Star home, many years ago, it was the right trail even if sometimes it was crooked and rocky and just hard travelling...like now when her best friend, her grandmother and her teacher was going on ahead, leaving that white girl and everyone else to carry on as best they could. And then that white woman knew that she was the grandmother now and it was her turn to tell the stories about where we come from and what those places mean, not that she could ever tell the stories like her grandmother, because for that old lady they weren't just stories, they were real.

And that white guy in the 1956 Buick, well he's old now, really old; a grandfather many times and a great grandfather, too. And he walks more slowly, talks not so rough. And that white woman grew up to see that the old white guy has his own stories and so she asks for those stories, too; so she can pass them onto her grandchildren, her brown grandchildren, the ones that old white guy does not know how to love.

Antoinette: The Transformation

Now, the moment at which I might expect a transformative experience to begin and a new story to emerge, I realize that something unexpected has happened: the transformation has already largely occurred. Acknowledging the nature of my own research and teaching practice and its difference from the dominant discourse has defused the opposition I have allowed for so long to dominate my life and shape my subjectivity as a university professor. By means of the writing undertaken for this project, my oppositionary stance has been transformed into one where I now feel that I can embrace the contraries and heal the split.

This transformation did not happen in the space of a few minutes, or perhaps it did. Likely it took two decades of reflective writing for the moment of the shift to arrive. As always happens when writing in a place of non-judgment from the midst of unknowing without a predictable outcome, what is expected is not what occurs and what occurs is noticed only in reflection.

CLOSING

As Marshall (1998) points out in his essay on the work of Foucault, "In speaking the truth one does not merely describe oneself but one makes it so because of the performatory function of language" (p.74). Performing this *métissage* of texts is a singular and collective act of re/creation. In performing our subjectivities, we assert the relevance, the legitimacy, indeed the necessity of including the full range of our humanness in our work of re/membering ourselves in/to the world, embracing the world, with all our relations.

PART II

COMMUNITIIES OF A/R/TOGRAPHIC PRACTICE

RITA L. IRWIN

COMMUNITIES OF A/R/TOGRAPHIC PRACTICE

I have had the privilege of working with quite a few a/r/tographic communities of practice even before the name was created (see Irwin, 2004a). A/r/tography, at its core, has been with us a long time. What is different now is that we have an identity and with that identity comes a chance to articulate what that identity has come to mean for many people. In this section, I explore what communities of a/r/tographic practice have come to mean and the commitments people carry or embody as they belong to these communities of practice. I begin by looking at the work of several philosophers before exploring four commitments that may underpin the work of practitioners within a/r/tographic communities.

A/r/tography begins with Being. Perhaps it is all about Being. Jean-Luc Nancy (1991/2000) claims there is no inherent givenness in our very Being, rather "*Being itself is given to us as meaning.* Being does not *have* meaning. Being itself, the phenomenon of Being, is meaning that is, in turn, its own circulation—and we are this circulation...*meaning is itself the sharing of Being*" (italics in original, p.2). He goes on to say: "Being cannot *be* anything but being-with-one-another, circulating in the *with* and as the *with* of this singularly plural coexistence" (p.3). Moving from common form to singularity are not events but rather moments of gradation in many directions. Meaning resides in circulations, multiple circulations traversing many directions simultaneously creating meaning in that which passes between us (see also Irwin, Mastri & Robertson, 2000). This "in-between" is neither consistent nor continuous nor connective but rather contiguous. "[A]ll of being is in touch with all of being, but the law of touching is separation" (Nancy, 1991/2000, p.5). There is no such thing as a single being for we are positioned with, among, beside and between other positions (or dis-positions) that leads to an understanding that all appearance is co-appearance. "The meaning of Being is given as existence" (p.12) for ourselves and for all beings. "It is the plural singularity of the Being of being. We reach it to the extent that we are in touch with *ourselves* and in touch with the rest of beings" (italics in original, p.13). With others we have access to presence, to singularities that are "coming to presence".

Giorgio Agamben (1993/2005) describes how language transforms singularities into members of a group whose meaning is defined by a common property that is the condition of belonging itself. Being is one singularity among others, not particular nor universal, but itself. Being is beside itself in an empty space in which life unfolds. It is the bordering of singularity to possibility that is a threshold, a point of contact within a space that must remain empty. It is in this access to an empty space where each can move freely that the arts offers as a way to experience "the plural touching of the singular origin" (p.14) through many different forms of

S. Springgay et al. (eds.), Being with A/r/tography, 71–80.

existence that is our creation. Being is known in an instant (an access, a shock, a look) when the coming together of singulars *is* singularity.

Nancy's (1991) work is instructive as we think about communities of a/r/tographic practice for he understands individuals to be constituted by being outside of themselves, the dimension of in-common is not added onto existence but is co-existent. In other words, "[O]nly a being-in-common can make possible a being-separated" (p.xxxvii). A/r/tographers recognize that no researcher, or artist or educator exists on their own, nor do they only exist within a community for, in fact, both occur. We are singular plural beings that are part of the whole of being singular plural. This is significant for a/r/tographers as they understand the need to be engaged in their own personal pursuits while they also recognize their pursuits are contiguously positioned alongside the pursuits of others, and together are becoming a whole constellation of pursuits. Moreover, their inquiries cannot be separated from others: artists, researchers, and educators as a/r/tographers are engaged with their own inquiries as well as the inquiries of others. Recognizing this positioning affords a/r/tographers working within communities of practice an opportunity to inquire together as they create deeper understandings and meaning making. Communities of practice are everywhere and many people belong to several. A/r/tographers, in particular, may belong to several communities of practice with each belonging to an educational endeavour, or an art world, or an academic culture, to name a few. They may also belong to a community of practice dedicated to a/r/tography (see Irwin, Springgay, & Kind, in press). A/r/tographic communities often come together around ideas that matter to a particular group of people. For instance, some groups are interested in social justice issues and deliberating collectively while others are interested in self-study and challenging themselves to engage with uncertainty and ambiguity. These interests can be theoretical, practical, artistic, and/or pedagogical and are situated within a living inquiry approach. In keeping with Nancy and Agamben's conceptions of community, a/r/tographic communities may be defined by the very act of coming together, the condition of relationality, of belonging. In this instance, community is a gift to be renewed and communicated, "...an infinite task at the heart of mortality and impermanence" (Nancy, 2004, p.35). This is the awareness with which a/r/tographers gather.

Reflecting upon the practices of a/r/tography affords me an opportunity to detail some of the commitments I have witnessed within a/r/tographic communities (e.g. Irwin et al. 1998, 2001; Irwin, Springgay & Kind, in press). The following commitments are not exhaustive and are presented here as openings to possibilities and potentialities rather than procedures. The commitments can be summarized in the following way: an a/r/tographic community of practice is a community of inquirers working as artists, researchers and pedagogues committed to personal engagement within a community of belonging who trouble and address difference. Let me try to elaborate by looking at four commitments embedded in this summary: a commitment to a way of Being in the world; a commitment to inquiry; a commitment to negotiating personal engagement within a community of belonging; and a commitment to creating practices that trouble and address difference.

COMMUNITIES OF A/R/TOGRAPHIC PRACTICE

A Commitment to a Way of Being in the World

An a/r/tographic community of practice is a community of inquirers working as artists *and* pedagogues. To be committed to inquiry is to be committed to a way of Being in the world. Inquiry embraces ambiguity and improvisation, and entertains uncertainty. Yet there is also a need to articulate what is unsaid, unknown, and/or excessive. "When we permit ourselves to entertain uncertainty, we are allowing ourselves to live dangerously with pedagogy—to invite chaos (uncertainty) suggests that we will trust the processes of complexity to resolve or manage the resultant problems" (Clarke, Erickson, Collins, & Phelan, 2005, p.172). In complex systems, phenomenon is self-organizing in that it is made up of and emerges in the midst of co-implicated activities of individuals (Davis, 2004). For a/r/tographical communities, this means the community of practice is flexible (even interdisciplinary) and may cross over several disciplinary units (for instance, artists, musicians, actors, dancers and educators who reside in different academic units and who work together as a/r/tographers). Members are committed to belonging to their community. They build relationships with others by offering an empty place of hospitality in which others can move freely and find their own interests that inspire learning within the community. Through dialogue, a repertoire of stories is created, one that can be used to negotiate interpersonal, theoretical and practical aspects of our lives and work. Furthermore, a/r/tographers address the explicit knowledge as well as the implicit or tacit knowledge shared among community members. This tacit knowledge may be difficult to identify but its power for the community is significant. For a/r/tographers, tacit knowledge may be found in intuitions, assumptions, embodied understandings and other implicit perceptions as well as in language, gestures and silence. Though tacit knowledge may seldom be articulated, a space of emptiness and hospitality provides a venue for self-reflection. This opportunity will likely become important to individuals choosing to become a/r/tographers and those choosing to continue as community members. It may be wise for some communities to pursue an ongoing articulation of some of these implicit perceptions in an effort to examine how they define, include and/or exclude individuals, ideas and processes in their a/r/tographic communities.

Ironically, becoming a practitioner is less about practice and more about becoming. For communities of inquirers, *becoming a practitioner of inquiry* includes the early introductions and commitments (perhaps unspoken) made by individuals within a community of inquirers. Yet the becoming never ends, for becoming is a continuous process inherent in the knowing-through-inquiry process. It is also an inescapable aspect of Being in that the individuation of a singular existence is not just a punctual fact (Agamben, 1993/2005, p.18). In educational circles, the transformative effect of learning in this kind of a community of practice is an integral aspect of how our own becomings relate to our educational practice. Learning is about a living curriculum, the *currere* of understanding (Pinar, 1975). Learning is situated to a particular place and time and the experiences that we have are not only as thinking beings but also as feeling, sensing beings (Ellsworth, 2005). Rather than a course, project, or goal, the emphasis for learning is on an awareness of our selves-in-the-making (Ellsworth). A community of practice is the site for weaving the personal and social aspects of our lives together, helping us make sense of our lives and the lives of others. The continual oscillation between potentiality to act, and from community to singularity creates our "ethos" (Agamben, 1993/2005), which coincidentally is also the same Greek root word from which the word "ethics" is derived. Practice is created through the negotiation and sharing of aesthetic and educational stories and understandings.

One important distinction should be made between an organizational unit and a community of practice. Although a community of practice may respond to external pressures, it is the individual and social responses made by members of a community that produce practice. Whereas organizational units manage people and their activities, some communities of practice invite leadership by focusing people on knowing-through-participation (e.g. Wenger, 1998, 2000) while a/r/tographic communities of practice invite knowing-through-inquiry (see Springgay, Irwin & Wilson Kind, 2005). Although some members of an a/r/tographic community of practice may wish to define a coherent holistic understanding of their inquiry, it should be that the community of practice is more complex than this. In fact, a community of practice typically exists as a rhizome of practices that reflects Nancy's "being singular plural." Members within communities of practice are related to one another through rhizomatic relations or complex networks and contiguous identities create, accumulate and disseminate knowledge within and among rhizomes of communities of practice (e.g. Irwin, et. al., 2006) in ways that other organizational units may not be able. For instance, inquiry within communities of practice may evoke a sense of what is important for each person as they share their knowledge in meaningful ways with a variety of people within or beyond an organization. Members also continually refine their knowledge through a living engagement with their practice and may begin to collaborate on innovative practices in an effort to enhance their professional and collective identities. Finally, a community of practice provides individuals with an exposure to other knowledge—to what is beyond ourselves (Blanchot, 1988). This experience of knowledge, as it is in the making, is also the experience of ourselves in the making; the self is what emerges from the learning experience (Ellsworth, 2005; Irwin et. al., 2001). An awareness of our own identity—our ever changing, ever learning self—helps to create, cohere, or transform a community of practice. Francisco Varela, Evan Thompson and Eleanor Rosch (1991) claim that it is this recognition from which ethical action arises. Members of these communities simultaneously attend to their own expertise and others while responding to the need to cross knowledge boundaries between communities. Both need to be sustained and nurtured.

For a/r/tographers, belonging to a community of practice is essential (see Irwin et. al., 1997, 1998, 2000, 2001, 2006; de Cosson et. al. in press). Although the arts as practice-based research is well established in the United Kingdom, and more recently so in Australia and Canada (e.g. Knowles, Cole & Luciana, in press), it is less so in the United States. At many universities, art schools, public schools, and informal learning environments, arts-based, arts informed, or practice-based research is still relatively unknown. Individuals or collectives wishing to pursue this kind of work may need to find, or create, their own community of practice (see also Irwin, Springgay, Irwin & Kind, in press; Springgay, Irwin & de Cosson, in press).

In this section, Barbara Bickel's chapter illustrates her commitment as an a/r/tographer to a way of Being in the world. In and through rituals, she awakens a reflexivity of practice, a way of knowing. For her, ritual is a way to engage in her own Being, and in a community of Beings. Working with other women, she co-creates a performance ritual as a spiritual aesthetic learning space. Her commitment to a co-creative process of inquiry is founded upon a relational sacred aesthetic that is negotiated and re-negotiated within a community of Beings. It is the commitment to inquiry that transforms each individual and the community. Moreover, Sean Wiebe's work is about a *way of being ourselves in poetry*. Through poetic inquiry he explores pedagogy in an array of images and words that attempt to engage us in his exploration of being in poetry. It is his commitment to poetic inquiry in a community of being that is always becoming, when poetic inquiry becomes living inquiry.

A Commitment to Inquiry

An a/r/tographic community of practice is a community of inquirers working as artists and pedagogues committed to personal engagement within a community of belonging. We need rich experiences in educational contexts and in artistic pursuits that recognize our "being singular plural" as artists and educators. Arts and education practice-based inquiry encourages an ongoing commitment to learning *in*, *through*, *with* and *from* the arts and education. A community of engagement is a group of individuals who are able to advocate for the merit and worth of their a/r/tographic work. This includes the ability to craft, refine and engage in work through artistic and educational means that employ a recursive, reflective and often rhizomatic process en route to evocative and/or provocative products or performances. It also means being committed to working singularly within a community of inquirers who are educators, artists and researchers.

How might we prepare ourselves to be personally engaged? A/r/tographers see themselves as artists and educators/learners continually developing their abilities, skills and expertise over time. A/r/tographers have rich experiences in teaching and learning that have called them to inquire into the world, to be curious, to seek questions, greater understanding, and meaning making as the sharing of Being. A/r/tographers are not necessarily professional artists or educators but they are committed to artistic and educational inquiry over time. This includes developing one's skills, curiosity, and understanding in a chosen art form and as a teacher or learner in a chosen educational pursuit. A/r/tographers see themselves as educators and learners committed to ongoing inquiry in and through time, and as artists committed to experiencing the arts within a community of artists. Being an a/r/tographer sometimes calls individuals to strengthen aspects of themselves that are not areas of strength: for instance, artists expand their educational interests, skills and abilities while educators enrich their artistic endeavours. Some arts-based educational researchers believe practice-based researchers need to have a professional commitment to educational as well as artistic practices (e.g. Irwin &

de Cosson 2004). This belief leads to the consideration of exhibiting, performing or sharing art forms with the public, while also being professionally engaged in education.

How might we prepare ourselves for a community of engagement? Inquirers need to understand a range of research practices and paradigms in order to help others understand what a/r/tography offers the field within a constellation of research practices. This will mean being well versed with a range of qualitative traditions, as well as quantitative traditions. For student a/r/tographers, this may mean taking courses that include an introduction to a range of research methods while also taking in-depth courses in qualitative research and if possible, arts-based educational research. A/r/tographers will also need to be knowledgeable about the theoretical work done in their areas of interest (in education and the arts), and be able to cite theorists, educators as well as artists in their work. An important aspect of this work is seeking out critical friends to provoke us to think critically about our work and creative friends who can inspire us to work creatively. Sometimes this is best realized by creating or joining study groups or other forms of learning communities that encourage theoretical and creative engagement among participants who share their research projects. At other times, this may be best realized by going to arts-based gatherings like exhibits & performances in order to understand contemporary trends in the arts and to inspire one's own artistic engagement. And finally, we need to be engaged in developing the field of arts and education practice-based research generally and a/r/tography more specifically. A/r/tographers need to have a creative life amidst the busyness of their daily lives, taking time for the slow and important work of contemplative and creative practice. A commitment to these engagements often involves a struggle in disengaging the questions of how to simply accomplish our goals and instead, equally consider socially based questions of what it means to be human and how we should then live together. Taking time to co-author or author articles, or co-create or create performances, and in so doing, participating in the development of a/r/tography as a field of inquiry may involve a careful analysis of what activities are reasonable to accomplish.

A/r/tographical inquiry has benefited enormously from technological advancement. Many forms of technology, such as audio or video recording equipment, musical instruments, the world wide web or other innovations, have advanced the arts and each of these can be used to bring image and text, sound and text, performance and text, or image, performance, sound and text together in ways that were not possible just a few years ago. This is especially evident in hypermedia. The community of practice within Marcia McKenzie and Nora Timmerman's research group were able to use "dialogues" in the form of visual, textual and aural data to link transcripts. More importantly, though readers could not change the website, they could add comments to the site that linked to any point on the site. This fostered dialogue amongst those in the project and those engaged in learning about the project. As a result, those in the community of practice who were creating the website found themselves writing in a space of collaboration, by writing in and through inquiry. They were also committed to negotiating with other members of their community including their readers. Also in this section is the work of David Beare and George Belliveau, who used dialogue as a way of representing data by writing a script for a play. An anti-bullying play is a play within a play about scripting data. Through this form, they weave in and out of questions and issues, negotiating their engagements within their preserve community and their own academic community.

A Commitment to Negotiating Personal Engagement within a Community of Belonging

Negotiating personal engagement within a community of belonging is part of the rhizomatic relationality of inquirers working together. A/r/tographers are continuously negotiating and renegotiating their foci as the community's research and inquiry evolves and shifts over time. This is an essential feature of a/r/tography for a/r/tographic inquiry does not set out to answer introductory research questions but rather to posit questions of inquiry that evolve over time. This feature is very important to inquiry and makes the research responsive to practice and to those involved in that practice (not just the researchers but also those who are impacted by the work). Yet, if the members of a learning community are used to organizational units, an evolution of research questions can also lead to confusion and ambiguity amongst members within a community. Even though communication and deliberation may be maintained and nurtured in and through time, there will inevitably be a messiness about the process. It is here that careful note taking, record keeping and meeting agendas can help to focus the activities of a group toward direction(s) that are of interest to members of the group. Individuals should record data collection strategies such as observations and interviews, as well as an initial analysis—all of which are important and should be carried out—if such strategies are used. Yet, they also need to record their artful, pedagogical, interpretive and critical analyses as they move toward a holistic understanding of the a/r/tographic inquiry process. Providing a few minutes of time within meetings for writing reflections may help members document their own growth and change. If these reflections are shared with the larger community on a regular basis and debated within the group (after analyses are carried out by individuals or collaboratively within the group), the research inquiry and research questions will evolve from within the a/r/tographic process. Furthermore, as these deliberations and analyses are juxtaposed with inquiries into the theoretical literature in education and the arts, the evolution of research questions becomes more recursive, reflexive, reflective and responsive. It may be that the introductory questions are addressed at various times in the whole a/r/tographic process but the subsequent questions will guide the rhizomatic relations of the overall project. As individuals share their own interpretations of knowledge, community members will engage in collaborative inquiry meant to reveal new understandings. Yet it may be that agreement within the community cannot be resolved. It is here that disagreements can lead to further understandings and engagements that may or may not be held by the collective community. It may be that in rhizomatic form, various individuals within the community will come to different understandings. If possible, these can be expressed, debated and taught from a rhizomatic position of multiplicity. After all, a/r/tographers are engaged in inquiry with a view toward deeper engagements and understandings over time.

Dónal O Donoghue's chapter in this section is an excellent example of how a group of men teachers explored masculinity and teaching as a life project that is constantly created and recreated, negotiated and renegotiated. A/r/tography became a space to "work in and work out" that which was observed, experienced, and analysed. O Donoghue's art examples are powerful metaphors that provoke viewers to rethink their very Being. The evocative images and embedded texts of O Donoghue's self-study complement the narrative inquiry of the men. As men spoke of living in "in-between" spaces, they began to speak more openly about other boundaries, boundary pushing, boundary crossing, etc. Their community was committed to personal and collective inquiry, and I might add, they were also interested in troubling how men teachers were perceived and how men teachers experienced the world. This leads us to the last commitment.

A Commitment to Creating Practices that Trouble and Address Difference

The fourth commitment suggests that a/r/tographic communities create practices that question yet re-imagine how we might live in difference. Each community of a/r/tographers seems to take on a life of its own. In fact, the communication of singularities in the attribute of their extension that is community—"... does not unite them in essence, but scatters them in existence" (Agamben, 2005, p.18). Each community begins to create its own rhythms of practice and engagement which lead to shared vocabularies and ideas. Over time, these communities may collaboratively create performances or exhibitions. Some communities will create shared rituals, sensibilities, and artifacts in and through time (Springgay, Irwin & de Cosson, in press). All a/r/tographic communities should be attentive to not only these habits (created over time) but also to the situations that emerge within the community and within the inquiry process itself. As John Dewey (1933) suggested, we find ourselves troubled or confused by a situation and it is on this basis that we seek inquiry into understanding or resolving the situation. These moments of instability are the experience of our changing, learning selves. Dynamic learning communities will inevitably experience situations (see also Doherty, 2004; Irwin et. al., 2006) that need to be attended to as a research collective either from within the community or as a result of the processes and/or products of the inquiry itself. These occasions spawn curiosity that leads to rich opportunities for understanding through ongoing living inquiry. It is here that education as an emergent pedagogy of practice honours the living curriculum, the living *currere* (see Doll, 2005, p.55), and reconceptualizes learning and inquiry through transformation. And, it is also here that Nancy and Agamben's concepts of community as having nothing to do with communion or with fusion into an ultimate identity seems most obvious. Community is made of what retreats from it: the essence of the "common" and its work. The retreat opens and continues to keep open this "strange being-the-one-with-the-other to which we are exposed" (Fynsk, cited in Nancy, 2004, p.xxxix)

Difficult situations not only lead to a reconceptualization of pedagogy, they also lead to a consideration of the ethical dimensions of community practices. It is here that we can learn from many artists who have been working in communities over the years. Hal Foster (1996) is critical and cautious about the community-based practices he has witnessed. His concern is that the authority of the artist is seldom questioned or even acknowledged. Artists and a/r/tographers have an opportunity to reclaim lost cultural spaces and even rewrite histories, yet their work still needs strong reflexivity in order to ensure that an ethically conscientious stance is taken and experienced by those with whom they work. As Miwon Kwon (2004, p.130) suggests: "community-based artists may inadvertently aid in the colonization of difference—for benevolent and well-intentioned gestures of democratization can have effects on colonialism, too." It is with this in mind, that all a/r/tographers need to appreciate that anyone with whom they work will be affected by their involvement, regardless of the extent to which the person is involved. Moreover, we must anticipate that the institutions in which we work also have an influence on our work. Communities of practice may become sites for reproductive practices and it is here that critique must occur. In fact, the conception of the community itself should be critiqued. The power of the community of practice is considerable and should not be under estimated. As a result of studying living systems, Kevin Kelly (1994) concludes that more is different and that a collective can accomplish much more than the sum of its parts. This returns us to the notion of being singular plural. We are contiguously connected and yet we belong to a singularity. As such, a community of practice can never be completely unified or be understood for the complexity of its singularity (see also May, 1997). Rather, with this impossibility of community comes the possibility of "collective artistic praxis" (Kwon, 2004, p.154). Whereas community-based art often has a *descriptive* nature, that is, when artistic expressions affirm rather than question coherent representations, collective artistic praxis is often *projective* in that a provisional group is created around specific circumstances (and the group is also aware of the conditions surrounding the circumstances) and grasps an unsettling working through of the collective process. According to Kwon, who has studied Nancy, a community is inoperative since "only a community that questions its own legitimacy is legitimate" (p.155). Communities are impossible to know completely and it is through continuous questioning that collective artistic and educative praxis can emerge to investigate and challenge the incoherence and uncertainty that such work projects.

A commitment to troubling difference isn't comfortable for anyone, yet each of the authors in this section show a commitment to creating practices that trouble or address difference. Bickel troubles the power relations within her community. Wiebe troubles the immediate successes teachers aspire to achieve and searches for lasting impact through poetic inquiry. O Donoghue troubles the notion of identity for men teachers against a backdrop of projected societal images and texts. McKenzie and Timmerman trouble the boundaries between form and content, author and reader, in the expression of research. Beare and Belliveau trouble the ways we represent data through form and interpretation. Each author's text is made more powerful through the use of metaphor, image, narrative, or hypermedia. Each author's text evokes or provokes us to rethink and re-imagine possibilities rather than probabilities.

RITA L. IRWIN

In summary, an a/r/tographic community of practice is a community of inquirers working as artists, researchers and pedagogues committed to personal engagement within a community of belonging who trouble and address difference. The four commitments explored here are not exhaustive but begin to illustrate the commitments a/r/tographers make to their practice. The commitments should not be seen as obligations but rather as beliefs toward a philosophy of community. An a/r/tographic community of practice is a community of inquirers working as artists and pedagogues committed to personal engagement within a community of belonging. The deeper commitments embedded in these engagements include: a commitment to a way of Being in the world, a commitment to inquiry, a commitment to negotiating personal engagement within a community of belonging, and a commitment to creating practices that trouble and address difference. These commitments, and likely others, provide a foundation from which to engage in a/r/tographic communities of practice, and indeed, to unwork these communities of practice so that they are truly collectives of praxis engaged in unsettling that which we take for granted, complexifying that which seems simple, and simplifying that which appears to be complex.

NOTES

[1] I wish to thank Valerie Triggs for her insights into Agamben's scholarship and more importantly, her editorial comments on an earlier draft of this chapter.

BARBARA BICKEL

UNVEILING A SACRED AESTHETIC: A/R/TOGRAPHY AS RITUAL

Prelude: Co-creation

The idea of ritual has previously emerged in the writing of a/r/tographers (Springgay, Irwin and Kind, in press; Wilson, 2004). This essay further addresses being with(in) and understanding ritual in the practice of a/r/tography. To do this I return to early experiences of ritual that emerged within my art practice. Through writing, I unfold aspects of ritual that continue to touch and in/form my practice as an a/r/tographer today. My present lens and practice as an a/r/tographer assists the reflective process and further illuminates these early ritual experiences, weaving together theoretical understandings of a/r/tography as ritual with the process of making and sharing art within community.

Becoming community is an ongoing process that requires an engaged practice of being aware of ourselves as "singular plural" (Nancy, 2000) beings. In the evolution of my practice as a singular artist, ritual has remained a vital element, encouraging a mutual relational aesthetic within art making, inquiry, teaching and learning within the plurality of community. This essay furthermore begins to articulate conceptual understandings of a sacred aesthetic within ritual and encourages others to reflect upon and explore these qualities and practices within their own a/r/tographic processes.

Within the two particular art exhibition openings and the co-created art I describe below, the relational, sacred, and aesthetic were re-united through conscious honouring of co-creation. This is in contrast to a predominantly individualistic and secular contemporary art world. Matthew Fox (1988) wrote, "...mutuality is presumed in the term *co*-creation. Divinity and we are co-creators, equally responsible...for the kinds of personalities, relationships, lifestyles, politics, and economics that we birth" (p.201). The mutual and sacred aspects of ritual require a compassionate awareness of the other as divine and calls for a caring responsibility within acts of co-creation.

The outcome of ritual is often "evocative and/or provocative," assisting each person involved to think critically, moving beyond patterned and comfortable ways of thinking and being with others, towards new perspectives and transformative learning[1] experiences. Ritual elegantly supports the practice of a/r/tography, which interweaves "the arts with scholarly writing through living inquiry" (Springgay, Irwin & Kind, in press, p.2). In doing so, it complicates traditional understandings of what art, research and education are. The essay concludes with ways of awaking to ritual within practices of art making and offers a simple structure for entering and implementing ritual within an a/r/tographic practice.

S. Springgay et al. (eds.), Being with A/r/tography, 81–94.

BARBARA BICKEL

Journal Entry Summer 1994:

It is a warm summer evening in Calgary and I am going to an art opening at a new gallery where the work of an artist, who is also a spiritual teacher and healer,[2] is taking place. Many people are gathered, conversations are raptly engaged with the art, and the wine is flowing. In the midst of this atmosphere the artist begins to address us. He ritually invokes cosmic spirit energies and begins to tell the creation stories of the art, honouring the people that have been involved with its birth. I listen with a sense of awe. He becomes in that moment an artist-mentor for me as I witness the reverence of ritual taking place at a commercial art gallery opening. My familiar notions of what an art gallery opening is supposed to be, transforms. This is how I want my art openings presented to the public.

Journal Entry Summer 1995:

I am working on my first major community art project since completing my fine arts degree. It is entitled *Sisters*.[3] I have just finished six weeks of working in a temporary studio in Victoria with six women friends from high school, including my younger foster sister. These women—who have had a significant impact on my life—upon invitation have agreed to join me in a collaborative art project exploring the theme of sisterhood.[4] This is the first of two travelling studio visits in this project. I am also travelling to my birth sister's home in the US where I will set up a temporary studio in her family room. The remaining twenty-two women, including my mother and stepdaughters, are working with me in my Calgary studio, where I currently live and work. Women friends[5] have been willing to travel from as far away as England, Ontario, Saskatchewan and neighbouring cities in Alberta to be part of this project. The significance of the bonds and desire for sisterhood are hard to ignore or downplay in the expressed effort of these women, some of whom I have not been in contact with for over ten years.

Tonight, on this unusually hot summer evening, we eat sushi and drink wine together with friends and family. We mingle amidst the six completed art pieces hung on the studio walls, celebrating—with tentativeness—our bodies and beings, as "sisters" represented in our co-created art pieces.

Following the completion of the art in Victoria, I returned to Calgary with the art. Each of us assumed, without question, that the completed art belonged to me. Once home, I found I was reluctant to show the art to anyone. After much personal reflection, I realized I had erred in not troubling the assumption that the art belonged to me alone. To exhibit this work, and a larger body of work I was in the midst of co-creating, required a greater awareness and permission on the part of the women to release the art to me and to the larger world. With this new understanding, it became clear to me that a further gesture needed to take place if this art was going to be shared with society. Five months following the small studio exhibition in Victoria, the gesture became a co-created gallery performance ritual,[6] on the opening night of the *Sisters* exhibition.

Returning Home. 1995. Barbara Bickel; co-created with Helen Bickel. Mixed media drawing and collage on wood. 48"x 36". Calgary AB: The Centre Gallery.

Reflections on Returning Home

Returning Home (see image above) was co-created with my mother. The symbols that she chose to represent sisterhood reflect our mother-daughter relationship. The fabric that she sat upon was a quilt that we had made together a few years earlier. The woollen afghan wrapped around her body was a wedding gift that she knit for my partner and I. The ball of yarn that she gazed into is a remaining remnant of that gift. Emerging from the dark background are the symbols of her Christian faith—a cross and three lit candles. Reluctant to expose her body as naked flesh she chose to cover herself in the relational warmth of her daughter's bedding. The experience of co-creating this piece was held within an unspoken sacred ritual space of mutual openness, appreciation and joy in creating and witnessing each other in the creative process. Reflecting now on the dark background from which her image emerges, I can see how it foreshadows the apophati[7] spiritual quest that I had begun to enter. The co-created art piece that affirmed her religious faith ran counter to my entry into a spiritual journey of unknowing and de-affirmation of a dogmatic Christian faith. Inviting my mother to participate in the public performance ritual illuminated signs of strain in our diverging spiritual paths. She was uncomfortable with the use of the word ritual in the art invitation as it represented taboos that her Christian faith warned against. Despite her discomfort she chose to participate and publicly affirmed her Christian faith at the unveiling of her art piece.

Warrior Mother. 1995. Barbara Bickel; co-created with Susan Nabors. Mixed media drawing and collage on wood. 48" x 30". Calgary AB: The Centre Gallery.

Reflections on Warrior Mother

Standing firmly, rooted in relationships with women, *Warrior Mother* (see image above) inspires the experience of sisterhood to step boldly forward. Susan's symbols of sisterhood where photographs of her female relations: her grandmother, her mother, her daughters, and herself pregnant with her second daughter, along with images of fruit representing female fertility. These images were embedded into the ground of her art piece, supporting and reminding her of her place in a lineage of beautiful women. She chose to wear only a bandana on her head to mark her identity as a warrior mother in a line of warrior mothers. I share this story as it reflects Susan's desire to extend her understanding of sisters into the world. As a surprise, her husband purchased the art piece and gave it to her as a gift. She was not happy with the well-intended gift, as she had fully let the art go in the performance ritual and preferred that it travel into the world, impacting others rather than staying with her. Her desire reflects the words of artist, researcher, educator, Kenneth Beittel (1985) who writes: "Art serves the evolution of consciousness because it serves the thirst deep in each soul for transcendence. The giving of one's art is a tangible symbol that we have not sold out" (p.51). In the end, she chose to accept the gift, allowing it to find a place within the entrance of her own home where she could firsthand hear the impact that it had on people entering.

Gathering Women: A Sacred Relational Aesthetic

In 1991, I began to question the artist-model relationship as an art student working with hired models in class settings. I could find little meaning beyond working with the body as an abstract, technical form to be rendered. As much as I loved the physical structure of the human body, it alone was not enough to give meaning to my art practice. Instead, I found satisfaction in the living relationship of a shared creative process and inquiry between myself and the person whose body experience I was witnessing[8] and drawing. I, in turn, was witnessed by the person with whom I was engaged in the creative process. Canadian artist and religious scholar Susan Shantz (1999) describes the feminine spiritual path as one of longing for a centre, a place of meaning; a sacred space where one's existence is opened up rather than confined (p.67-68). My longing for shared creative experience has led me to a mutually collaborative practice of art making with others. It is here I have found that my personal desire to co-create often runs parallel to the desire of others to co-create. For a short period of time, we consciously live the existence of "being-with-another" in a "singularily plural existence" (Nancy, 2000, p.3). I am called to work with community in my art and to openly engage in a co-creative and sacred process of inquiry. A sacred and relational aesthetic (Bourriaud, 2002) feeds the core of my art practice.[9] By sacred, I mean honouring, receiving, and holding reverence for the spirit of mystery that is ever-unfolding between humans, the environment, and the cosmos (Wilber, 1996).

   In an effort to honour the gifts that I receive as an artist working with others, I have, over the years, acknowledged those who have allowed me to photograph and

BARBARA BICKEL

draw their bodies, as co-creator (Fox, 1988), collaborator (Irwin *et al.*, 1999; Roberts, 1981; Torbert, 1981), and co-researcher (Heron, 1981). The degree to which my co-creators are collaborative[10] and directly part of the art making process varies, from allowing me to fully guide those involved by making the decisions in the process, to collaboratively making decisions on the image and the materials to be used, and in some cases, to working directly on the art piece with me. A relational aesthetic involves a negotiated co-creative practice of give and take, connection and disconnection, while striving to be mutually honouring and supportive.

Rupture: The Politics of Representation

Some of the women in the *Sisters* project struggled with the representation arrived at in the co-created art piece. They had trouble accepting the visual image that was reflected back to them, despite the fact that we had mutually agreed upon the pose and or photograph that was to be drawn. These were often painful struggles of an undeniable power relationship between me as the artist and the women as models. It was further complicated by a criticality of self-image on the woman's part as model, and my trained critical eye as an artist for a quality aesthetic in the art product. Artist-educator Susan Stewart (1993) wrote of the potential transformative power of collaboration that can address power relations directly:

> In this process of grappling with power relations rests the means of transforming them, both at a personal level, and socially and politically. Collaboration is an alternative and highly resistant model of creative interaction. It is a process that demonstrates a method of art making which can be democratic, transformative, and empowering, and which has the potential to renew and build community. (pp.43-44)

The co-creative process within the *Sisters* project required a dialogue that was unfamiliar to myself and the women. I was inviting participation in an art process where the women did not necessarily feel confident. I, in turn, had to work creatively to solve artistic problems that, as a trained artist working independently, I would not have encountered. Honestly sharing our feelings about the art piece in process and at completion was, at times, a great challenge.

In situations where there was an obvious struggle regarding the art being created, my co-creator and I made every effort to communicate and work through the rupture. In terms of her representation, one woman experienced great difficulty in the co-creative process. She could not be satisfied with her choice of how she was to be represented. Following numerous conversations, we eventually resolved the dilemma by representing her "real" self by ritually erasing the art piece together. Trinh Minh-ha (2005) addressed these appearances and disappearances of the "real", writing: "In this realm of the immaterial the accent is not so much on the spectacular appearances as on the underlying disappearances that happen with every appearance" (p.16-17). As our ritual destruction of the drawing left her without art representation in the project, I suggested that she choose a piece of plain wood that could be framed and hung in the gallery. We titled this blank piece

Death of the Image. In the gallery performance ritual,[11] she was able to verbally and symbolically share her journey of appearance/disappearance/reappearance that took place through the letting go of her physical image, while being witnessed by those attending.

The performance ritual—the unveiling of the art by the women and myself at the art opening of *Sisters*—was an extension of the emergent private rituals that took place in the studio. Within the gallery, each art piece was covered with a veil. A walkway was left clear around the circumference of the gallery. A co-created altar[12] was in the centre of the gallery. It held objects that represented sisterhood and that were brought by the women. The audience members were seated around the altar and were not able to see the art prior to the performance ritual. During the performance ritual, I walked with each woman to her art piece and we unveiled the art together. Once the art was revealed, the woman spoke, read poetry or stood in silence, offering her art to the audience. The gallery performance ritual gave the women a location to publicly present their personal responses and their understanding of the art to those witnessing the unveiling. In some cases, the discord between myself as the artist and they as the models were resolved through this ritual, in others the conflict was acknowledged, yet remained present.

As an artist, my professional standards were often challenged as I found myself having to let go of the impulse to edit the final pieces that did not meet my aesthetic and artistic discernment. I had to work hard to come to a place of resolve that honoured the relational co-creative process of the art project, the quality of the final art piece, and the exhibition. This experience was fraught with anxiety and questions—what is art for—and ultimately expanded my understanding of art as a relational community-based experience. Collaboratively working with twenty-nine women was an amazing gift that simultaneously included transformative intimate relationships and personal artistic and relationship anguish. The art exhibition ultimately represented the failures and hurts of sisterhood, as well as its beauty and power. Each woman's experience brought to the fore prior unspoken or unformulated thoughts regarding female relationships.

Performing Ritual

[Ritual is]... neither a detached contemplation of the world nor a passive symbolization of it but is the performance of an act in which people confront one kind of power with another, and rehearse their own future. (Driver, 1997, p.188)

Ritual has been a deeply engrained part of my life since my birth. As the daughter of a Christian Minister, my life was punctuated by cyclical sacred holidays, or what are called liturgical rituals (Grimes, 1995). Anthropologist Victor Turner has expanded the traditional image of liturgical ritual and extended the imaginary of ritual to "threshold-crossing" (cited in Grimes, p.60). I was re-introduced to rituals framed in this way, through women's circles that celebrated women's biological cycles as well as earth-based rituals that follow the cycle of the year. My spiritual journey opened anew with this threshold crossing into non-discursive and creative bodily and earth-based ritual practices that were free expressions of mystery.

Concurrently, I crossed a career threshold and committed myself to a full-time art practice.

Unfolding in the 1990s, I eventually found validation for my art practice, which resonated with the feminist art of the 1970s. This art movement emerged out of the North American Women's Movement (i.e., Ana Mendieta, Mary Beth Edelson, Judy Chicago, and Hannah Wilke) and challenged the Western art canon by incorporating body art, ritual, and the expression of a female self (Gloria Fenman Orenstein, 1987; Lucy Lippard, 1995). I recognize in retrospect the importance of choosing to practice art full-time and how that activated a ritualizing spiritual practice in my personal and professional life.

I acknowledge that ritual is also a word that can illicit a response of mistrust, as it can and has been used to silence and control others. Mistrust emerged most profoundly in my mother's response to the use of the word outside of a sanctioned religious ceremony and institution. Because of its power and transformative ability, ritual can be used destructively as well as productively (Driver, 1997; Pryer, 2002). Yet when performance rituals have the intention of affirmation, expressing our experience of mystery, letting go, transformation and a re-inscribing of female experience, it can function as a subversion to limiting cultural norms.

To assist in theoretically understanding the form of ritual that has evolved within my art practice, I turn to the work of ritual scholar Ronald Grimes (1995). Grimes acknowledged the consistent role that artists play in bringing "emergent ritual" into society through art and artistic performances, acting as vehicles to awaken reflexive consciousness in society. "Ritual enactment at once awakens the reflexivity of consciousness and tranquilizes the anxiety provoked by doing so" (p.69). He illuminated an understanding of "nascent ritual" or emergent ritual and challenged the study of ritual to focus not only on historical and established rituals, but to study the new creation of ritual in postmodern society. He positioned rituals not as set structures but as "structurings" that "surge and subside, ebb and flow" (p.62). Grimes credited ritualizing as an important mode of knowing. Within ritualizing, the "'knower and known' are conjoined" (p.69). He reminds us that research happens not just on ritual but in ritual. Ritual is a structuring that we can create, explore, learn, and teach within.

The *Sisters* project was my initiation into public performance rituals, which have since become a vital component of each of my major art projects. It is through collaboration with co-creators, with other artists, and in sharing my art with the public in a sacred context, that I have expanded my understanding of the world and myself. I am a relational learner, and ritual offers a sacred place for relational learning. Educator Allison Pryer (2002) wrote, "[r]itual is a catalyst for processes of innovation and creativity, and thus generative of new knowledge" (p.144). Ritual has been the sacred container that has allowed me to take risks and extend my art practice beyond the limiting modernist notions that question what is art and who is an artist. Entering ritual allows one to engage in what can be a profound inquiry. The emergence of ritual that has occurred within the inquiry practice of a/r/tography is not surprising then, and further assists us in moving beyond traditional notions of research and knowledge.

Emergent ritual as described by Grimes offers a fluid structure that can augment the creative process. In its simplest form, ritual offers a structure[13] that includes: 1) an intention which grounds and clarifies the purpose of the work to be done within the ritual, 2) a chosen and or created sacred space which acts as a container within which to do the work of the ritual, 3) an intentional form of witnessing that may or may not include other human beings and, 4) some form of closure that allows one to step outside of the ritual process and return to ordinary life. Ritual enacted within this simple structure has the ability to contain and hold with reverence what may seem disturbing, unfamiliar, too complex, too simple, or too special to enter into the ordinary reality of everyday life.

Through the process of co-creating in the *Sisters* project, I came to realize that I was not in ordinary reality with the women. Upon reflection, I recognize the unfolding structure of the ritual process with each woman's co-creation through: 1) having a clear intention of our work exploring sisterhood, 2) entering the sanctuary of the studio space together, 3) co-witnessing each other in the act of creating and, 4) deciding when we were complete, sharing some of our feelings about the art created and our experience together, and leaving the studio space.

The performance ritual in the gallery became an essential gesture to honour and extend the co-creative learning aspect of the art project. I wrote letters to the women in Victoria, sharing my insight of needing to release their art images into the world ritually and inviting them to take part in the performance ritual—if not physically, then in writing. A few of the women did share in writing their experience and what they learned through the co-creation, and these were read at the opening performance ritual.

The co-creation of the performance ritual itself offered an opportunity for all of the women that I had been working with individually, to come together as a group. Some knew each other well, others did not. During this next layer of the co-creative process, the women were able to share their experiences with each other and support each other in preparation to present a collective experience of sisterhood to the public. The intention set for the performance ritual was to release their images to the larger world. Simultaneously, it was a celebration, an honouring, and a place of closure for what had been a nine month creative process. Due to space restrictions, the audience attendance was limited to friends and family. Each woman invited supportive witnesses to be present for the ritual unveiling of the art, which for some represented a wound. Following the performance ritual, the gallery opened its doors to the general public and a celebration ensued. Ronald Grimes (1995) wrote of the significance of the responsive presence of a community of witnesses for ritual transformation into a sacred experience:

> For ritualizing to occur, the surroundings must expose a vulnerable (*vulner* = wound) side. Whether the vulnerability stems from a human or divine face does not seem definitive, but some aspect of the cosmos must appear to be responsive in order for ritualizing to gestate. The more deeply an enactment is received, the more an audience becomes congregation and the more a performance becomes ritualized. "Sacred" is the name we give to the deepest forms of receptivity in our experience. (p.69)

My notion of presenting art to the public was forever altered by this opening performance ritual experience. I participated in and was profoundly transformed by this sacred ritualizing of art, which included exposing the vulnerability of beauty and wounds.[14] The transformative gift of art was offered and received because of the willingness of the women to participate and the responsiveness of the witnesses that congregated.

A/r/tography as Ritual within Community

In reflecting upon and sharing the relational art and ritual making process in the *Sisters* project, I hope to amplify our understanding of the relational practice of a/r/tography. Within a community, this process can be a profound yet unsettling experience. It requires that we work consciously with differences, question the inevitable power relationships between ourselves, as artists, researchers, educators and learners (Irwin *et al.*, 2006), and open ourselves to questions of ethics[15] when working with others. When roles are enacted without questioning the underlying power structures, voices within the community are often silenced and lost. We then run the risk of repeating comfortable and often oppressive patterns of learning, teaching, and making. Consequently, we lose the opportunity to transcend our partial understandings of knowing, being, and doing, which are most available to us when working within community.

The power of working and practicing within community is that we are taken outside of ourselves through the interrelational connections that develop. Despite this, we each remain individuals with diverse experiences and particular focuses within the act of inquiry. Art theorist Carol Becker (2002) solicits a sociological framing of the purpose of art where art assists in the growth and well-being of community.

> We need to see art as it is—a sociological phenomenon, representative of human evolution and expression;...a link with our own collective unconscious and with out spiritual development as a species... It is through such a process that one comes to understand how art functions in the society and how important it is to society's well-being. (p.57)

This is certainly a position to be embraced by artists and a/r/tographers. By incorporating a ritual practice within my work as an artist and now as an a/r/tographer, I have a sacred structure and container that can support the entry into the collective unconscious. I am not left adrift with the intensity and diversity of the new understandings that may surface for myself, or those with whom I am working. I can bracket the rich time that is spent entering the realm of the arational,[16] which is brought forward through the act of entering a creative process. I can then anchor it with the understanding that I will return to the rational and ordinary world to begin to decipher and articulate it (Beittel & Beittel, 1991).

Engaging the practice of a/r/tography—the integrated practice of art, research and education—with a sacred aesthetic of ritual can bring us closer to the ancient mysteries that mystic educator Rudolf Steiner (1964) wrote of:

The Mysteries which fostered that unity [a consciousness of the common source of art, religion and science] were a kind of combination art institute, church and school. For what they offered was not a one-sided sole dependence upon language. The words uttered by the initiate as both cognition and spiritual revelation were supported and illustrated by the sacred rituals unfolding, before listening spectators, in mighty pictures. (p.83)

Through a sacred pedagogical practice (Lincoln & Denzin, 2005), we may counteract the alienation and fragmentation of a world that is "suffering from its loss of center" and assist in the development of a new age that the late Kenneth Beittel (1989) passionately articulated:

The practice of art as seen here is a spiritual discipline that offers a powerful antidote to an age of suffering from its loss of center...In this coming age we will see a big shift in human consciousness, away from the mental, egoistic, toward more spiritual ways of being and knowing...to practice thus is to work at self-transformation: a transformation of one's entire being-not by increments, but by a quantum leap. This is art for a new age. (p.ix)

Although rarely articulated by artists working with community or on their own, emergent ritual as a spiritual discipline has much to offer the practice of a/r/tography.

A/r/tography is the interdisciplinary location from which I have begun to articulate and find support and inspiration for the sacred and relational aesthetic elements of an art practice that is community-based, educative and transformative. It is a practice that is alert to intersubjective awareness and an awakening of consciousness that is not dependent on transmission of knowledge alone. Mary Richards (1962/86), a potter, mystic, and teacher, makes the important distinction between knowledge and consciousness.

[K]nowledge and consciousness are two quite different things. Knowledge is like a product we consume and store...By consciousness I mean a state of being "awake" to the world through our organism. This kind of consciousness requires...an organism attuned to the finest perceptions and responses...When knowledge is transformed into consciousness and into will, ah then we are on the high road indeed... (pp.15-16)

A/r/tography as ritual offers the structure to combine intuitive relational art-practices with qualitative research. Arts-based practices and research can assist in the expansion of society's understanding of itself by extending knowledge into consciousness.

Practicing A/r/tography as Ritual

[I]ngrained in modern social interaction and political performance; ritual is not compatible with industrial speed; to perform a ritual one must slow down. (Trinh Minh-ha, 2005, p.99)

Trinh's words offer essential advice for those interested in practicing a/r/tography as ritual. The pace at which the world of academia operates has become similar to industrial speed driven by corporate production and consumerism. A/r/tography as ritual takes us out of the normal confines of linear time and space and transports us into altered spaces where intuition leads us, the cosmos witnesses us, and where the sacred is valued and engaged. A/r/tography as ritual has parameters that permit us to enter time-free states of unknowing, and to return when decide to a rational discourse of knowing. New understandings of consciousness gained through a/r/tographic research are limited if they cannot be translated back into the language familiar to others. But first we must slow down and take time to enter ritual space.

Becoming familiar with a/r/tography as ritual as an individual is an important first step before undertaking a/r/tography as ritual with others. To come to a personal understanding of emergent ritual, a/r/tographers must begin to reflect on our creative processes and look for signs of the four elements of emergent ritual within: 1) intention, 2) sacred space, 3) witnessing and 4) closure. Once we begin to recognize these elements in our creative process, we must attend to aspects that may be missing and begin to practice them with conscious awareness. As the ritual container for entering the unknown is consciously created and worked within over time, self trust will inevitably begin to grow. Practicing a/r/tography as ritual with a solid sense of trust in the self can contribute to work that stretches individual limits and moves towards a greater depth of understanding.

Once we become practiced and confident with a/r/tography as ritual individually, we next need to extend the practice into working with community. This may mean reflecting anew upon previous work done with community. Moreover, it is necessary to find the places where we have already been utilizing elements of ritual and notice the elements that may be missing in our community practice. Practicing a/r/tography as ritual with others is a risk that may venture to places of conflict and misunderstandings. Yet it is within the practice that there is an opportunity to move through the differences to mutual acceptance, respect, and—at times—transformation of the differences.

Acting with awareness and reverence for the sacred within a practice of a/r/tography as ritual assists in gathering community together in a way that is transformative, non-traditional, and emancipatory; it challenges oppressive societal structures. Through sharing my experience of a sacred relational aesthetic of art making and ritual in the *Sisters* project, I have demonstrated a story; a sacred way to bring community together through art—questioning oppressive ways of artistically representing and being with each other. Within the *Sisters* project, we encountered the lived experience of singular plurality, individually witnessed and witnessing within the larger context of witnessed and witnessing women.

A/r/tography as ritual results in the combination of years of developing ritual in an art practice with the educational arts-based inquiry of a/r/tography (Bickel 2004, 2005). A/r/tography as ritual assists in bringing forward what I experience as the liminal (Sameshima & Irwin, 2006), spiritual world of the ancient mysteries. It is through the interrelational dance of the three identities of artist/researcher/educator partnered with the institutional realms of art/science/religion that the gift of sacred aesthetic art has the opportunity to express itself most powerfully in the world. The work of an "initiate" who chooses to practice a/r/tography as ritual within community will be to bring forth the relational and sacred aesthetic of art and education into greater visibility and practice—within the academy, the art community, and the world.

NOTES

[1] Transformative learning (i.e. Meizerow, 2000; O'Sullivan, 1999; Tisdell & Tolliver, 2003; Vella, 2000) has been theorized by numerous adult educators. For my use of the term, I draw from the work of adult educators Elisabeth Tisdell and Denise Tolliver. They, in turn, draw from and extend the transformational learning theory as mapped out by Meizerow and O'Sullivan, which they find limited in its individual psychological focus. They combine the work of religious and sociological scholar David Abalos (1998), whose community-based, social justice work extends beyond personal transformation as focus, to societal transformation. It is within the combined personal and societal understanding of transformative learning that I work.

[2] Dwayne Rourke lived in Bragg Creek, Alberta at the time.

[3] Poet Jan Sheppard collaborated on this project with me. As each art piece was completed, she interviewed myself and each woman, and followed by writing a poem that reflected upon both the woman's experience and the art itself. The poems were displayed on the wall beside each art piece in the galleries where they were exhibited (The Centre Gallery & Art is Vital Gallery in Calgary, Alberta & the Richmond Art Gallery in Richmond, British Columbia). We also self-published a limited edition of hand-bound books of the art images and poetry. (See Bickel & Sheppard (1995). The art and poetry of sisters. Calgary, AB: In Search of Fearlessness Press). For the purpose of this essay, I will not focus on this part of the collaborative project.

[4] Each woman chose a pose they wanted themselves to be represented in for the drawing. I invited them to bring an object that represented sisterhood for them, and a shawl or piece of fabric that they could drape however they liked on their body. They would be naked under the shawl but could choose how much their bodies were covered or not. Some chose to be fully draped and others sat or lay on their shawl.

[5] There was a wide age distribution amongst the co-creators: the young girls included my 11 and 13 year old stepdaughters, a 6 month old baby, and a 5 year old neighbour. The oldest participant was 62 years old. For the sake of flow in the writing I will call them all women.

[6] Twenty-two of the twenty-nine women were able to be part of this co-created performance ritual.

[7] Apophatic is known as the *via negativa* form of theology where one knows through unknowing. (Shantz, 1999, p.65).

[8] Through choosing to consciously witness the person that I am in co-creation with (rather than experience them as an object to be rendered for my own artistic and aesthetic ends), I have come to hold reverence for the role of art and testimony as theorized by Felman and Laub (1992). They wrote of art as inscribing or artistically bearing witness to "what we do not yet know of our historical relation to events of our times" (p.xx) and suggests, like the philosopher Levinas, that the artist as witness gives testimony to "the vehicle of an occurrence" (p.3) that is a reality beyond the artist herself.

[9] My writing practice is also fed by a relational aesthetic. I would like to acknowledge here the gift of critical and supportive conversation and editing that my partner, R. Michael Fisher, and Rita Irwin have contributed to this essay.

[10] In my master's thesis (Bickel., 2004), I addressed the practice of collaboration in art and found four different levels of collaborative involvement that I have experienced in art projects. Developing a working relationship of vulnerability, honesty, mutual respect, and trust that is willing to address differences and power relations is key to successful collaboration. If you want to know more about these levels, the thesis can be accessed on line at barbarabickel.com.

[11] As an artist, I distinguish between the term performance ritual and the term performance art as the aspect of sacred intention through ritual is essential to my practice and is often not present in contemporary performance art.

[12] An altar is a small table placed in the centre of a ritual with objects of offering placed upon it.

[13] For those interested in an analogous process that includes a social therapeutic aspect of ritual inquiry, see Bickel and Fisher (2006), which synthesizes the four moments of currere (e.g. Pinar & Grumet) and the art of qualitative thinking (e.g. Beittel).

[14] Hongyu Wong (2005) wrote of wounds and the source of creativity they inspire in curricular meaning-making.

[15] The question of ethics emerged for me again in the writing of this essay where my view as the artist is written without the input of my co-creators. I acknowledge that my writing reflects my story and may not accurately reflect theirs. In particular, acknowledging the names of my co-creators in the two art images felt important yet was crossing an ethical line of appropriating their experiences into mine. I have addressed this by sharing the essay with the two co-creators and inviting their responses to the writing that reflects my experience and have made changes where they have felt needed to best honour them.

[16] I draw understanding of the term *arational* from the Swiss philosopher Jean Gebser (1984). The arational includes mystical states, intuition, body knowledge, and emotions and is often accessed through the making of art and ritual. It includes the rational and irrational in its embrace.

SEAN WIEBE

A/R/TOGRAPHY: RESONATION IN WRITING

The a/r/tographer develops an aesthetic interaction with the world, an artistry of words, living inquiry, and teaching, and simultaneously develops a community of relationships around that aesthetic. My a/r/tographic story is one of poetry: I write poetry in that same compulsive way that I bite my fingernails. Spontaneity rules, and yet so much of my poetry comes back to classroom teaching; even though I write from chance and in those unforeseen moments, my poetry often explores the idea of creating transformative memories in the classroom.

Despite their apparent obscurity, my poems are an attempt to linger on the artistic moment that can bring self and other together, whether on the beach or in writing with students. Often that moment appears common place, but every art depends on nuance details and lingering spirit. When poems inquire into these moments and develop them as moments of significance, those lingerings often hold more transforming energy. The beauty is in the motion of picking up the moments while all around the classroom events continue to unfold.

For half my life now I have worked with student writers: writers of all ages, talents, and interests. The most consistent thing I have done over the years is teach writing to writers, not to students. Students often find it difficult to make the leap from student to writer—often the only impediment to writing well is belief in the identity of being a writer. Students wonder whether they are real writers, whether they will become writers, whether their writing is any good, and by extension, whether they are any good.

Once self-identified as a writer, a student can carry with her the commitment and care of writing practice, that tireless scrutiny and rumination of the world around her. This commitment carries over to one's sense of self, even to confidence as a human being, and to a resonance in writing that is artistry in craft, but also artistry in an aesthetic living. As a teacher, I have influence on how and whether a writing identity is taken on. For adolescents in particular, the notion of being is in flux and one's identity can be discovered, even given, right in the classroom community. For writing teachers, this is why the classroom needs to become a writing community. Creating that community is not a complicated science, but it does require an amazing openness of heart. From that place of openness, writers can take real writing risks (however momentary) and from these moments when writers are being writers with one another, a writing community emerges right in the classroom. This is where I like to linger in my teaching: it is where the energy lies. And it is why, I suppose, that I now call myself an a/r/tographer: the name has been given to me, though it is clear I have been an a/r/tographer from the very beginning.

In thinking of David Jardine and Sharon Friesen's (2006) paper on *The*

S. Springgay et al. (eds.), Being with A/r/tography, 95–107.

akin to emphasizing the actual practice or discipline of writing. I always feel more alive when writing poetry, like I am an explorer striking out, in love simply with adventure, and willing to go places I'd never intended to go. I like to share this feeling of poetry, this discipline of poetic living. So in the classroom with my students, we quickly get on with the business of ideas and observation, of journaling that spills over into passion, of writing workshops that simmer and hiss, of stuffing envelops with the promise of plenty, and of licking stamps for the sheer enterprise of communication. Our success rate is as low as can be expected, but that is only publishing success.

The success is in learning to live poetry, that ethereal life with its vain assertions and emotional falls: to dance naked or walk on water or disappear before the mirror. I mean that the poet lives carelessly so that there is no limit, so that nothing which is not life-giving will survive. This is the immediate success, the one that provokes passion, but there is also a success that lingers: this one not so stereotypically adolescent or youthful folly. It is the desire to create some kind of lasting influence, some lasting community spirit that lives on past its present members. I wrote the following poem with Jonathan, a student who graduated last year. We remain in contact in words, in poetry, and somehow in our lives too.

THIS WEB OF LINES

We are all given something

 to compensate for what we have lost (Alexie, 2005, p. 143).

poetry poetry poetry

broke her virginity in university

the empty eyes

sloked with some dope

her tongue has moved

doped out and broke

three lays for a smoke

everyone in the mouth of her stain

poetry poetry poetry

whisperings within the soul

the forgotten smile

like a jaded 40 year old

entangled in this web of lines

her hands with many lines

we see her acquaintances drive by

because they hate her

poetry poetry poetry

transformation in the baking sun

the summer oil on her legs so slick

hers is the most beautiful soul

she writes poems like mannequins

lost in another era

poetry poetry poetry

so much a beautiful girl

floating idly back in time

off this roof into the sky

finding party favours that rhyme

with her body

While I might give to some students the writing identity, I have discovered that not much depends on me in sustaining it. Really, it is the words that sustain. For example, in teaching with a kind of mentorship emphasis, there is a sense of responsibility to keep and maintain relationships that keep us writing, both student and teacher. And within this role or responsibility, there can be so many relationships, so many students to stay in contact with, that it is possible to feel overburdened. But with the Leggoian reminder that it is possible to love everyone (see Sameshima & Leggo, 2006), I learn that the words themselves take us the rest of the way. This lingering legacy may begin at first with the teacher's enthusiasm, her own sense of writing, or his own sense of living unburdened and enlivened, or perhaps with just the right encouraging words to inspire some confidence (Wright, Horn, & Sanders,1997), but it is the writing which brings completion to what a teacher begins.

I DO NOT EXIST IN TIME

I've sent you off

and cannot call you back

SEAN WIEBE

sounds from lips
these words
so silent on the page
cannot embrace
or quench the distance

I've been chasing cars
looking for you
behind the wheel
so certain you have driven by
beauty in another time
If only I could dream again
the whys and hows
of where we've been

my love is only here
lonely here
between the lines of rhyme
yours too
our bodies ever locked
and intertwined
as threads woven
in another time

trace the letter L
along my cheek
keep your breathing
body close
when morning comes
beside me
you will be here

arm under waist

a single moment

full and fragile

teetering towards a timeless place

that knows no taming

through some incantation

my heart has summoned you

and here now

top down

my heart is finally at rest

So much depending on the teacher to keep up with a constant output of positive personal energy cannot be possible. What happens is that writing is exciting enough to keep this process going without much help. Writing becomes the teacher. Writing becomes the maintainer of the relationship.

Writing sustains, writing keeps the heart warm, the words warm, and writing brings us back to remember the first writings that we had. Trusting the writing allows me to accept my own limitations. When I believe less in the writing, when the writing is not affecting my own heart (see Neilsen, 1998), it is then that I try physically to do more, try to connect more, and am most susceptible to burnout. It is imperative that I let the writing do the work. The writing brings the connections.

This refreshes me as a writer too. For in a relationship of writing, I am writing, which is always what I want to do more—to build relationships in writing, our writing keeps us together.

This notion became more solid for me in witnessing my son's desire to write and make stories. He writes. He writes mostly when I write. His enthusiasm carries on past my own, but it peaks and grows in some kind of correlation to my own writing habits. I've suspected this to be true in teaching as well. There is nothing better for getting a class back on track than to publish something myself—to take to class a poem in need of work-shopping, make those revisions together, and bring it back to them showing how their input has mattered.

The poetry speaks not so much about me, or us, but the journey I like to call *ourselves in poetry*. This approach allows the artistic material to speak, and affords us the opportunity to question and play with the loose ends of inquiry (of poetry), the unexplored places of pedagogy (in poetry), and to consider the overlap of living in and out of classroom contexts (by poetry).

I need this heightened, poetic appreciation when I step into the classroom, so I've been reading more poetry! Names like Jeanne Walker, Frank Orr, Richard Cecil, and Stephen Dunn come to mind. Somehow my reading of poetry, more so

SEAN WIEBE

than reading in other genres, brings me closer to the appreciation of beauty in the world and in the word.

WITHOUT PROCESSION

With sunshine

we make our own trail

you and I unfenced

against a cloudless sky

as steps to the unknown

This day I learn to

resist the need to mark it

but to let words free

as I bend branches

you are saying my own thoughts

in code language

I need this heightened, poetic appreciation when I step into the classroom. Otherwise, the familiar takes over and my interaction with those around me falls into the realm of objectification and the enacting of routines and stereotypes. There is a vigour in poetry that balances the rigor of research (Leggo, 2004a).

Stephen Dunn (1994) reminds us that our journey happens while travelling elsewhere. While we are chasing the poetry, an acceptance letter may appear. The stop points along the way are unanticipated, appearing while we are focal to something else entirely.

Robert Creely (1985) reminds us to "drive". To simply "get in a big, old, god-damn car and drive". Creely, that old magician knows, however, that while we drive, while we experience that freedom of wind blowing through our hair, while we are distracted with our own pleasure of the art, out of no where comes—blindsiding us—look out—we must swerve—alas it is too late—we run into a governmental examination.

Billy Collins (2001) reminds us to find a melody in, of all places, the barking dog. Yes, there is a melody here. But how does one copyright a "barking dog solo"? The poetry of living is symphonic, like barking dogs.

Howard Nemerov (1991) reminds us that the light in the darkness is only temporary. We must learn to see in the dark. The poetry that unfolds in a classroom can be dark. It is distracting, distractive, an abstraction, abstracting.

100

SEQUEL

before him all his pawns

are ready to command

lined up rank and file

how powerful

his chest becomes

this otherwise ordinary man

is dangerous when

he thinks he understands

how great the oz

with whom we must contend

who imagines

the structures and the movements his

the victory his own

injured and unskilled

we admit that

when the pieces move

to some other plan

when the beginning is

or where it ends unknown

we are upset

But the king is ready to defend

his head

on this it all depends

What I have felt in poetry is an enthusiasm for a kind of living much needed, much more needed than I had realized. For example, after this last spring break holiday, I shared with my Creative Writing 8 class a feeling of my life changing while I was lying still: on a holiday that included the appealing dazzle of *Disneyland, Universal Studios,* and *6 Flags,* I was surprised about my favourite part of the

SEAN WIEBE

trip—lying on Laguna beach—not to tan, or even to ogle my surroundings, but to lie there, dead, in jeans, jacket over my face, slipping in and out of consciousness.

WITHOUT A TRACE

Morning laughter calls

warmly dressing me to share

a cup of coffee

our lips sip gently

sunshine peeks through the shutters

sitting together

we want to linger

longer but the day's plans take

shape.

Lying there, like so many other unplanned curricular moments, was restful and beautiful. I know its beauty because I recall this story with longing, while the story of *Disneyland* has been summed up in a photograph, already framed and fixed to the wall.

Still curious to me is how 13 year old boys, lovers of basketball and junior high dances, have reacted to this story, to this moment of living poetically. They too have need of rest, of lingering moments that last, and of finding the beauty of poetry to offer some balance to the rigour of their own studies.

HEART AND FINGERS

my heart beats

that same old song

blood pumps

my fingers punch

these keys

beats skipped

irregular rhythms

too crisp

sounds something like

m yhea rt is brok n

my fingers punch

everything dishes

flying cupboard doors swinging

the heart still beats its

illusory last passions

oh, the blood can flow

through holes in the wall

back to bed

to fall asleep

and dream the peaceful dream

the saints surely dreamt of

in jail or while on fire

fingers now curled

over the blankets

pulled up to my chin

here it all started

and here finally parted

my fingers can relax

and let others punch

those keys for me

My students know tests, standards, competition: they know at 13 the unemployment statistics, the university entrance standards, and the heavy weight of parent expectation. Rigour comes to them like rigor mortis to a body (see Leggo, 2004b).

THERE WAS A TIME WHEN THESE THINGS DIDN'T MEAN ANYTHING

I'm becoming more comfortable

at funeral homes

meeting dead people is easier

than the living

who also know

it is difficult

to be a human being

alive people want

something

coming up close

like perusing footnotes

look into my past

look for the real man

underneath the veneer

ask if there is any purpose

under there

the words

make no-sense so

alive people stare

and take stock

decide if my clothes

are too old

want small talk

looking down my throat

searching for any

dreams stuck

in the esophagus

alive people probe
and peer and want
me to care
and I get the distinct
feeling that what I'm saying
is being "interpreted"   (as a cry for help)
stepped on
ground into blood
drying in the sun
under the sole of their feet   (he's so weak)

anyway
alive people
offer a few condolences
like the coughing up of oil
on my engine:
what really is there
what is
there to say or think or do
or believe
they are grease
clogging the arteries
the pistons

is it really worth it
the whole
effort to not be
concerned with what
alive people will say
or write on

my permanent record

as if

the impressions they

leave are so important

I rarely remember even

in my heart

this freedom

now I want them

whoever they are

to say something

more meaningful

than the dead

Let me conclude with another story: I was recently travelling with our school's senior-boys tennis team. Driving down the highway on route to a tennis match, these boys, these seniors, were belting out James Blunt's "You're Beautiful". Moments like this remind me that beauty is cherished more than ever, and I have some idea that the enlivening of poetry can help. Like beauty, poetry brings together some kind of collaborative aesthetic in the shared space of words. The poetic aesthetic is with, among, beside and between us—we can feel the resonance. And by being in touch with our own being, our own writing resonance, we also touch others, and become part of their shared space of words.

This is a process of creativity, an artistic moment that can bring self and other together while remaining separate. In community my *Being* is always among others, and in that shared space *being* is always becoming. With poetry I am searching for myself, and yet, in poetry, I am othered to myself. This is true among persons, and is also true within persons, and it is true of, in, and by poetry. With others we have access to ourselves. In other words, within me is self and other. It is a creative process outside the body but also within the body. As an a/r/tographer I recognize that I do not work alone, but within a community of art, there is a creation which is my process of becoming, not only an artist but a human being.

I call myself an a/r/tographer because in the classroom the multifaceted identity overlaps with others who in the classroom are also discovering the relationship of self and other. Here, in the in between spaces of being, life unfolds. Somehow, it is the poetic process that brings collaboration and unity within the divided me—the artist of a/r/tography. We reach out our hands and can feel the resonance of writing.

The a/r/tographer lives in the multiplicity of a community of discursive relationships; the a/r/tographer, writer of unauthorized (even collaborative), autobiographies, creates fictions—reproductive and resistant—intimate textual intertwinings that tell of both self and of culture and of writer and reader. To date, I still call this poetry. It is, surely, a ruthless and loving poetry of destroying the self while simultaneously writing the self into being.

DÓNAL O DONOGHUE

"THAT STAYED WITH ME UNTIL I WAS AN ADULT": MAKING VISIBLE THE EXPERIENCES OF MEN WHO TEACH

This chapter is about men who teach at the elementary level. The chapter, which draws on a study of fifteen men teachers in Ireland, is neither written nor presented in the format that is familiar and characteristic of ways of writing about the experiences of men teachers (see Allan, 1993; Coulter & McNay, 1993; King, 1998, 2000; Lahelma, 2000; Mills, Martino, & Lingard, 2004; Sargent, 2000, 2001, 2005; Thornton, 1999). It comprises images and texts presented independently, simultaneously, and together, in an effort to make visible social constructs of male elementary teachers—constructs which are neither uniform nor universally generalizable. I write and create a text where two different structures of expression (graphic and linguistic) give form to these men's experiences of living, performing, negotiating and embodying multiple (and often contradictory) identities as teachers, men, and male teachers.[1]

As educational researchers, we are trained to look towards the practices, processes and understandings generated by other educational researchers, scholars and theoreticians in our field as signposts to what and how we should inquire. Rarely, in the process of conceptualising or doing educational research, do we look towards or at the work of artists, their practices and processes of art making, and their methods of representing and giving visual form to concepts and ideas. As an artist, researcher, teacher, and scholar engaged in the practice of a/r/tography, I am interested in exploring what the processes and practices of writing and art making—in particular that which presupposes an attention to form, medium and representation, and especially contemporary art practice—can offer in conceptualising, doing and representing research about men teachers. There is much we can learn from paying close attention to the way artists work and represent. Much like research, artistic creation is a collective process within which the individual artist is but one of many persons who brings a work to fruition (Becker, 1982; Bourdieu, 1996; Crane, 1989). A piece of work is not only produced by the artist, but by all those who come in contact with the work subsequently and who have an interest in it. As Bourdieu (1996) observes, an artwork is "in fact made not twice, but hundreds of times, thousands of times by all those who have an interest in it, who find a material or symbolic profit in reading it, classifying it, decoding it, commenting on it, reproducing it, criticizing it, combating it, knowing it, possessing it" (p.171). Much like art, how we do and represent research is inseparable from what gets communicated, and the opportunity for understanding and meaning making that is made possible. Ever since Modern Realism, artists have attended to the relationship between medium

S. Springgay et al. (eds.), Being with A/r/tography, 109–124.

argued that artists have always attended to these relationships). Willie Doherty's installation *Same Difference* and the interpretations of that piece make visible this relationship.[2]

Same Difference was first installed in Matt's Gallery, London, 1990. It was later shown at the Irish Museum of Modern Art, Dublin on the occasion of the exhibition *Willie Doherty: False Memory October 2002-March 2003*, where I came to view it. The installation deals with issues of conflict, representation, and identity as lived and experienced specifically in Northern Ireland, but also in life more generally. Using two projection screens placed in a dark room and positioned diagonally opposite one another, Doherty projects the image of Donna Maguire's face on both screens. He photographed Maguire's face from a TV screen following her arrest by the Dutch authorities as a suspected IRA terrorist (Mac Giolla Léith, 2002). Using slide projectors, Doherty projects onto this image of Maguire's face (on both screens) words, descriptors, and terms that construct and story Maguire. The words/descriptors/terms come and go, always being replaced by another. The image of Maguire's face remains. On one screen (which I call Screen A here for the purposes of description), pejorative terms drawn from the "anti-Nationalist popular press" (murderer, pitiless, murderer, misguided, murderer, evil, murderer) are projected. On the other screen (Screen B), words/terms of pro-Republican (volunteer, defiant, volunteer, honourable, volunteer, committed, volunteer) are projected (see Mac Giolla Léith, 2002). On Screen A the term murderer is projected every second time. The same applies in the case of the term volunteer, which appears on Screen B every second time. *Same Difference* tells the story of what it must be like to exist in a divided space, to live, to be observed, seen and constructed by communities from both sides of that divide—one being the Nationalist Republican side (where she is constructed through notions of heroicism, bravery, daring and courageousness), the other, the Unionist loyalist side where she is anything but brave, heroic or courageous, and is instead a misguided, pitiless murderer. It tells a story through the act of projecting, and this story is made sense of through the memory and knowledge of the viewer. The act of projection speaks of an identity that is constructed out of and through projection. This is not an embodied identity. It is one generated from projections—carefully selected and collated projections.

The sequence of the words tells me, the viewer, of who I am looking at, of whose presence I am in. So, are these projected identities, projected constructions, projected imaginings and classifications? Does this work speak of disembodied identities—identities that are constructed outside and beyond the person, identities that are constructed by others? Does the identity of Maguire change depending on who is doing the projection? Is this work about the possibilities of living different identities or of living a particular identity that generates another? As a viewer, I am drawn into this piece of work and I become part of the work. I am positioned in the work, not outside, or looking in from the outside, but right in the middle of the work. I move from viewer to participant. It requires me to become bodily involved, turning my head back and forth between both projections. And in the work, I began to feel what it might be like to live in such a space, a space of conflict and tension, where choice isn't choice as we understand it in a democratic society. The work forced me to choose a side, to align myself with one of the two sides. For me, being in the middle was certainly not a comfortable space. Being neutral is difficult. It got me thinking about the impossibility of being neutral under these conditions. I began to question and ask which group I would align myself with if I lived in that space, because *Same Difference* forcefully tells me (without telling me in the usual way) that it would be impossible to remain neutral. And while I was positioned in a gallery space and not in a contested terrain per se, it became a place of contact, a place of conflict, and place of choice.

The kind of reading and understanding that I secured from this art work is influenced in great part by the means through which Doherty has selected to make and present *Same Difference*. The meaning of the work is thus constituted by and in the form, medium, and mode of representation. Is Doherty transforming data (lived, remembered, or researched, or does it matter) into a public form that others can understand? Is he telling it as it is (from his perspective)? Is he engaging in representing data to advance or increase our understanding? Does he succeed? Is he simply provoking the viewer? What kind of questions does this work pose, what kind of questions can we generate from viewing and participating in this piece— what forms of knowledge are being presented, constructed, contested, and reformed? As Elliot Eisner (1997) argues, "Alternate forms of data representation promise to increase the variety of questions that we can ask about the educational situations we study...we can expect new ways of seeing things, new settings for their display, and new problems to tackle... put another way, our capacity to wonder is stimulated by the possibilities the new forms of representation suggest" (p.180-181). This is evident in the work of the French artist Sophie Calle, especially her work *Suite Vénitienne* (1980), *The Hotel* (1981), *The Detachment* (1996), and *Appointment with Sigmund Freud* (1998). She creates "factual narratives with fictional overtones" and combines them with her photographic works, thus creating a form that is neither "auto-fiction" or "photo novel"; material that provides opportunities to consider how to do inquiry that attends to living experience (see Macel, 2003). Work such as this provides opportunities to ask how we might represent experiences in a visual form through visual narrative, especially those instances experienced in non-verbal, non-linguistic modes.

I am interested, then, in the kinds of possibilities, the kinds of questions, and the kinds of representations and interpretations that this work makes possible for doing and representing research about men teachers, as well as the processes involved in making, representing and receiving such work. It is at the intersections between art and research, living and performing, knowing and doing, that I focus my attention. I believe that research should not only enlarge and advance our understanding of that which is being examined, but that the process/es and the outcome/s of the inquiry itself should make a space for the creation of new knowledge that is individually and culturally transformative (Sullivan, 2005). To what extent can the processes and practices of art making lead us to research practices that are open and attend to multiple ways of coming to know, of re/presenting, and of meaning making—to research that is transformative? How we might explore issues of living, performing and teaching through artistic and aesthetic processes?

The study of fifteen men teachers,[3] on which I draw for this chapter, is an a/r/tographical inquiry shaped and structured in accordance with the theory and practice of a/r/tography (see Irwin & de Cosson, 2004; Irwin, 2004a; Springgay, Irwin, & Wilson Kind, 2005). It simultaneously draws on the practice of other forms of arts-based educational research methods, including both narrative inquiry and autoethnography. The way in which we came together as researchers and researched enabled the fifteen men and I to construct a community of a/r/tographic practice. This was particularly evident in the processes of mutual engagement alongside one another in our own inquiries and in the inquiries of each other and others, in our developing, charting, debating, negotiating and out creative practices of doing, reflecting and knowing, We were in constant negotiation about our focus as our understanding, knowing, and doing developed, evolved and shifted over time. As Rita Irwin claims in the introduction to this section, "Negotiating personal engagement within a community of belonging is part of the rhizomatic relationality of inquirers working together".

The study grew out of sentiments expressed by James King in the preface to his book, *Uncommon caring: Learning from men who teach young children.* Following his research with seven men teachers, King (1998) writes "I realize that we have begun something that still begs for more attention. The culture's constructions of 'teacher' and 'male' both hold a great deal of potential energy. Unpacking the beliefs is continuing work" (p.viii). This study is located within social constructivist, feminist informed, and poststructuralist theories of masculinity (see Connell, 1995, 2000; Kimmel, 1994; Lesko, 2000; Mac an Ghaill, 1994; Martino & Pallotta-Chiarolli, 2003; Messner, 1997). Central to the study is the idea that masculinities are constructed, performed, and regulated, but they are not uniform and universally generalizable to all men in our society. Masculinity is conceptualised as something that is not "singularly possessed or something that 'is'" but something that is continually created through a series of repetitive acts. These stylised and embodied performances are "naturalised" through repetition and regulation and are shaped by other dimensions of identity such as race, age, sexuality, disability, together with institutional factors (Renold, 2004). As Michael Kimmel and Michael Messner (2001) put it, "our identity as men is developed through a complex process of interaction with the culture in which we both learn the gender scripts appropriate to our culture and attempt to modify those scripts to make them more palatable" (p.xv). The construction of masculinities is specific to particular sites (Martino & Frank, 2006). Schools and their social and discursive practices legitimate and authorizes particular versions of hegemonic masculinities by providing the space for these masculinities to be performed and enacted.

The research for this ongoing study of men teachers in Ireland is characterised by its multimodal reflexive processes of inquiry. Data is generated and collected at different points and employs a range of diverse methods, including narrative writing, journaling, observations collected through digital video and still images, recorded interviews and group discussions, written assignments, and researcher-created art works. These men engage in narrative processes—keeping journals, writing their stories, and reflecting on doing teaching and doing masculinity. They tell stories, they write stories, and they live stories. These became stories that story them—stories of them as men, as teachers and as male teachers teaching. Such stories are open, partial and relational. While teaching, both as practice teachers and as class teachers, each man kept a journal which included renderings of the spaces they encountered—of the spaces they created, disassembled and reassembled. They wrote of the conversations they initiated, to which they contributed and they overheard, and of the observations they made and were made around them. We met on a number of occasions, both as a group and in pairs. Initially we set out to explore what King (2000) describes as the troubled relationships between the socially constructed categories of "men" and "teacher" (p.3).

While the inquiry developed in a non-linear manner, we started by exploring issues around our individual and collective identities as men, as teachers and as men who are teachers. We focused in particular on the experiences, places, and spaces that inform, form, and reform these identities and on the borders, boundaries, and openings within and across these sites. Individually, we photographed places and spaces where our identities were played out, enacted, performed, affirmed, challenged, and contested. We explored masculinity and teaching as a life project constantly constructed and reconstructed, and lived. Together, we collected images, newspaper cuttings, and journal articles to read and share. Drawing on these, we analysed the prevailing societal discourses about male teachers as expressed in recent media and we wrote narratives about our lives as teachers, as men, and as men teachers. We constructed life histories and personal narratives both visual and written. And in these autoethnographic visual and written texts, as Carolyn Ellis and Arthur Bochner (2000) put it, "concrete action, dialogue, emotion, involvement, spirituality, and self consciousness are featured, appearing as relational and institutional stories affected by history, social structure and culture, which themselves are dialectically revealed through action, feeling, thought and language" (p.740).

I made art throughout this process—art that was influenced, guided, and shaped by our questing, both individually, together, and in pairs—art that attended to, articulated, and made visible explicit, implicit and tacit knowledge. As Stephanie Springgay, Rita Irwin and Sylvia Kind Wilson (2005) observe: "Through attention to memory, identity, autobiography, reflection, meditation, story telling, interpretation, and/or representation, artists/researchers/teachers expose their living practices in evocative ways" (p.903). This multifaceted approach seeks out multiple voices, multiple forms of knowing and coming to know, and multiple ways of coming to understand and experience and represent. It provides opportunities to do what Irwin describes in the introduction to this section, to uncover, make visible, and address the explicit, implicit, and tacit knowledge shared by community members. Our questing was not about getting to the bottom, rather it was about bringing us in touch with our own lives and the lives of others, and deepening our understanding of the world in which we live and experience (Eisner, 1997). It was about recognising that we are contiguously connected while yet belonging to a singularity; not alone in our community of a/r/tograhic practice but also in the lives we live.

A number of issues already identified in studies of men teachers and their experiences of teaching emerged in this study. Issues such as teaching as care, the problems of touch and being bodily present with children, questions of discipline, surveillance, and monitoring all emerged as key issues. That teaching, particularly at elementary level, has been constructed as an act of caring, devoid to some extent of real intellectual and abstract thinking was troubled and troubling in our inquiry. These men articulated ways in which historically shifting cultural definitions of masculinity have excluded men from teaching when it is constructed as care. And yet, they described themselves and their characteristics using terms of care and nurturing: "I think of myself and my friends, Keith and John in particular, we're all the same, as in we're all kind of caring and sensitive too" (Michael).[4] The research, however, is not limited to these issues, insights, confirmations, and outcomes. It provides a space for these men, these fifteen men, to be present, to be with, to think about and articulate why they entered teaching. It offered them ways to examine who they are when they teach, why they act in particular ways, at particular times, in particular places and under particular circumstances, how they perform masculinity and masculinizing practices, how they deal with expectations and demands, and so on. "How I ended up in front of a laptop pondering the issue of men in the primary teaching profession has indeed caused me to question how I ended up teaching in the first place and what it means to teach", writes Pete.

As I mentioned earlier, throughout this inquiry I engage in art making and writing processes. To do so, I use field notes, recorded conversations, observations, interpretations and understandings, together with the participants' autobiographical and narrative texts. I look, I observe, I seek out, I make choices (aesthetic and intellectual), and I photograph. I take many photographs. I photograph spaces, places, people standing, looking, walking, thinking, feeling, acting, wondering, performing. I focus on positions and positioning, points of connection and points of departure, lines that demarcate and lines that reunite, shapes that lead and mislead, points of entry and exit, boundaries. I record surfaces, textures, forms, light, shadows, presences and absences, colours, details. Later, I combine elements from some of these photographs as I work with image creation. I include some and discard others; I sometimes repeat the same image several times; I crop; I trim; I position; I join; I create; I make patterns (visual and textual); I add text; I take text away. I position text in images, sometimes beside an image, other times under, over, above, or below an image. And I do this to make visible the lived experiences of fifteen men teachers in Ireland. I do this to re/present, to un/settle, interrupt, disrupt and extend normalized ways of inquiring into, thinking about, understanding, and representing the issues that confront men as they become elementary teachers.

This process, the outcomes of the process, and the artworks presented (a selection of eight) in this chapter provide a space to work in, work out, and make sense of—as well as position, place and untangle—that which I come to hear, experience and name during the research process. They are records of recursive, reflexive and reflective analyses and reanalyses. They provide a place and a means for "learning to perceive differently," where "learning to perceive differently requires that one engages in practices that in some way, removes one from the comfortable habits of the familiar" (Carson & Sumara, 1997, p.xvii). I view these works as texts, as a tangle of texts, as texts that are being written, rewritten, read and reread—texts that integrate knowing, doing, and making—texts that have transformative potential. The texts attend to absences, to the things that are not said. They make visible the many things that are said, but in ways that are revealing, and rely on both image and text. As artworks to be looked at and read, interrogated, decoded, critiqued, and classified. They provide a space to think critically about how teaching and gendered identities are constructed, negotiated, lived and relived. In doing so, these artworks might serve to disrupt or rupture that which we think we know about what it means to be a male teacher at elementary level. They provide an opportunity for a reengagement with ideas about men, masculinity, teaching, and living. And yet, neither artworks nor texts presented below can ever fully describe the lived experiences of these men teachers, the process of coming to know, name, understand, and re/present encounters of recognition, acknowledgement, and approval as well as encounters of resistance, conflict and struggle.

As we spoke and wrote and discussed collectively and in pairs, the men began to acknowledge the highly complex and contradictory nature of what they do when they perform teaching and perform masculinity. The self is elaborate, complex, and formed by multiple discourses of power/knowledge. "When I was invited to become involved and contribute to this research project I immediately thought that this was going to be an easy account to give and it would not be too taxing. However the more I thought on the subject and the more people I spoke to, the fuzzier the picture became" (Anthony). Understandings/renderings/representations are presented throughout the paper in the form of text and image. Some of these understandings/renderings/representations are critical, some are descriptive, but all strive to reveal, to uncover, to emphasise and draw attention to that which is often regarded as familiar and known. While the understandings/renderings/ representations presented may not offer definite conclusions, they do present new ways of thinking about and inquiring into the making of men who teach and knowing men who teach—a making and a knowing which is never fixed, always in the state of becoming continuous.

In-between # 1. 2006. Dónal O Donoghue. Digital print on paper. 36" x 36". Courtesy of the artist.

Living a life of "in-between" (in-between spaces of practice and possibilities, in-between private and public, in-between the socially constructed categories of "teacher" and "man") was how the professional life of the beginning male teacher was often described. In-between implies a middle ground. The idea of the "in-between" presupposes a space created and spatially defined by its relationship to that which gives it meaning and form in the first instance, that which enables it to exist. And yet, a change in this in-between alters that which defines it as such. In-between spaces can be spaces of exposure, spaces that restrict and limit, spaces that are always altering shifting and always in the process of becoming something else—tangible but un/known.

In-between # 2. 2006. Dónal O Donoghue. Digital print on paper. 36" x 43". Courtesy of the artist.

These men spoke about living in the in-between, in relation to what is expected and what is possible. It was assumed that they would be great disciplinarians without much experience in the practice of managing behaviour: "On a few different occasions I have been asked by female colleagues to speak to certain individuals who had misbehaved. Some of these women have been teaching for up to thirty years. Is my gender more powerful than their considerable experience?" (Colm). They tell of how they are expected to act as role models, disciplinarians, and enforcers of discipline; it was presumed that they would be principals without ever expressing a desire to be.

It is assumed that every male teacher wants to, and will become, a principal some day…comments like 'when you're a principal of your own school' have been directed towards me, some in sarcastic or joking manner, however, they have been made nonetheless. (Michael)

Assumed that we are all the same # 1. 2006. Dónal O Donoghue. Digital photograph with text on paper. Diptych, panel I, 36" x 11"; panel II, 36" x 28". Courtesy of the artist.

As a man who teaches I am expected to show an interest and aptitude for sports and training of school teams, especially in the games of the Gaelic Athletic Association (GAA). There is a lot of pressure to conform to this norm and this puts undue pressure on me at least, with little or no experience of GAA coaching. (Glenn)

I think that if you don't fit that mould, the school will feel they're missing out because they've gone out, I don't mean out on a limb, but they've gone to the trouble of employing a male teacher, on the kind of on the assumption that he'll look after the sports side of things and if they're not looked after, the teacher isn't seen to be looking after this side of things, it's a bit of a let down for the principal. I feel I have to change or evolve in order to fit this mould, therefore feeling immense pressure. (Michael)

Assumed that we are all the same # 2. 2006. Dónal O Donoghue. Digital print on paper.
36" x 54". Courtesy of the artist.

As teachers and men we talk about living in the in-between, always and simultaneously being projected into the spaces that generate and sustain this in-between, but never fully inhabiting any of these spaces. Our identities as teachers (and men) are never this or that, but constituted of partial identities and contradictory positions located in spaces of in-between. We are assumed to be all the same; produced and repeated entities.

Viewed through #1. 2006. Dónal O Donoghue. Digital print on paper. 24" x 52". Courtesy
of the artist.

As men teachers we are seen as safe and dangerous all at once and we are positioned and placed between both constructs. We are often viewed with suspicion; enduring noticeable levels of surveillance and scrutiny not alone in our dealings with children but in our sexual and social behaviour more broadly. "You see that's why there are so few men that enter teaching, you are very aware that it is a caring profession" wrote Daniel in this study. As in Mary Thornton's (1999) study, these men articulated their concern that they might be perceived as perverts or potential child abusers for wanting to work with children. Many men spoke about being projected into an in-between space regarding their sexuality. Preferred as heterosexual, but often viewed as homosexual, these men talk about the effort spent establishing, policing, and making visible the boundaries between both. That in-between space between public and private identities, between how this space is managed, negotiated, and lived, is made visible by Michael's remarks when he writes of a recent event:

> It was during Cheltenham and my sister texted me with a tip so it came up to break time so I told the teacher, I'd to go back down to the house, it was during break time anyway. I ran back down…and I felt like a child. I stopped in the village and there was a bookies [turf accountants] there. It was like a dart across the road to about ten yards beside the bookies door and then I found myself looking around to see did I recognise anyone. I didn't and it was madness. Anyway it was 33/1 and I won and it was well worth it. I'm not trying to be funny but it's true, I went near enough to the bookies and I had a good look around to see if there was anyone and that particular day we were training after school and on the days we train, I'd wear a tracksuit and I felt they mightn't recognise me anyway so off I went, went in, placed my bet, came out and back to school.

In a similar vein Daniel wrote,

> Unlike the other staff members I live close to the school, therefore I would occasionally socialise in the village during weekends. Strangely, I find myself being very conscious of my behaviours, not that I would usually be swinging from the rafters. However, I always ensure that I do not drink too much and have my wits about me as I feel it is part of my duty as a teacher. Parents expect teachers to be perfect citizens; again one has the fit the mould in this regard also.

It is often in these in-between spaces that power is played out, contested, and takes form; where identities are formed, reformed and transformed; where an othering take place; where boundaries are imagined, articulated and lived. Located in the in-between denotes living within and between boundaries.

Openings and closings. 2006. Dónal O Donoghue. Digital print on paper. 24" x 57".
Courtesy of the artist.

As a group we conceptualise performing teaching and masculinity as acts of boundary pushing, of boundary crossing, of boundary negotiating, of boundary maintenance, of boundary dismantling and re/assembling and of boundary shifting. For these past weeks now I have been listening to stories that tell of boundaries, stories that are boundaries, and stories that come from boundary encounters. Boundaries hem these men in and keep them out. Boundaries provide openings and closings; boundaries are spaces of translation, sites of struggle and sites of resistance.

Viewed through #2. 2006. Dónal O Donoghue. Digital photograph on paper. 36" x 27".
Courtesy of the artist.

For us, boundaries dictate, limit, constrain; they lead, guide and direct. But boundaries are also porous. We live in a world of boundaries. Boundaries provide openings and closings; boundaries are constructed, maintained, monitored and surveyed. Boundaries are sites of possibility. Boundaries are for crossing. Boundaries protect, disrupt, they divide; they inhabit in-between spaces, marking out and establishing one space from another. Boundaries encompass, take in, and cover over. Boundaries can be and are dismantled and reassembled many times over. They shift, disappear, and reappear. Boundaries are policed. Boundaries define and are defined. Boundaries separate private space from public space, unused space from used space; they overshadow. While boundaries dictate, limit and constrain men and boys in schools, they too create boundaries and are involved in spoken and unspoken ways in safeguarding, disassembling, altering and re constituting boundaries—boundaries of knowledge, boundaries of practice, boundaries of being with. As Brian explained:

> They wouldn't expect a man to take part in auditions for the musicals they stage here. Maybe one or two did go in for auditions in the past simply because they needed fellows in the musical. I remember one of the lads did because I went to see this musical with a girl (a couple of her friends were in). If I went for an audition and I told the lads they would fall over laughing. All the lads in this college are kind of, the majority of them are always going around with hurleys and we're always going playing soccer or rugby down the field, and I suppose to go and do a musical would be kind of going against the grain. You know, what I mean?...Yes, I feel restricted sometimes, but I suppose half the time it wouldn't bother me like I couldn't be bothered going doing that, even though I like it and I like teaching drama. I'd like to act but I don't think in college I'd be bothered. I'd say I would, maybe join the drama society if I got a job somewhere where I didn't know people. (Brian)

In schools and colleges of education, boundaries were built around these men, boundaries that protect them yet lock them in certain spaces. Boundaries by which they define and are defined. Boundaries that limit, keep in, retain, release and enable their consciousness, real, imagined or experienced.

MAKING VISIBLE THE EXPERIENCES OF MEN WHO TEACH

Concluding Remarks

Looking right. 2006. Dónal O Donoghue. Digital print on paper. Panel I, 24" x 10". Panel II, 24" x 10". Panel III, 24" x 46".

Research into the experiences of male teachers is not new, yet in recent years there has been an increased focus on men who teach. This focus stems largely from the growing concern with the fewness of men teachers in our schools, particularly at elementary level. Efforts to attract, recruit and retain more male teachers have become more widespread, more visible and more cogently planned and staged. Over the past decade or more, this recruitment and retention drive has more or less framed the debate about male teachers with the result that the space for exploring issues relating to the men who teach, such as the formation and contestation of male teacher identities and the construction, negotiation and renegotiation of masculine identities of men teachers, has been curtailed significantly; issues such as those identified have been silenced and overlooked as a result. As Janet Smith (2004) claims, "in particular attention is seldom paid to the experience of male primary school teachers" (n.p).

Scholars have broadly responded to the drive to increase male participation in teacher education programmes and in schools in one of two ways: one by engaging in an identification and profiling process, and two by critiquing the assumptions that underpin and drive government policy and practice—namely sex role socialisation theories and the normalization and homogenization of male teachers that is likely to occur as a result. For example, studies that profile the characteristics of male entrants into teaching in terms of age, social class, reasons for making career choice and so on, are plentiful (Johnson et al, 1999; Mulholland, 2001; Reid and Thornton, 2001; Thornton, 1999). Also common are studies which suggest, as Rebecca Coulter and Margaret McNay (1993) put it "that the call for more men elementary level teachers especially oversimplifies complex issues and leaves unexamined the political nature of that call" (p.398). In addition to this work, there is a growing body of literature that explores what King (2000) calls the troubled relationships between "the socially constructed categories of 'men' and 'teacher' (p.3)." The complex and often contradictory experiences of men teachers have been probed mainly through ethnographic studies of the lives and work practices of practising teachers (see for example Allan, 1993; King 2000; Sargent, 2001; Smith, 2004).

In this study, and indeed in this chapter, I go where studies of men teachers have not gone before (methodologically at least, but also I believe conceptually). Locating, situating, and conceptualising this inquiry in contemporary art practice, and the theory and practice of a/r/tography more specifically, has offered possibilities (that other research methods close off) for inquiring into, coming to know, and re/presenting experiences of men who teach—experiences of living, performing and embodying multiple and often contradictory identities as teacher, man, and male teacher. It offers opportunities for a visceral knowing and a visual knowing, and for ways of sharing and re/presenting that resonates with the lives we live, in all their richnessess and complexities.

ESTHETIQUE DU MAL

And out of what one sees and hears and out

Of what one feels, who could have thought to make

So many selves, so many sensuous worlds,

As if the air, the mid-day air, was swarming

With the metaphysical changes that occur,

Merely in living as and where we live

—Wallace Stevens (1945)

NOTES

*   I wish to thank most sincerely the fifteen men who participated in this inquiry. They gave freely of their time, thoughts, experiences and energy. I am truly indebted to them. Without them this work would never have seen the light of day. I also wish to acknowledge the College Research Directorate Mary Immaculate College University of Limerick for the grant support given for this research.

[1]   Experience is conceptualised as relational, temporal and lived.

[2]   Willie Doherty is an artist who has spent most of his professional working life making art about the Troubles in the North of Ireland: the political and religious conflict between nationalists and unionists; republicans and loyalists.

[3]   This ongoing research study is located in a college of education and liberal arts within a university in Ireland. It has been in operation for almost a year at this stage. It involves men who are in their final year of a teacher education programme and men who are certified teachers in their first year of teaching in elementary schools. The men range in age from 21 to 37. All are white and middle class and one is married.

[4]   For purposes of anonymity, participants' names have been changed and replaced with pseudonyms.

MARCIA MCKENZIE & NORA TIMMERMAN[1]

RELATIONALITY IN WEB-BASED HYPERMEDIA RESEARCH: A WORKING EXAMPLE IN TEACHER EDUCATION

I think one of the things [that would support my work] is…an understanding of entry points that's helpful and is contextualized enough…the old deep description kind of thing about understanding the contextual stuff, and understanding how people go about doing things. The possibility of bringing people together and having conversations. I mean, the ability to say, "yeah, so how do you understand that," or…"what do you do that works?", or "what do you do that offers entry points?", or "how do you see"—not even best practices, but "what is it about the intersections of the systemic, the programmatic, and the, the bodies, both of the instructors and students, that make this a good, possible space?" (teacher educator, DATL Project transcript #8-1, p.17-18)

This year's been—maybe it's just that I've taught it now for five or six years, or whether it's this group [of students], or my own kind of sense of frustration, I'm not sure, but it seems like I'm at a loss right now for trying to figure out how to get them, what angle to take to get them to notice these things, to question some of these things…I get resistance whichever way I go. I do feel pretty much alone in it…So, you know, is there a way of bringing people together to kind of really ask these questions? (teacher educator, DATL Project transcript #6-1, p.5, 9, 11)

As the above comments suggest, being a teacher educator can mean working in relative isolation. This is particularly the case when, like these teacher educators, you are one of few who are exploring discursive understandings of knowledge and identity with pre-service teachers in relation to socio-ecological issues. Geographical distance and lack of time can mean that there is little opportunity to meet with similarly-focused colleagues to share and further develop understandings and teaching practices. In addition, though a small body of more general theoretical literature exists (e.g., Boler, 1999; Kumashiro, 2004), as well as a range of subject-specific theoretical work (e.g., Weaver, Morris, & Appelbaum, 2000), little practical information is available on how other teacher educators are going about this work (Kumashiro, 2001). It was with hopes of providing opportunities for collaborative and on-going learning focused on enabling teachers to integrate discursive understandings into their own socio-ecologically focused teaching, that the world wide web-based *Discursive Approaches to Teaching and Learning (DATL) Project*[2] was developed (http://www.otherwise-

S. Springgay et al. (eds.), Being with A/r/tography, 125–139.

Using this project as an example, we respond in this chapter to Irwin and Springgay's question included in the introduction to this volume: "How might we begin to think of research methodologies as relational situations that provoke meaning through contemplation, complication, and as alternative models of space and time?" (p.1). In envisioning the creation of opportunities for collaborative inquiry and learning with the DATL Project, we were inspired by the potential relationality of web-based hypermedia space and time. Encompassing notions of relational inquiry, relational learning, and relational aesthetics, web-based hypermedia research offers unique opportunities for exploring the porous boundaries between art, research, and teaching. Rooted in our overlapping researcher/teacher/activist/artist identities, as well as in interests in methodological issues of representation, legitimation, and politics in the post-post period (McKenzie, 2005), the choice of venue for the DATL Project encourages simultaneous focus on the form and content of research that aims to be a socially useful activity.

We begin the chapter with some further background on the objectives of the study before turning to explore in greater depth the relational potential of web-based hypermedia space and time. Though it is in its early stages, we hope that the working example of the DATL Project provides insight into some of the possibilities and challenges of web-based hypermedia research.

Contingency and the Socio-Ecological in Teacher Education

In recent years, a number of educators have advocated for an explicit emphasis on the contingency of knowledge as a useful access point for teaching and learning about social and ecological issues. Countering the press towards "neutrality" typical of K-12 education (Kelly & Brandes, 2001), their work shares an interest in the possibilities that discursive understandings of the world offer for addressing socio-ecological issues in education in more in-depth ways. Created and reinforced through practices such as language use, traditions of family and culture, and institutions such as school and media, discourses can be understood as having different degrees of authority, with dominant discourses perpetuating existing power relations (Foucault, 1980). In contrast to understandings of agency as the capacity for choice and self-determination, this suggests the limitations of reflexivity and resistance in processes of discursive constitution. However, with subjectivity viewed as more than the sum total of discourse positions (Walkerdine, 1989), agency can be considered a matter of "positioning": not freedom from discursive constitution, but the capacity to recognize that constitution and to "resist, subvert, and change the discourses themselves" (Davies, 2000, p.67).

While indicating that there is no panacea for successfully attending to socio-ecological issues in K-12 education, Kevin Kumashiro (2001) suggests that by taking up a discursive understanding of the world, teachers may be in a stronger position to work with the various "partial knowledges" that are brought to the classroom, including their own. Similarly, Megan Boler (1999) calls on students and educators to hone their awareness of how our modes of seeing have been shaped by dominant discourse, and to engage in the process of questioning cherished beliefs and assumptions. Despite the potential of the discursive approaches for addressing socio-ecological issues suggested by these and other educators (e.g., Gough, 1993, McKenzie, in press; Sumara, 1996), little research has explored attempts to introduce these ideas in teacher education programs, or subsequent efforts of teachers to intentionally integrate discursive approaches to teaching into K-12 classrooms. Indeed, Kumashiro (2001) proposes in particular that research needs to be done on how to prepare teachers to teach in these ways.

The DATL Project responds to this call for research with a particular focus on collaborative inquiry. Interested in eventually generating complicating knowledge and possibility for a broader audience through the web-based site, the initial stage of the study is centred on the work and learning of a small subset of Canadian teacher educators.[3] Considering themselves to be introducing pre-service teachers to discursive understandings of knowledge and identity in relation to socio-ecological issues, these educators joined the study with an interest in sharing their questions, insights, and teaching practices with similarly-focused colleagues. Through a web-based hypermedia environment, the DATL Project seeks to create opportunities for this interactive work.

Relational Space and Time

The origins of hypermedia are typically traced back to Vannevar Bush, a scientist and engineer who in 1945 proposed the memex as an interactive encyclopedia or library which would provide a dynamic system for organizing information (Bolter, 2001). In the early 1960s, Ted Nelson (1992) coined the term "hypertext" to describe "non-sequential writing—text that branches and allows choices to the readers, best read at an interactive screen" (p.2). Hypermedia extends the notion of hypertext by including photographs, video, graphics, sound, and other forms of data, and the terms are used interchangeably by some (e.g., Landow, 1997).

Both hypertext and hypermedia function using a number of key features (Dicks, Mason, Coffey, & Atkinson, 2005), including textual, visual, and/or aural entities ("nodes"), and a means of enabling the reader to move between entities ("links"). Any node may have multiple links to other nodes, with nodes able to be designated depending on which side of a link they are on ("source" or "destination"). Links can be named in order to help identify relationships between nodes, and can function by closing one node in order to open another ("basic link"), or by opening a secondary node as a subpart of a primary node ("anchored link"). Links can also have different targets depending on whether certain conditions have been met ("conditional" or "dynamic"), and basic links can be used to create a default route through the hypertext. The most common use of hypertext and hypermedia is on the world wide web, with options to hyperlink from one website or webpage to others.

Authors of fiction and non-fiction have also begun to make use of hypertext to explore alternative literary forms, with new landmark books including *Afternoon: A Story* by Michael Joyce (1996), *Victory Garden* by Stuart Moulthrop (1995), *Socrates in the Labyrinth* by David Kolb (1994), and *Cyborg: Engineering the Body Electric* by Diane Greco (1995). To date, few empirical research projects have been undertaken using hypertext or hypermedia, with notable exceptions in the fields of anthropology and sociology. Sometimes termed "digital ethnography," these projects include work by Peter Biella (1997), Sarah Pink (2003), Michael Wesch (2006), and research undertaken at the Cardiff School of Social Sciences by Bella Dicks, Bruce Mason, Amanda Coffey, Paul Atkinson, and others (2005). A relatively well-known example of hypertext research in the field of education is Wendy Morgan's electronic re-working of the data from Lather and Smithies' (1997) monograph on women living with HIV/AIDS (Morgan, 2000).

Almost without exception, these examples of hypertext/hypermedia writing and research have been created using the software *Storyspace* (www.eastgate.com). Described as enabling the creation of rich hypertext structures, the software uses visual maps to show each hypertext writing space along with its links. Able to add, link, and reorganize by moving writing spaces on the map, author/researchers can develop complex, yet carefully thought through, hypertext/hypermedia structures. Limited by the multimedia capabilities of *Storyspace*, some researchers have used this software in order to work with their textual data and then moved into other software, such as *Authorware* or *Director*, in order to incorporate photo, video, and sound elements (e.g., Dicks et al., 2005). Also, almost without exception, this work is then made available in CD/DVD form, with only a few hypertext/hypermedia research studies currently existing on the world wide web (e.g., Wesch, 2006). An increase in theoretical work in this area in recent years suggests that interest in hypermedia research is growing (e.g., Barbules & Lambeir, 2003; Coover, 2004; Dicks & Mason, 1998; Dicks et al., 2005; Mason & Dicks, 2001; Pink, 2004; Voithofer, 2005), no doubt in part as a result of the shift in much social science research towards recognizing and representing complexity.

Described as "postexperimental" and of the "post-post period", much current social science research is typified by multivoiced texts, researcher reflexivity, cultural criticism, and experimental works; characteristics in keeping with poststructurally-informed understandings of social science research as contingent, evolving, and messy (Alvesson, 2002; Denzin & Lincoln, 2000; McKenzie, 2005). As Irwin and Springgay suggest in the introduction to this volume, "meaning and understanding are no longer revealed or thought to emanate from a point of origin, rather they are complicated as relational, singular, and rhizomatic" (p.xv). Davis and Sumara (2006) tell us that *implication*, *complicity*, and *complexity* all derive from the Indo-European *plek*, meaning "to weave, plait, fold, entwine" (p.16). Indeed, it quickly becomes evident why the relationality of hypertext and hypermedia research is intriguing in its potential to represent the complexity now commonly theorized as inherent to our objects of inquiry. The following sections outline in more detail some of the possible relational qualities of hypermedia space and time, including intertextuality, multiply threaded text, overlap in form and content, blurred author/reader boundary, and the new poetics of hypermedia design.

Intertextuality

The interactive character of reading any text is highlighted with a hypertext, in which the primary text is a gateway into a much larger, complex network of material to be explored. In a hypertext, any information item should be seen, not as simply an isolated "fact" or a discrete reference point, but as a node of multiple intersecting lines of information...Hence the text is not simply a collection or list of entries, but also a system of interrelationships; and in fact its value as a knowledge tool may be primarily in how and where it proposes these links. (Burbules & Callister, 1996, p.27)

As Nicholas Burbules and Thomas Callister (1996) suggest above, hypertext muddies the notion of a "primary text", instead promoting an intertextual conceptual space. Whereas a print text can suggest that there is a separation of one text from others" (Landow, 1997), in a hypertext, related materials can be more explicitly and fully available. Links infer connections within and between texts (and other media), bringing the texts together and blurring the boundaries among them (Landow, 1997). The visual underlining of links in hypertext also contributes to this blurring of boundaries, fostering a sense that meaning is always incomplete—deferred until the next link is followed (Dicks et al., 2005).

In the representation of research, hypertext and hypermedia allow for connections to be easily made among sections of textual, visual, aural, and other data, as well as with larger portions of data (e.g., full interview transcripts), researcher interpretations, articles, and a range of other electronically-available material. This enables a more contextual representation of the data, and the potential for more complex linkages and understandings to emerge (Dicks & Mason, 1998). As Mason and Dicks (2001) suggest, "Data are no longer considered to be a series of quotable excerpts but are coherent networks of associative links. Hypertext thus potentially enables a more holistic interaction with the data" (p.447).

> "Cognitive Overload"...
> One of the challenges presented by the intertextual possibilities of hypertext or hypermedia research is data oversaturation (Voithofer, 2005). Computer capacity means that large amounts of data can be stored and potentially integrated into a research project, with the potential outcome of overwhelming the reader. As Burbules and Callister (1996) write, "In hypertext, the premium can be on drawing more and more sources in, multiplying the number of data points and diversifying the direction of meaningful associations—to a potentially limitless (and perhaps at some point counterproductive) degree" (p.33).

However, Burbules (1998) points to the importance of problematizing the seemingly neutral character of links. Suggesting that links define, enhance, and restrict access to information, he writes, "the use and placement of links is one of the vital ways in which the tacit assumptions and values of the designer/author are manifested in a hypertext—yet they are rarely considered as such" (p.105). An important part of hypertext "critical literacy", Burbules proposes, is evaluation and critique of the various types of rhetorical moves inherent in links, including metaphor, metonymy, synecdoche, antastasis, identity, cause and effect, and catachresis (pp.110-117). While these tools of rhetoric may be most common on the world wide web, Dicks, Mason, Coffey and Atkinson (2005) suggest that they are not necessarily the ones that are most likely to be used (or the most useful) in hypermedia research. They ask whether link-types should be project-specific or whether a common set of links could be established for shared use, suggesting that some combination of both is most likely (p.175).

Some of the link-functions that Dicks, Mason, Coffey and Atkinson (2005) identify as more useful to hypertext and hypermedia research include expansion (e.g., elaboration, exemplification, exception), as well as the use of bricolage and juxtaposition to suggest alternative or conflicting representations. Burbules (1998) also expands on the rhetorics of bricolage and juxtaposition, suggesting that although they may be more in keeping with the rhizomatic character of the world wide web, they are just as much rhetorical forms as are metaphor and hyperbole, and thus imply just as much responsibility in the selecting and ordering of information. Likewise, Dicks, Mason, Coffey and Atkinson (2005) contend that hypertext as a data analysis tool has the potential to focus the researcher on the explicit relationships among elements of the data.

As with other forms of social science research which have begun to explore intertextuality, hypertext and hypermedia facilitate a break down of the space and time of the research "field". Considering her own ongoing experience and writing to be integrally connected to the focus of her research, Elizabeth St. Pierre (1997) comments, "it is not just that I don't know where the field is, I don't know *when* it is either" (p.368). Unlike the bounded entity of the anthropological site of old—which could be entered and exited and considered objectively, "concepts such as intertextuality and intersubjectivity have suggested that ideas, images and discourse overspill the confines of any one [location or] set of texts...Thus the field no longer equates to a temporal, spatial and social unity—instead it is flexible, accessible, ongoing" (Dicks & Mason, 1998, p.4).

Multiply threaded texts

Rather than abandoning linearity, one is offering the reader an environment in which to pursue multi-linear lines of enquiry... a more deterritorialized and multi-layered field of meaning can emerge as the object of study. (Dicks & Mason, 1998, p.10)

There is nothing about hypertext or hypermedia that ensures more complex ways of relating information (Burbules, 1998). However, closely connected with issues of intertextuality, hypertext is more amenable to lateral linkages and the creation of multiple organizational threads in contrast to the linear and sequential organization of traditional text. Drawing on Deleuze and Guattari (1987), some have suggested that hypertext is *nonlinear* and noncentred—a rhizomatic structure versus the root structure of more linear texts. Indicating that hypertexts actively invite and facilitate multiple readings of the same material, Burbules and Callister (1996) write that, "this rhizomatic structure can be seen as both a feature of the organization of text, and as a way of reading any text nonlinearly and nonhierarchically—the difference is the degree to which a hypertext, by explicitly representing such a nonlinear, nonhierarchical structure, encourages such readings" (p.30).

Dicks, Mason, Coffey and Atkinson (2005), however, propose that *multilinearity* or *multiply-threaded* may be more suitable as a metaphor for hypermedia research, suggesting that hypertext allows for a number of "paths" or "trails" to interweave without any one being singled out as the defining argument (p.160). Concerned with the tension between the urge to complicate research and the countering urge to offer some intellectual coherence, Dicks and Mason (1998) propose that hypermedia be used as a means to explore these tensions rather than to sidestep them.

"Lost in Hyperspace"...
A challenge of abandoning linear text is "the disorientation" experienced by some readers (Conklin, 1987). How can authors ensure that the multiple choices do not make the text impenetrable?

In response to the potential dilemma between offering structure versus freedom to the reader of hypertext or hypermedia, Burbules and Callister (1996) suggest that it is not necessarily an either/or matter. They propose that hypertext systems can be developed that incorporate "capabilities for both pre-structured and personally structured readings" (p.43). Applicable strategies include those related to links (conditional vs. static links; paths; link naming and other rhetorical functions), as well as those related to hyperstructures (new multisequential narrative structures such as the cycle, pyramid, map, other metaphors) (Burbules, 1998). In allowing the writer to organize nodes according to both associative and hierarchical links, electronic writing can encourage *both* rhizomatic and root structures (Dicks et al., 2005). Indeed, in order to enable meaning-making for the reader, Dicks, Mason, Coffey and Atkinson (2005) propose that the enforcement of some sequentiality is necessarily in any text, with every hypertext (so far) including, "some form of imposed internal structure, usually implemented through navigation and metaphor" (p.65).

The merging of form and content

> Hypertext is more than just a new way of organizing existing information; it influences the kinds of information it organizes. As the organizing system of a hypertext grows and evolves, the structure of the information itself changes. Form and content are interdependent. (Burbules & Callister, 1996, p.25)

As researchers across the social sciences have come to realize over the past several decades, the form of research determines what content is presented to the reader (Clifford & Marcus, 1986). This is particularly the case with the hypertext form, in which the processes of "analysis" and "writing" are largely collapsed (Coffey, Holbrook, & Atkinson, 1996). By selecting data to be included in nodes, establishing linkages among nodes, and structuring the overall organization of the material, researchers are simultaneously undertaking analysis and representation. In addition, as developing communication technology enables processes of research design and implementation to become more collaborative, the distinction between doing and reporting research may increasingly blur (Voithofer, 2005, p.9).

Linking materiality to the relationship between form and content, Voithofer (2005) suggests Kathryn Hayles' (1992, 1999) term "technotext" for research in which form and content are co-designed, and in which the textual structure provides a sense of its constructedness. Not the exclusive domain of electronic media, Voithofer (2005) proposes that the design of all forms of research/writing can benefit from approaching the text "as being not simply words on a page, but material elements that shape the reading experience" (p.8). Indeed, he suggests that human-computer interfaces (such as keyboard and screen, the metaphors through which media are presented, and the many modalities through which digital information is accessed) indicate the various embodied ways that individuals interact with media. Acknowledging the differences between culture and interface, he proposes however, that, "consistent with theories of materiality, the two can never be totally separated. To change the interface is to change [culture], and vice versa" (pp.7-8).

Blurring the author/reader boundary

> It could be claimed that hypertextual reading is a practice of agency, a performance of active intervention—and sometimes a tussle with the structuring already set up in the authored links. In "constructive" hypertexts (Joyce, 1995), it is possible to go further: readers can literally become writers, adding materials, commentary, and links that can be saved for other readers in turn. (Morgan, 2000, p.143)

Another key feature of hypertext and hypermedia is the radical interactiveness afforded by the breaking down of the reader-writer distinction. Instead of an author-controlled textual environment where words are fixed on the page in a top-down, left-right, beginning-end, format, hypertext offers the reader more control over the construction of the text through their selection of different pathways through the material (Peters & Lankshear, 1996). Morgan (2000) explains the distinction as follows: "In a word, the difference between print and hypertext is between place and space. The one fixed in place; the other a space intersected by mobile elements... Print is presented as a product; hypertext is necessarily a reader's performance, an event" (p.131).

In addition, in some hypertext systems, readers can create their own links

"The Fantasy of Representation"...
Dicks and Mason (1999) write, "there can be detected in these experiments a fantasy of direct, transparent representation, in which all power relations have been overcome through an innovation which is merely textual" (p.3). Instead they propose we need to continue to recognize that research inevitably involves mediation, translating one form of knowledge into another. Indeed, "there is no textual format that pictures the social world as a perfect simulacrum" (Atkinson, 1992, p.7).

and add comments and other material, moving into the "backstage" area of the data to create their own interpretations (Mason & Dicks, 2001, p.453). Whereas "browsers" are more casual and curious readers and "users" are seeking specific information from the hypertext, Burbules and Callister (1996) describe "co-authors" as requiring "the means to actively – and perhaps permanently—change and add to the system in light of their own active reading" (p.38). As readers create their own associative references, the distinction of author and reader breaks down even further. Indeed, recent developments such as wiki technology and other emerging social software platforms are enabling readers to more easily add, remove, or otherwise "co-author" content on the world wide web.

Despite this potential of hypertext and hypermedia to blur the line between author and reader, it is clear that researching does indeed still mean authoring. Jørgensen and Phillips (2002) warn that representing the world in one way or another is unavoidable in any production of meaning. Also skeptical of the assumption that "better" methodology will necessarily mean better research, Kamala Visweswaren (1994) proposes that deconstructive ethnography attempts to "abandon or forfeit its authority, knowing that it is impossible to do so" (p.79). Similarly, Maggie MacLure (2003) suggests that "despite the search for more 'innocent' forms of representation, in which the voices and concerns of subjects might be heard without distortion, issues of power and authority will always return to haunt research writing" (p.104). Taking up these concerns in relation to his web-based ethnography *Nekalim.net*, Michael Wersch (in Dicks et al., 2005) writes,

> The "burden of authorship" is great in hypermedia ethnography, precisely because the subjects and their voices can seem so near (and therefore can be so easily misunderstood). My argument here has been simply that providing space for the subject's own words does not equate to giving them voice. (p.64)

Reflexivity in hypermedia research, then, is not about pretending there is no difference between the voices of participants and those of authors, but involves foregrounding the inevitable processes of selection and interpretation that make "authoring" what it is (Mason & Dicks, 1999, p.22).

Burbules and Callister (1996) suggest that "the very virtues of hypertext—complexity and comprehensiveness—make implicit authorial, organizational choices all the more essential for the usability of texts, and yet all the more difficult for the reader to detect" (p.44). As a result, hypermedia researchers have a responsibility to articulate how data and methodologies have been selected and transformed. Instead of brushing over contentious questions of authorship and validity, these issues need to be openly addressed in relation to the dynamic and intertextual form of hypertext and hypermedia research (Morgan, 2000).

The new poetics of hypermedia design

> A... feature of the digital text is its integrative power and its radical convertibility, realigning alphabetic, graphic, and sound components into a single common denominator... Thus the notion of disciplinarity, of separate, distinct subjects each with its own textual time-space—its separate learning-

teaching space and its own canon—begins to look problematic. One might talk speculatively here of a new interdisciplinarity or multidisciplinarity, of a great synthetic unity of humanities, arts, and sciences. (Peters & Lankshear, 1996, p.62)

Even more so than with hypertext alone, hypermedia allows the researcher to explore multiple representations of the field of study. Beyond illustrative, archival, or documentary functions, the inclusion of visual and aural data in hypermedia environments ushers in a new orientation to representation and research. Working in conjunction with a broader "turn to the visual", this orientation has "writing being pushed to the margin", and calls for a new focus in textual practice on design (Kress, 1998, p.56, p.62). For hypermedia researchers, this means exploring how we design the representation of data not only textually, but also visually, aurally, temporally, and artistically.

Arrangement and display of data become key in the new poetics of hypermedia design (Kress, 1998). Dicks and Mason (1998) write that hypermedia research involves "undertaking a form of authoring which is collage-like in nature," potentially merged with a "more authored kind of meta-narrative," resulting in hybrid forms of representation (p.13). Recognizing the unique opportunities afforded to authors of hypermedia and other related types of research representations, Springgay, Irwin and Kind (2005) have referred to the "doubling of visual and textual" as a place of possibility "wherein the two complement, extend,

> "The Burdens of Design?"...
> "The challenge for ethnographers choosing to present their work on the computer screen is that their choice of modes and media is always going to contribute to the making of meaning. Different modes afford meaning in different kinds of ways, even though those differences may not be easily and straightforwardly specified. If every screen-design choice that the ethnographer makes is redolent with meaning, then those choices become burdened with a significance that is as yet largely uncharted." (Dicks et al., 2005, pp.166-167)

refute, and/or subvert one another" (p.900). Barbara Duncan (1997) also suggests that this juxtaposition of different forms of representation is a key aspect of electronic work and "one which allows for refreshing forms of art and literature as well as other forms of research" (p.5).

A unique function of combining different forms of representation in hypermedia is the range of relationships to time and space that they offer. Whereas still images exist in space in similar ways to print text, aural data exists in time and only becomes tied into space through its representation on the computer screen (Dicks et al., 2005). Likewise, data that takes the form of moving images exists in both space and time. Concerned that readers/viewers will conflate "seeing" (or "hearing") with "knowing," Pink (2001) asks how this might be taken into consideration in hypermedia design. Suggesting there is no such thing as "multimedia analysis," Dicks, Mason, Coffey and Atkinson (2005) indicate that each medium must be considered on its own terms before being integrated into a hypermedia project. Accordingly, they propose that the objects of hypermedia design can be read aesthetically and/or scientifically, depending on content and context (p.83).

As Clifford Geertz (1980) indicates, the blurring of, so called, "art" and "science" has a relatively long history in social inquiry. Philosophical inquiries that look like literary criticism, parables undertaken as ethnographies, and other such meldings, have become increasingly common across the social sciences over the past several decades (Barone 2001). Duncan (1997) suggests that the multiple connections that can be achieved by mixing media can serve to bolster the possible associations that can be attached to any one topic, broadening perspectives and working to break down disciplinary boundaries (p.5). Embracing interdisciplinarity "not as a patchwork of different disciplines and methodologies but as a loss, a shift, or a rupture where in absence, new courses of action un/fold," Springgay, Irwin and Kind (2005) are among those complicating traditional divisions between art and science through the use of art as a research methodology in itself (p.897).

It is perhaps within the intentionality and practice of design that hypermedia research overlaps the most with arts-based and arts informed theories. Interdisciplinarity, alternative relationships to space and time, and the "turn toward the visual" (Kress, 1998) are all elements of design that point to the intersections among these areas of inquiry. Identifying this commonality, Voithofer (2005) suggests that "because materiality is a central concern of arts-based researchers, the design resources of this community offer numerous theories, methods, and evaluative principles for the creation of research technotexts" (p.10). Indeed, as we are discovering, in multiple ways hypermedia research "already defines a collaborative possibility" (Burbules & Lambier, 2003, p.6).

The Working Example of the DATL Project

Quoted in the introduction to this volume, Graeme Sullivan (2005) writes, "If a measure of the utility of research is seen to be the capacity to create new knowledge that is individually and culturally transformative, then criteria need to move beyond probability and plausibility to *possibility*" (italics in original, p.72). We are indeed inspired by the transformative possibilities enabled by the relationality of hypermedia research—the possibilities for relational inquiry, learning, and aesthetics fostered through hypermedia intertextuality, multilinearity, merging of form and content, blurring of author and reader, and multimedia design. As we design the web-based hypermedia environment of the DATL Project, we work to encourage these possibilities.

In contrast to most other hypermedia research to date, the DATL Project is a live site on the world wide web. After a great deal of research, trial-and-error, and communication, we decided upon two software programs for use in the creation of the site. To enable careful attention to the data content of each node, the types of relationships among nodes, and the overall structuring of the site, we are using the software *Storyspace* for data analysis/design. As described earlier in the chapter, this program facilitates the design process by providing an easy space to explore links among the data, as well as different map views to help make decisions on data representation. However, because *Storyspace* shifts to straightforward linking pages when uploading the data to the web, we needed a second type of software to offer the more-than-textual layering capabilities that we had in mind.

Although tempted by wiki technology and other developing software that promotes collaboration and dissipated control among users, we knew the available time of other participants would likely inhibit learning to use new software and getting significantly involved in the development of a website. In addition, the time and costs involved for us to learn to use more complicated web development techniques, such as *Ajax*, were also factors. In the end, we decided to go with the already familiar *Adobe GoLive* software for the creation and maintenance of the website. With a platform that allows for the incorporation of various media, and a host of tools that create varied interactive actions (e.g., user or time-triggered actions that open up new windows, make images appear/disappear, float layers), *GoLive* also includes capabilities for some co-authoring and collaboration within comment boxes and discussion boards.

Through the use of these software, we have created a project website that is organized around three different research "dialogues." These comprise text drawn from the transcripts of telephone and in-person interviews, and are structured in the form of performative dialogues. Focusing on the questions of "what and why," "how" and "well?" these dialogues are in effect each an entry way into separate sections of the hypermedia project.

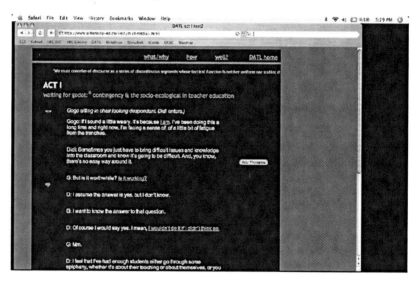

Hypermedia screen: Stand-alone Text. 30 March 2007. Digital Snapshot.

Layered onto each of the three dialogues are other visual, textual and aural data, including related photographs, paintings, transcript excerpts, sounds, discussion notes, and comment blurbs. Wanting to support the deepening of participant and others' inquiry and learning into the topic at hand, the dialogues can be read as stand alone documents (see image above), or readers can choose to select links to engage with other related material (see image below). Link-type is indicated by the form of the linking mechanism, including an eye symbol to link to images, a comment blurb to link to previously entered comments of readers, an asterisk to link to larger transcript excerpts which provide more context, and underlining to indicate links to other pages of analysed textual data. In the linking of text to image, text to text, image to sound, and also in the combined effect of presenting all of these links and layers simultaneously in one site, we aim to represent and generate complicating knowledge. Indeed, the design of the site revolves around the metaphor of layering: layering thought, layering images, layering data, layering knowledge.

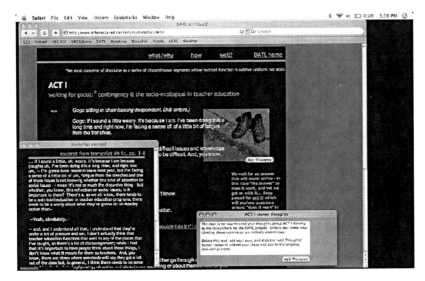

Hypermedia Screen: Layered Representation. 30 March 2007. Digital Snapshot.

While readers are not able to immediately make changes to the site; central to its design are components which enable readers to provide their comments as they view the data. A floating "Add Thoughts" button on the right side of the page follows the reader as s/he scrolls, allowing for the submission of various reactions, questions, or notes in relationship to specific parts of the website. In addition, a discussion board that readers can link to at any point in their explorations allows a space for ongoing conversations among readers, participants, and authors. As Dicks, Mason, Coffey and Atkinson (2005) suggest, web-based hypermedia research has the added advantage of enabling a forum for readers' comments, which can "foster a dialogue that may prove a valuable resource in its own right" (p.63)—valuable both for the readers' immediate learning, and as an additional data source that can be layered back into the ever-deepening web of material on the site.

Theory, ability, time, emotion, and various other contextual factors unite in complex and situated ways in the practices we undertake as researchers, and inevitably, as decision-makers in hypermedia design. As Mason and Dicks (2001) suggest, "a hypermedia-based project is probably too complex for one person" (p.447). Working with two or more researchers facilitates the research, design, learning, and utilization of the software programs that make this type of representation possible (Anderson, 1999; Kress, 1998). To provide a sense of our own community of practice (Irwin, this volume) in the creation of the hypermedia website for the DATL Project, we have compiled a short series of quotes drawn together from research meetings, phone conversations and emails. Though taken from various points in time and accordingly ranging somewhat in content, they render a "behind the scenes" understanding of the day-to-day practice behind our theory:

> MM: ...The priority now is to focus on figuring out what we should use to do what we want and how we are going to design the site, etc. I want something that looks multi-layered with text boxes, images, videos, etc., and space for dialogue...

> NT: ...Okay, so I'm starting a list below of things that I know we can do with the website. There's four different categories of tools that I will explain below. I've found out about three of them from three different phone calls...

> MM: ...After fooling around in *GoLive* a bit, I'm wondering if we might not be able to just use *GoLive* to do what we want if you do some more reading on what the various functions in *GoLive* offer, etc... Ideas? Next steps??...

> NT: ...With *GoLive* we have access to interactive images & text (pre-programmed). ...And when I refer to interactivity, it would be something like the appearance, shifting and disappearance of pre-programmed objects to pre-programmed places. The actions can be triggered by either time lapse or by user activity (i.e. clicking mouse, moving mouse over the area, etc.)...

> MM: ...I'd like to create a page with links to images at appropriate spots through the dialogue using some sort of consistent image (giving people the option of linking or not); we can do the same thing with layering in sounds and text excerpts from the transcripts. These would be images, sounds, video clips, text boxes, etc. that would open as small boxes on the side of the screen, layering beside/over the main Act I page...

> NT: ...I'm working now on two pages that I think will be a bit different, but are both along the lines of what you seem to be looking for. I'm learning how to do forms (this seems to be a way for us to get comments), various actions and layers. It's a steep learning curve now, but I think if we stick with what *GoLive* has to offer, it will be relatively easy to build the pages once I figure out all these tools...

> MM: ...I like the look that the site is developing into...

Conclusion

[With new technologies] the writing space becomes the site of collaboration, and the text that is being produced facilitates and instantiates this collaboration. (Burbules & Lambeir, 2003, p.4)

In their recent book on complexity and education, Brent Davis and Dennis Sumara (2006) describe a number of conditions of collective work that encourage the emergence of the "as-yet unimagined:" neighbor interactions, distributed control, internal diversity, internal redundancy, randomness, and coherence (pp.135-136). With the overlapping, yet disparate interests and commitments that participating teacher educators bring to the DATL Project, we are optimistic that the conditions of rich diversity and internal redundancy are well satisfied. The project website, in turn, provides a space and time for neighbor interactions—an intertextual, multilinear, and multimedia environment in which these geographically spread out teacher educators (as well as others) can interact. Encouraging reader engagement through the potential for layering in comments, concerns, and other additional data, the website also enables a limited distribution (or partial sharing) of control. And finally, the DATL project website seeks coherence through carefully structured form and content, as well as the potential for randomness or "the emergence of unanticipated possibilities" (Davis & Sumara, p.149). The DATL project is an in-progress endeavour, and we are at work discovering the challenges and possibilities of representing and generating complex and collaborative web-based hypermedia research—we welcome your input.

NOTES

[1] Nora Timmerman is a Ph.D. student working as a research assistant on this project.
[2] The DATL Project is funded by a Social Sciences and Humanities Research Council of Canada Standard Grant (2005-2008).
[3] Nine teacher educators based in the Canadian provinces of British Columbia, Saskatchewan, and Ontario are participating in the first stage of the project. Their involvement includes an initial 90 minute semi-structured interview, and then opportunities for response and discussion through in-person focus groups and online interactions.

DAVID BEARE AND GEORGE BELLIVEAU

DIALOGUING SCRIPTED DATA

Introduction

*[David and George are at a table discussing ways to engage in a writing project
that addresses issues of scripting data for research purposes.]*

David: George, as a way to further our understanding about scripting research
data, how about we engage in a dialogue about each other's work on this topic?

George: You mean *construct* a script that examines our experiences of
dramatizing data in research?

David: Exactly. Through dialoguing we'll share key moments in our script-writing
process as we researched our students' play-creating process: you with your pre-
service teachers and me with my secondary students. In the end, this will be a
reflective script about creating research scripts that were based on our students'
creations of scripts.

George: A play within a play within a play—meta-metadrama! Talk about
multiple layers! Let's begin!

Setting the Scene

David: In my multiple roles as teacher, artist and researcher of high school theatre
education, I am interested in studying theatre for positive youth development.
Based on research data spanning several years, I developed a theoretical model
linking theatre with youth development (Beare, 2002). While the model was useful
to academically frame the process, I felt compelled to breathe life into the research
and to share the essence of the data in an artistic way. I did this by transforming the
data into a series of monologues and dialogues. Below, Mike (*all character names
are pseudonyms*) shares a major theme—vision—which I discovered in the
research and he describes the interaction between art and people.

Mike: The purpose of art is to question ourselves, to question how the world
operates, to question how to make the world a better place. This questioning, this
dialoguing between people, within ourselves, is not limited to a theatrical creative
process, of course, but this is my tool of choice. For me, everything I create is a

S. Springgay et al. (eds.), Being with A/r/tography, 141–149.

that I exist, that I am not alone. It makes me feel like I am a part of something, part of humanity, part of the universe. I feel this on a very primal level. So when we work through a collaborative play-creating process, the aim is to not reproduce art, but rather to create art...to work organically, starting the entire creative process at its grassroots.

George: As an artist, researcher and teacher in theatre education, I constantly try to find ways to weave these areas in meaningful ways for my university students and myself. The latter part of a research project in drama and social justice involved the creation of a research script. The project involved 12 pre-service teachers collectively creating an anti-bullying play to be performed for elementary students. After writing four traditional papers about the learning and meaning that emerged from the drama research (Belliveau, 2004a; 2004b; 2005; 2006b) I decided to closely examine the pre-service teachers' journals, my field notes, and the script they developed, to then create a dramatized script of what emerged during the play-building process (Belliveau, 2006a). Tracey took on the leadership role of playwright in the collective writing process.

Tracey: After sharing our respective tableaux, we reworked them by expanding them further using dialogue. Oh, by the way, I'm Tracey, an elementary teacher, and one of my tasks during the project was to pull the group's ideas together into one script. I guess I'm the playwright of the collective, if that's still the term to use in a collective?

Writing Around an Anti-Bullying Theme

David: I was amazed at the different parallels between our scripted data. In both cases our students wrote scenes around anti-bullying, and we both dramatized the research of the play creation process. When I read your piece, the inner voices of your pre-service teachers resonated with my experiences with the collaborative play-creating process.

George: That's how I felt, too, when I read about your students' inner voices. Let's first look at what our students created. Below is a section from the pre-service teachers' script where Suzy bullies Lauren.

LAUREN: I'd be happy to share some of mine with you. (LAUREN sets her lunch down on the table and goes to sit down. As she does, SUZIE grabs the bag of chips that was from LAUREN's lunch.) Wow, this is great. We haven't had lunch together since grade 6... (SUZIE stands up and inspects the bag of chips, opens it up, takes 2 or 3, then crumples the bag and throws it over her shoulder onto the floor and walks away.)

SUZY: Are you comin'; Courtney, or what?

COURTNEY: (hesitates) Yeah, I'm comin. (looks back at LAUREN feeling guilty) Wait up Suze! (LAUREN obviously upset runs off stage.)

David: This scene represents what typical high school students would create on the subject of bullying. While the practices of democratic decision-making and critical inquiry are essential to learning (Gonzalez, 2006; Lazarus, 2004; Rohd, 1998), I question if this type of script is too stereotypical for performance purposes.

George: I agree that some of the scenes created by the pre-service teachers edged on stereotypes and they could no doubt have been pushed further. However, there's the question of what is the goal of the activity and who are the participants. In your case, you're working with theatre students who have a desire to perform. My setting consisted of teachers with very little theatre experience who wanted to expand their comfort in communication and had a desire to address bullying in schools. So, from the outset, the issue (bullying) was driving the process (Goldstein, 2001; Gray & Sinding, 2002). In addition, because the project took place within a teaching practicum, I felt it was important for me to guide *their* work rather than impose my theatre vision.

David: I agree. It comes down to intent (Jackson, 2005). Last year a group of my students created a similar three-person scene on bullying. Yet, in our case, the artistic storyline took higher priority over the subject of bullying (Schonman, 2005). For example, in the scene below, the Master of Badlands finds a lost teenage girl showing her sister's ring to a homeless woman, known as the Mad Bride.

Master: Don't listen to her rubbish, she's insane. (MAD BRIDE panics, grabs the ring from LADY VENGEANCE and attempts to hide it.) Now if you don't mind Mad Bride, I'll be takin' that. Come on, hand it over. (MAD BRIDE reluctantly gives MASTER the ring. MASTER pockets the ring.)

Lady Vengeance: Give me back my ring! (Holding her back.)

Master: You must be confused. This is my ring. Crazy here works for me. She's the half-time show. Completely lost her mind. The Mad Bride is pure comedic genius.

Lady Vengeance: But it's mine. I mean, it's my sister's. I gave it to her. See the engraving. She must have found it.

Master: Uh-huh. But is your sister here to claim the ring?

Lady Vengeance: No, she's dead.

Master: Sorry kid, finder's keepers, loser's weepers. (She takes out the ring, blows on it, and rubs it on her sleeve.) But if you want it you'll hafta earn it.

David: This play continues by showing how this abused girl eventually turns into Lady Vengeance. Our intent was not to *teach* about bullying, but rather to *capture the essence* of the topic.

143

George: So are you questioning how strong the playscript (and performance) needs to be in order to have a positive affect/effect on the participants?

David: Yes, and the audience, too!

George: So, it's a question of intent and audience. For instance, in our current dialogue that we are presenting in a reconstructed script form, our intent is not to entertain necessarily, but rather we wish to inform and share with our audience aspects of dramatizing data. Whereas in a play geared towards performance, we would likely include theatrical elements such as rising tensions and climax, in this work our interest lies primarily in the scripted data. Generally, theatre scripts are blueprints for performance, meant to be lifted from the page. So, can our current engagement be called a play (Saldana, 2006)?

David: Not really. If we wish to engage an audience on various levels, we need to consider performance aspects. For instance, this script lacks conflict – our dialogue is likely too cooperative to become a play. It might be more interesting to read this script if our ideas were more at war with one another. In effect, do not people turn to theatre to watch someone prevail or falter over excruciating circumstances?

George: Perhaps we are not creating a playscript, but rather a carefully constructed transcribed conversation. If that is the case, then maybe we need to prepare our audience for the didactic, rather than artistic, nature of this work. Because in essence, our primary intent with this dialogue, and with our research scripts on collective creation processes, is to be informative (Mienczakowsk, 2001).

David: With our secondary intent being to engage (and perhaps entertain) as much as possible with the reflective and research material.

Writing Scripted Data

David: Whether our playscripts are didactic or artistic, I found that one of the biggest challenges of writing scripted data is remaining true to the essence of the original data. For instance, each of my characters represents a mixture of several sources. No character speaks for one participant, but instead, each is an integration of many voices linked by themes. In order to connect the voices together, I took some artistic license to *fill in the blanks*. Sometimes I changed words, shortened a long, rambling sentence, or even added a sentence. Should I have been totally faithful to the data?

George: What's fascinating about your question about the debate (tension) between original data versus verbatim is that we are currently engaged in it. This script is an edited version—the essence of what we have developed over a few months of dialoguing, e-mailing, and phone conversations. As Saldana (2005) would suggest, we're looking for "the juicy stuff" (p.16) and we have left the so-called boring stuff out. Plus, our playbuilding work with our students—the actual plays they developed—constantly involved the editing of their stories to find the essence. Your point about merging various voices resonates with my research script as well. The fictional character, Tracey, represents at least three voices within the group who played significant roles in the writing process.

Tracey: I sometimes wonder how close the play we created relates to us as a group. We've invested so much in this as teacher/actors that we're maybe writing our story, without realizing it. The bullying we're presenting, which we think is based on research—what we read and experienced in schools—may be bullying tendencies and bullied experiences from inside us.

David: I noticed in your research play that you used monologues more than dialogues. Why's that?

George: I guess that since the original data was based on individual journal responses, interviews, and field notes, this naturally matched the one-way directional flow of monologues (Saldana, 2005).

David: My research script, as you noticed, is mostly monologues, and these sections seem to remain truer to the spirit of the original data. The dialogues, on the other hand, appear more disconnected. In hindsight, I maybe should have interviewed small groups or conducted more focus groups in order to capture the natural dialogue between people. This would possibly help in adding more believability and dramatic tension to the dialogue components of the script.

George: The approach I took to build tension, for dramatic effect, came through the use of a chorus (Prendergast, 2003). I used this device for a variety of reasons, most importantly because the pre-service teachers actually created a chorus in the play. In addition, the device allowed me to represent dramatically a number of perspectives in a short time frame. Historically, choruses in plays, in particular Greek plays, tended to have a dialogic voice within them. The dialogic tension represented the spirit of our group, in that there were varying views working in the collective. As I have argued elsewhere (Belliveau, 2006), this tension can be used productively for play creation.

Chorus: The scene in the lockers is much better now that we have the calculator in it.
The movement is confusing. We seem to be losing lots of the words.
I like the action—kids will prefer that to too much talking.
I don't know if I can memorize all those lines.
I'm glad all those long monologues are cut.
We only have two weeks to rehearse this play!
I thought including the parents was a good idea...but that's cut.
The play is way less confusing with only six characters... we needed to nix the parents.

Multiple Voices

David: Your use of chorus lends itself nicely to multiple voices. I chose to introduce the characters and central theme of the collaborative play-creating process in a similar fashion.

> Daniel: It is HELL!
> Mike: It's incredible!
> Steven: It's so gay.
> Pam: It feels satisfying, challenging, and invigorating.
> Daniel: It is meaningless, frustrating, and tedious. Can't we for once do a normal play?
> Kristy: It's hard.
> Steven: It's boring.
> Shelly: It's FUN!
> Karen: It's not fun when your friends hate you for getting a part.
> Pam: I have all these ideas buzzing around in my head.
> Mike: It is the most incredible feeling!
> Shelly: Of course, if I don't get this part, I will simply die!
> Karen: Maybe I should just let her have the part?
> Paul: What? You're changing the script again!
> Steven: Again?
> Kristy: I wish I could say I love it but it's really stressing me out.
> Mike: I love it!
> Shelley: I absolutely love it!
> Daniel: I hate it! Despise it!
> Pam: It has really opened me up.
> Paul: It changed me.
> Mike: It changed my life.

David: Even though I want to provide many perspectives, I see how the rearrangement of data shows my bias on this subject. I sense that I am trying to persuade the audience in certain directions. Notice how the first half of the dialogue focused more on negative comments, but by the end, there is a shift towards more positive ones.

George: I think it's inevitable and essential for us to manipulate the data as we shape our scripts, because in the end we are playwriting, turning the research into an art form (Saldana, 2005). However, there is an ethical obligation to stay true to the essence of what was said or recorded during the research. For instance, if 80% of the responses were negative thoughts towards the process, then I think we're ethically obligated as researchers to represent that within our scripts. If not, we'd not only be creating a script, but fabricating data. Our goal is to represent dramatically the multiple voices of participants' experiences in an honest, truthful, and efficient manner.

David: To that end, I tried to capture the spectrum of students' lived experiences during the process, by including shadow voices—moments where students shared what *did not* work in the play-creating process.

> Daniel: Writing this script was so bloody tedious! We were all over the map, with no sense of direction, everybody fighting over these petty power struggles... I mean, I had this real cool ending where the main character disappears after a big fight and the audience is left wondering if he's dead or not. Now that would have gotten the audience talking. Isn't that the point of art? To get people talking, stir things up? (He locks his locker and continues walking.) Whatever, it doesn't matter, most of the people in the group voted for Karen's ideas. Don't you see what's really happening here? In the end, after all the talking, after all the wasted hours spent on writing, after everything! It's still [the teacher's] ideas that are being expressed, not ours. If you ask me, this whole process is one big cliché.

George: The shadow voices not only offer another perspective of the process but they breathe life into what took place. They offer some of the tension you suggest should take place within a script. So, as we dramatized our data within our research scripts, did we seek the controversy within the data for dramatic effect, or were we trying to represent the lived experience of the participants?

Diverging Perspectives

David: I think your script partially addresses this question, in that it represents the lived experiences as well as the inner tensions of the pre-service teachers in their process of co-creating an original script.

> *Chorus: Great to have our first draft.*
> *We can finally start rehearsing.*
> *I can't believe she cut out Lauren's monologue.*
> *It was one of the best parts of the play.*
> *She didn't incorporate any of my suggestions!*
> *The guy parts are pretty slim.*
> *All our ideas are nicely meshed in this script, but we still don't have an ending.*
> *We need something at the beginning.*

David: Still, is the inner tension created for dramatic effect?

George: By positioning diverging voices side by side, I no doubt aimed for dramatic effect; nonetheless, that's what was happening—their visions, feelings, ideas, etc. often did collide in the collaborative process.

David: The colliding of ideas is echoed in my research script, especially through Karen and Pam who discuss the process of deconstructing and reconstructing ideas to shape a scene.

Karen: I kept at [script-writing] because I like the idea of creating something from nothing—a bunch of people sitting around brainstorming ideas, playing mental volleyball. You know, exploring options, trying out different things until you come up with something new. Brainstorming in a group is like an engine piston reaction—there's an explosion at one end and this force is sent to the other end and it fires back and so on, you know, a chain reaction setting ideas into motion.

Pam: You know, it's really about sharing ideas. And knowing that ideas aren't bad; they either fit or don't fit. It's really "Survival of the Fittest of Ideas"—where the weak ideas get weeded out and the stronger ones move forward. It's just a matter of not taking it personally, even though it's extremely personal. It's a matter of trusting the vision.

David: The freedom you gave your pre-service teachers to figure out the scripts for themselves is striking. Joan Lazarus (2004) advocates for learner-centred practice and for high school theatre teachers to view theatre as a learning laboratory. I struggle with my role as theatre teacher/artist, and often wonder if I am too involved in the students' learning process. I edit and workshop the students' work numerous times. Pam describes how 90% of all writing never makes it to the stage.

Pam: ...most of the ideas were just there in order to get to better ideas, and then to get to even better ideas after that. It's hard to do this without hurting people's feelings—we get so attached, you know. Sometimes [our teacher] even had to override our decisions and cut something we all liked or add something we didn't like and he'd say, "You know what guys, you're just going to have to trust me on this one." Some didn't like it when he did that, but for me, I really appreciated his leadership. His guidance and honesty somehow challenged me. It forced me to think differently about art. It forced me to go places I wouldn't have gone on my own.

David: Often I question: "Do I let students figure the script out for themselves and progress from there, or do I challenge them and impose my expertise and experience?" Which is more pedagogically sound?

George: No doubt there's a balance of guiding the process and allowing the participants to discover the process. Jonathan Needlands (2006) shares similar concerns regarding sharing power and knowledge: "How do I ensure that my work is progressively challenging so that there is a movement, over time, from teacher-led to individual autonomy?" (p.18) It seems to me that while you inspire your high school students to go outside of their comfort zone, I encourage my pre-service teachers to do this for one another.

Tracey: From the various ideas generated through the interactive tableaux, we developed some dialogue. One member of the group wrote a first draft, then e-mailed it to someone else in our small group, and so on, until all four of us that were working on this scene had a chance to give our insight. It's amazing how rich our scene became after that one session and some e-mail exchanges! And, it was truly collaborative.

David: A similar collaborative spirit emerged with my high school students, but it occurred more through peer-mentoring.

Mike: When I was in grade 9, I thought Derek was the coolest actor in the entire play! I idolized him. I loved everything about his style. Everybody wanted to be like him. Me, I even dressed like him...It's funny, as I'm talking about this, I'm just starting to realize that as I'm going into my final senior year, that I'm going to be a Derek for someone else. It's weird to think that I'm going to be this role-model and someone's going to look up to me and, for better or worse, I am going to have all this power to affect them, the way Derek impacted on me. Weird, huh?

George: It seems to me that the dialogue between participants is crucial, not only for ownership in the work, but also to foster sustainability of such creative endeavours. Collaborative creation environments foster leadership, and isn't our role as educators to share knowledge but also to create environments where learners can discover and build knowledge and understanding!

David: And create a community. Dialogue seems to be at the root of all our multiple scripts. We use dialogue to create our scripts, and we use scripts to express our dialogues. We write dialogue about our dialogues. As artists, researchers, and teachers we mix, reposition, shape, bend, play with, and tear apart dialogue to examine, highlight, question, honour and inspire further dialogue.

George: Let us temporarily end our dialogue and give voice to Tracey and Mike. I think their process of co-creating scripts resonates with the challenges and rewards of scripting data as a form of research and art—and this might hopefully inspire further dialogue on this topic!

Tracey: I feel kind of like what I assume George must feel like. I know he has ideas about what the play might look like, yet he is holding back on his vision in order to allow us to create it collectively. I'm finding it incredibly challenging to let go of my own ideas and include all the other voices. There are so many great ideas, and...I can't include them all. Yet, I fear others won't feel validated if I don't use their suggestions. Somehow, I have to funnel and blend all the ideas into our 30-minute piece.

Mike: You see, we're actually experiencing what art wants us to do—unifying people to discuss and exchange ideas—to question ourselves. And the questioning and dialoguing is happening as we're creating the piece itself. It's a double whammy! It's a multiplication of something that is already great! You're multiplying everything by the number of people involved. You're connecting minds, connecting hearts, connecting ideas... all coming together to create a play all squished into a two-hour show.

PART III

ETHICS AND ACTIVISM

STEPHANIE SPRINGGAY

AN ETHICS OF EMBODIMENT

A lone body moves along the shore of an industrial beach near Vancouver, British Columbia. The cold, grey winter day adds to the bleakness of her surroundings. The solitary figure flails in the water near the shore, struggling with a bucket. She then kneels and holds the vessel beneath the surface of the water, only to rise and walk, again, along the beach. She stops abruptly and throws the contents of the pail outwards, so that it splashes up against a screen. What at first appears distant and separate from the viewer becomes immediate and intimate, conflated by the fact that the water has turned to thick, red blood. The blood oozes and drips along the skin of the film (Marks, 2000) fragmenting and distorting the image. The action is further altered as the viewer watches this performance-based video installation through, quite literally, falling water. The scene described above is experienced as a video installation, where the video projection is seen through a wall of falling water that ends in a rectangular and minimalist fountain. This work, by First Nations-Canadian artist Rebecca Belmore, entitled *Fountain,* was conceived for the Canada Pavilion of the 2005 Venice Biennale.

As a basic element of nature, water can be a symbol of human destruction and control. The fountain, a public sculpture that contains and generates water, signifies prosperity (Martin, 2005). Historically fountains in Europe were commissioned by the nobility and papacy as monuments to their own strength and power (Martin, 2005). Today fountains are often commissioned by banks, corporations, and governments as a promise of economic stability. While great fountains help to memorialize colonial relations, Belmore's installation *Fountain* is an exposure that ruptures the embedded violence of colonizing that took place over, through, and across water. The blood that splashes and dribbles along the screen is a powerful metaphor for the burden of First Nations' history. Likewise, her actions speak of the blood of all people whose sufferings are caused by greed and power.

This opening chapter on "ethics and activism" engages with *Fountain* and other works created by Belmore in order to examine a/r/tographical research from the perspective of an *ethics of embodiment*. While the field of arts-based educational research and its constitutive variations has exploded in recent years, scant attention has been paid to the question of embodiment and the possibilities of arts-based educational research as an ethical approach to teaching, learning, and being (Slattery, 2003; Springgay, 2004a). Belmore's work embodies the qualities and features of a/r/tographical research and teaching, and thus serves as a conceptual and theoretical example.

As an introductory chapter, I begin with a brief examination of ethics from a feminist/social standpoint (see Ahmed, 2000; Jaggar, 1994; Todd, 2003), a position that contends that ethics is distinct from morality, where morality is a set of codes and behaviours. For instance, feminist cultural theorist Sara Ahmed (2000) offers that: "Ethics is instead a question of how one encounters others *as* other (than

S. Springgay et al. (eds.), Being with A/r/tography, 153–165.

by the regulative force of morality" (p.138). As such, ethics involves a "being-with". Following this section on ethics, I turn to introduce the features of a/r/tography with an attention to the in-between—a space that I argue is necessary for the generativity of being-with. It is being-with and the in-between, I argue, that enables the possibilities of an ethics of embodiment. The paper opens to a discussion on the implications of "doing" a/r/tography in educational contexts, and introduces the four exemplary—and diverse—chapters included in this section.

An Ethics of Embodiment as "Being-with"

In understanding the term "ethics," I draw on feminist cultural theorist Sara Ahmed (2000) who argues that ethics is distinct from morality, where morality is a set of codes and behaviours. "Ethics," she offers "is instead a question of how one encounters others *as* other (than being) and, in this specific sense, how one can live with what cannot be measured by the regulative force of morality" (p.138). When education takes up the project of ethics as morality, it is interested in particular principles that govern bodies such as regulations, laws or guidelines (Todd, 2003). In this instance, ethics or morals is designed to assist students in learning how to live and act. It is made into concrete practices, duties, and systems of oppression. Ethics becomes a particular acquisition of knowledge that is rationalist in its features.

In contrast, educational philosopher Sharon Todd (2003) suggests that an ethics understood through social interaction, and where knowledge is not seen as absolute, gives importance to the complexities of the ethical encounter. This, Todd and Ahmed both claim, insists on transitioning from understanding ethics as epistemological (what do I need to know about the other) and rather problematizes ethics through a relational understanding of being. Embedded in feminist/social ethics, relationality rests on a complex view of everyday experience "in terms of human relations and social structures" (Christians, 2003, p.223). For example, in discussing Luce Irigaray's account of sexual difference, Judith Butler (2006) argues that an ethics premised on "imagining oneself in the place of the other and deriving a set of rules of practices on the basis of that imagined and imaginable substitution" (p.111) assumes a symmetrical positioning of subjects within language. This substitution "becomes an act of appropriation and erasure" (p.111) and thus ethics is reduced to an act of domination. Rather, the ethical relation emerges between subjects when one recognizes that self and other are incommensurable.

> I am not the same as the Other: I cannot use myself as the model by which to apprehend the Other: the Other is in a fundamental sense beyond me and in this sense the other represents the limiting condition of myself. And further, this Other, who is not me, nevertheless defines me essentially by representing precisely what I cannot assimilate to myself, to what is already familiar to me. (Butler, 2006, p.111)

Such an understanding discloses the impossibility of putting oneself in the place of others.

In another performance-based video entitled *Vigil*, Belmore embodies and bears witness to the missing women from the downtown east side of Vancouver since the 1980s. In the eyes of the authorities, these unnamed missing women were insignificant because they were native and worked in the sex trade. When questions of a serial killer where proffered, the police responded that there were no bodies and that the women who led erratic lives were impossible to trace (Watson, 2002). In 2001 an intense examination of a pig farm in the lower mainland of British Columbia revealed DNA from numerous missing women. The list of DNA findings continues to grow.

Vigil is a thirty minute performance (and subsequent video installation) acted out at the corner of Gore and Cordova Streets in the downtown east side of Vancouver, the site of many of the missing women's abductions. In the performance, the women's first names are written in black marker on Belmore's arms. Screaming these names she rips a rose and its thorns through her teeth.[1] Through her own body Belmore embodies the crimes committed against the native body, the woman's body, and the social body. Her performance does not claim to speak "for" the missing women, nor about their lives and experiences, but rather weighs heavy with the flesh of the body. It is not possible to assert a feminine kinship with Belmore, or with the women whose lives are implicit in her work on the basis of identifying with some universal female experience. What we as viewers/co-participants experience is an awareness of the importance of the knowledge of the body as we engage in relations of bodied encounters.

In *Vigil*, a red dress is pulled taut over the weight of a woman's body. Repeatedly, it is pulled to a point of unendurable tension. This is not representation of the body but the phenomenology of flesh, of nailing and tearing; the body as meaning as opposed to a container of meaning. Belmore's performance does not re-enact the violence against the unnamed women, nor does it lecture on the moral victimization of the colonized, but rather through the physicality of the body, of touch, and sound it undoes meaning. This could be further expressed through the words of feminist philosopher Elizabeth Grosz (2001) who writes:

> The space in-between things is the space in which things are undone, the space to the side and around which is the space of subversion and fraying the edges of any identities limits. In short it is the space of the bounding and undoing of the identities which constitute it. (p.93)

As Allison Jaggar (1994) writes in the introduction to the anthology on feminist ethics, how we engage with bodies/subjects cannot become simple applications of moral principles. Ethical principles, she argues, are not understood prior to or independent of identity or of individual's actions, but rather derived from the very contradictions, ambiguities, and multiplicities of encounters between bodies/subjects.

Feminist/social ethics also critiques and disrupts the conventions of impartiality in research and teaching, disavowing norms, rules, and ideals external to lived experience (Heller, 1990). A feminist/social approach to ethics asks questions about power—that is, about domination and subordination—instead of questions about good and evil. Such an approach to ethics is centred on action aimed at subverting rather than reinforcing hegemonic relationships (Jagger, 1992). Art educator Candace Stout (2006) urges educators to reconsider their responsibilities with regards to research participants, and asks the question: "How shall I be toward these people I am studying?" (p.100). Such a question approaches ethics from the point of view of behaviour. How must I behave, and what actions will this entail in order for me to ethically treat Others? This assumes that the ethical behaviour is something already known prior to the encounter with the Other. Yet, Butler (2006) in her re-visitation of the work of Irigaray contends that the ethical relation is premised on the "*never yet known*, the open future, the one that cannot be assimilated to a knowledge that is always and already presupposed" (p.115). Ethics does not claim to know in advance, "but seeks to know who that addressee is for the first time in the articulation of the question itself" (p.115). This argument, Butler (2006) suggests, poses a more difficult question: "How to treat the Other well when the Other is never fully other, when one's own separateness is a function of one's dependency on the Other, when the difference between the Other and myself is, from the start equivocal" (p.116). It is the *never yet known* that Todd (2003) argues is at the heart of pedagogical (and here I would also add research) relationships, stating that "our commitment to our students involves our capacity to be altered, to become someone different than we were before; and, likewise, our students' commitment to social causes through their interactions with actual people equally consists in their capacity to be receptive to the Other to the point of transformation" (p.89).

Thus, ethics shifts inquiry from "getting to know the other" to research grounded in bodied encounters that are themselves ethical in nature. Instead of "getting to know the other" I want to consider an ethics of embodiment from the perspective of being-with, where ethics is figured around bodied encounters. Todd (2003) explores this sense of lived ethics in her discussion on teaching. I extend her words on the pedagogical encounter to include research and lived experiences.

> Teaching would not be focused on acquiring knowledge about ethics, or about the Other, but would instead have to consider its practices themselves as relation to otherness and thus as always already potentially ethical—that is, participating in a network of relations that lend themselves to moments of nonviolence. (p.9)

We cannot create a simple list of expected behaviours and have them function as ways of being ethical, rather ethics itself involves a rethinking of embodiment as being-with. This, argues Todd (2003), moves us from empathetic understandings where the Other is ultimately consumed, to openness and risk, attention to ambiguity and to what we cannot know beforehand, and "to be vulnerable to the consequences and effects that our response has on the Other" (p.88).

The philosophies of Maurice Merleau-Ponty (1968) locate the body as the expressive space by which we experience the world. In his theories of intersubjectivity, each body/subject participates with other body/subjects, co-mingling and interpenetrating each other. Bodies bring other bodies into being without losing their own specificity, and each materializes itself without being contained. Rather than an understanding of self and other as oppositional, intersubjectivity becomes imbricated and reciprocal. One is always already both self and other at the same time. Such a conjecture is similar to Nancy's (2000) theories of "being-singular-plural". For Nancy (2000), to be a body is to be "with" other bodies, to touch, to encounter, and to be exposed. In other words, each individual body is brought into being through encounters with other bodies. It is the relationality between bodies that creates a particular understanding of shared existence. Relationality depends on singularity. A singular body, argues Nancy (2000), "is not individuality; it is, each time, the punctuality of a "with" that establishes a certain origin of meaning and connects it to an infinity of other possible origins" (p.85).

Peter Hallward (2001) substantiates this definition with: "The singular proceeds internally and is constituted in its own creation. The singular, in each case, is constituent of itself, expressive of itself, immediate to itself" (p.3). Criteria are not external but are determined through its own actions. Nikki Sullivan (2003) provides us with a further explanation: "Each "one" is singular (which isn't the same as saying each "one" is individual) while simultaneously being in-relation" (p.55). Singularity as a theoretical construct demands that self and other no longer hold opposing positions. Bodies/selves cannot exist without other bodies/selves, nor are the two reducible to one another. In other words, my uniqueness is only expressed and exposed in my being-with. This being-with is not defined through the common (I am not "with" because I have the same characteristics i.e. *all* women or *all* students), but a with that opens the self to the vulnerability of the other; a with that is always affected and touched by the other. This openness propels us into relations with others; it entangles us, implicating self and other simultaneously creating a network of relations. Clifford Christians (2003) re-iterates this when he writes:

> This irreducible phenomenon—the relational reality, the in-between, the reciprocal bond, the interpersonal—cannot be decomposed into simpler elements without destroying it. Given the primacy of relationships, unless we use our freedom to help others flourish, we deny our own well-being. (pp.225-226)

Being-with constitutes the fabric of everyday life and the ethical encounter. Through bodied encounters body/subjects create lived experiences together and nurture one another's ethical relationality.

It is these acts of engagement as being-with that are taken up and embodied in Belmore's actions. Another of Belmore's installations also makes reference to "missing bodies" and likewise enacts the theories of flesh that it also interrogates. *blood on the snow* evokes the massacre by the United States Calvary at Wounded Knee Creek, South Dakota. On December 29, 1890 some three hundred unarmed Sioux, mostly women and children, were killed. The bodies, frozen under a blanket of snow, lay obscured for four days before being buried in mass graves. This slaughter is marked as one of the most violent incidents in the history of the American settlement of the west.

The installation includes a chair enveloped and surrounded by an expanse of white quilted fabric onto which blood red pigment seeps. The comfort and purity of the white quilt is violated; white violated by red blood. However, it is not a static representation of the massacre itself, nor the people whose lives it commemorates, rather it exists in-between, in the encounters between bodies/subjects, and between our own singularity.

A research methodology that insists that research participants are static objects to be studied also assumes that particular descriptions of the Other can be concretely defined. An ethics of embodiment counters this with: "Particularity then does not belong to an other, but names the meetings and encounters which produce or flesh out other, and hence differentiate others from other others" (Ahmed, 2002, p.561). In other words, an ethics of embodiment as being-with is concerned with the processes of encounters, the meaning that is made with, in, and through the body not discernable facts about a body. Feminist philosopher Moira Gatens (1996) argues that:

> Reason, politics and ethics are always embodied; that is, the ethics or the reason which any particular collective body produces will bear the marks of that body's genesis, its (adequate or inadequate) understanding of itself, and will express the power or capacity of that body's endeavour to sustain its own integrity. (p.100)

Ethics is not dictated by a rational and universal mind but rather embraces notions of bodied particularity.

In turn, any understanding of ethics always assumes a complex body. Therefore an ethics of embodiment is complex and dynamic; open to challenge and revision. An ethics of embodiment "opens the possibility of engagement with others as genuine others, rather than as inferior, or otherwise subordinated, versions of the same" (Gatens, 1996, p.105). Ethics, argues Gatens (1996), is not just different forms of knowing but different forms of being, and it is this complicated and responsive understanding of lived experience that is at the heart of a/r/tographical research.

A/r/tography

A/r/tography[2] is a research methodology that entangles and performs what Gilles Deleuze and Felix Guattari (1987) refer to as a rhizome. A rhizome is an assemblage that moves and flows in dynamic momentum. The rhizome operates by variation, perverse mutation, and flows of intensities that penetrate meaning, opening it to what Jacques Derrida (1978) calls the "as yet unnameable which begins to proclaim itself" (p.293). It is an interstitial space, open and vulnerable where meanings and understandings are interrogated and ruptured.

A/r/tography invites educators to contiguously bring together the various elements that constitute our creative and educative selves. For example, rather than thinking of teaching, learning, art making, and researching as disparate and fragmented entities, a/r/tography is engaged in the process of actively folding and unfolding such multiplicities together.[3] As such, a/r/tography attends to the spaces between artist, researcher, and teacher. This is not to suggest that it privileges one form over another, but allows for these dynamic practices and identities to interface and collide with one another so that meanings, understandings, and theories generated become multiple, tangled, and complicated.

Drawing attention to a/r/t (artist/researcher/teacher) is not intended to single one identity out, rather it is an encounter between bodies that releases something from each. It is in this disjunction that meaning is made. Similarly, the slash is the place of negotiation. It is a place to move and a position from which to create a rupture. According to Deleuzian (1994) principles, in a/r/tography binaries are not abandoned, but played off of each other, rendered molecular, so that their realignments in different systems are established. Likewise, a/r/tographical inquiry punctures artistic meaning, research, and pedagogical practices.

A/r/tography is a process of living inquiry (see Irwin & de Cosson, 2004). Immersed in action research, hermeneutics, and phenomenology, a/r/tographical research insists on contemplative practices. In other words, a/r/tography is embedded in living experience. How we perceive ourselves and our world sensuously and creatively impacts how we examine educational phenomena. Moreover, because it is a research methodology informed by the arts, it is necessary that encounters with contemporary art as theory become part of our constitutive understandings of self, other, community, and education (Rogoff, 2000).

While many forms of arts-based educational research focus on the creation of artistic products as representations of research, a/r/tographical inquiry is constituted through visual and textual *understandings* and *experiences* rather than visual and textual *representations* (Irwin, 2004). A/r/tographical research may culminate in an artistic form (e.g. art installation, poem, or dramatic monologue), however it doesn't need to. While many arts-based methodologies focus on the end result, a/r/tography is concerned with inquiry—the mode of searching, questing, and probing—insisting that these elements be informed by and through the arts. Likewise, a/r/tography interfaces art and scholarly writing not as descriptions of each other, but as an exposure of meaning pointing towards possibilities that are yet unnamed. Neither is subordinate to the other, rather they operate simultaneously, as inter-textual elements and often in tension with each other.

On many occasions, I have noticed that the best conversations happen when my video camera is buried deep within my backpack, raising the question: *when is data?* Yet for all the absent tape recorders, video cameras, and failures to write legible field notes, the constructed nature of data and the research encounter needs to be further questioned. It is not a matter of consideration of which method is better suited to extricate "experience" but rather the realization of the impossibility of ever understanding the other's experience. Rather than viewing experience as a concrete reality with a fixed essence that can be simply reflected by language (text and/or image), a/r/tographical research argues that experience is itself constituted through relational encounters, and thus constituted by and in language. Thus, the representation of research cannot be seen as the translation of experience. Instead a/r/tographical research as living inquiry constructs the very materiality it attempts to represent. In other words, engaging in a/r/tographical research constructs the very "thing" one is attempting to make sense of. Thus, a/r/tography is both a methodological and ontological strategy—one that is reflective of the ongoing practices of identification. As such, it emphasizes that the stories of identification are unfinished, multiple, and conflicting.

The features of a/r/tography include six renderings through which research can be imag(e)ined, enacted, and understood: *living inquiry, contiguity, openings, metaphor/metonymy, reverberations,* and *excess* (see Springgay, Irwin & Kind, 2005). Renderings enable artists, researchers, and teachers to interrogate the interstitial spaces *between* things, and to convey *meaning* rather than facts. To be engaged in a/r/tographical research means being open to a continual process of questioning. Renderings are not criteria. Rather, through the inquiry process and the space of representation one needs to become attentive to these renderings; to contemplate experience in light of living inquiry, contiguity, and so on.

Subsequently, a/r/tography radically transforms the idea of theory as an abstract system distinct and separate from practice, towards an understanding of theory as a critical exchange that is reflective, responsive and relational. Theory *as* practice becomes an embodied, living space of inquiry. Theory is not pre-determined nor a stable interpretive scaffold, but part of a relational encounter, itself capable of creative change and development (Meskimmon, 2003). Thus, meaning finds its place in the in-between where language hesitates and falters, where un/certainty cannot be represented, and where knowledge remains unspoken.

It is precisely this *in-between* of thinking and materiality that invites researchers to explore the interstitial spaces of art making, researching, and teaching. According to Elizabeth Grosz (2001) the in-between is not merely a physical location or object but a *process*, a movement and displacement of meaning. It is a process of invention rather than interpretation, where concepts are marked by social engagements and encounters. Concepts, argue Deleuze and Guattari (1994), "are centres of vibrations, each in itself and every one in relation to all the others. This is why they all resonate rather than cohere or correspond with each other" (p.23). Meaning and understanding are no longer revealed or thought to emanate from a point of origin, rather they are complex, singular, and relational. As such, a/r/tographical texts are not places of representations where thought is stored "but [are] a process of scattering thought; scrambling terms, concepts, and practice; forging linkages; becoming a form of action" (Grosz, 2001, p.58). As living inquiry, a/r/tography expresses meaning as an exposure—*never yet known.*

Opening to the Never Yet Known

Belmore's art highlights the need to find alternative ways of re-conceptualizing the body outside of the binaries that reduce it to an object; to an Other. In her performative-installations we are offered flesh filled singular gestures that place the body of the artist, the bodies of the women, and the body of the viewer at the in-between. The implications of such a way of thinking are bound up with understanding the relations between identities rather than in terms of describing identities, intensions, or acts of individuals or groups. Her art, I argue, maintains the alterity and unknowability of the Other.

In 2002, when Belmore performed *Vigil* on the streets of Vancouver, fifty-one women had been "identified" using DNA. Many more women were still "missing".

Slaughtered body parts were still being unearthed on a pig farm. Fifty-one roses slashed through screaming teeth. Fifty-one names articulated, opened, and embodied. Understood in this way *never yet known* becomes an interstitial space, the in-between, the space of perverse mutation and force. The possibility, or impossibility, of the *never yet known* invites us to face the Other not through particularities that are descriptions of her body, but as bodied encounters. As Sara Ahmed claims: "Particularity then does not belong to an other, but names the meetings and encounters which produce or flesh out other, and hence differentiate others from other others" (Ahmed, 2002, p.561). Beyond the veil of blood, *Fountain*, *Vigil*, and *blood on the snow* offer the power to conceive of knowledge and research as embodied and as being-with.

A/r/tography materializes the in-between and thus effectively invites researchers and teachers to move beyond static dualisms which pit theory against practice, self against other, and mind against body. A/r/tography is deeply rooted in corporeal theory (Meskimmon, 2003), where the body's immersion and intertwining in the world creates meaning. It is a way of living in the world as being-with, of touching the other not to know or consume the other, but as an encounter that mediates, constructs, and transforms subjectivity.

A/r/tography is a mode of thinking about or theorizing multiplicities. It is not about framing rules or understanding principles, but about the possibilities of intertextual relations. Instead of requiring logical certainty and the guarantee of universal validity, a/r/tography is embedded in imagination, experimentation, uniqueness, and conjecture. It seeks to provoke, to generate, and to un/do meaning.

Likewise, embodiment, according to Grosz (2001), is an attitude of endless questioning. Thus, a/r/tography as an ethics of embodiment is a "thinking [that] involves a wrenching of concepts away from their usual configurations, outside the systems in which they have a home, and outside the structures of recognition that constrain thought to the already known" (Grosz, 2001, p.61). Such thinking is situated in the in-between.

However, while scholars like Homi Bhabha (2004) and Trinh Minh-ha (1989) have examined the liminal place of hybridity and uncertainty, as a place where one might go beyond the contained grid of fixed identities and binary oppositions, other scholars like Ien Ang (2001) worry that there is a romanticizing tendency in the valorization of the in-between. Such concerns are based not only on the assumption that the deconstruction of binary oppositions is subversive, but that we overstate the power of the in-between. Moreover, as Sara Ahmed (2000) argues, there may be ways in which relations of power are paradoxically secured through the very process of destabilization. Examples from popular visual culture include the iPod advertisements where fragmentation, fluidity and marketing through the exploitation and exoticization of difference are central elements. Therefore, rather than assuming the in-between as inherently subversive, there is a need to pay attention to the different ways in which specific forms of liminality are positioned and to the possibility of their different effects (Gonick, 2003). What I mean by this is that it is not sufficient to make claims that understanding the body as unstable, fluid, productive and in-between enables its resistance, rather we need to examine the in-between as a space where intercorporeal encounters and the relationality between beings produces different knowledges and produces knowledge differently.

Issues of race, class, gender, sexual orientation, and multiculturalism (bodied identities) are now being discussed as essential to postmodern education and in many cases have advocated particular understandings of liminality, uncertainty, and the in-between. I believe that such pronouncements are necessary and important but what a/r/tography adds to this already redolent space is a pedagogical practice and a research methodology that is located at the in-between, where the *never yet known* is interrogated and ruptured.

Likewise, as educational researchers, many of the questions we grapple with take into account how we conduct research with others; how do we negotiate diverse voices and how do we re-present their stories? A/r/tography maintains that the representation of research (which we all do by imaging and writing about research) does not reproduce violence towards the other, but rather looks to a network of relations that are continuously being produced in and through the inquiry itself. A/r/tography refuses to locate ethics within a rational, autonomous body/subject but rather in the "very forms of relationality that structure our encounters with other people, ones that are frequently infused with powerful feelings and emotions" (Todd, 2003, p.141). As educators and educational theorists, we need to recognize that the very things we seek to understand are produced in the moment of inquiry and hence slip from our ever knowing them fully. From an ethical point of view, being-with cannot be a matter of policy but is a fundamentally a personal, practical matter where our encounters with difference and otherness are brought fully to bear on us, and for which each of us is responsible.

Once again I return to Nancy's (2000) writings. Nancy contends that excess is not a numerical equivalent (10, 400 or 2 million) but discourse in its totality. Excess is not a degree of magnitude. It is being-with; an unheard of measure. In other words, being-with is not qualifying something against something else—the setting of criteria or an established norm. Rather the conditions for being-with are contingent upon and exist within the structure itself—an absolute measure. In this sense an a/r/tographical act is its own possible measure. Instead of thinking of our actions, encounters, and thoughts—our living inquiry—as substance that can be arranged in discrete moments, counted, and subjected to normative evaluations, we need to understand living inquiry in education as *never yet known*. What I am suggesting is a complex understanding of the ways we participate in attending to difference within institutional contexts, and also to the ways that education and research as practices already contribute to the conditions that create difference. Thus, what I am proposing is an ethics committed to ambiguity, uncertainty and to the never yet known.

CHAPTERS INCLUDED IN THIS SECTION

The chapters included in this section are not intended to offer a single framework for understanding ethics and activism. Each author(s) addresses the ethical relationship between self and other through different intellectual traditions, intermedia practices, and embraces the "call to a/r/tographical relations" in divergent and sometimes discordant ways. Rather than fall into the trap of harmony, stability, and normalizing discourses, the cacophony produced by these dissonant voices demonstrates the complexities of a/r/tographical acts. Writing about interpretation, David Jardine (2003) says:

> Interpretation does not begin with me. It only begins when something happens to me in my reading of a text, when something strikes me, tears me open, wounds me and leaves me open and vulnerable to the world, like the sensitivities of open flesh. (p.59)

Our interpretation of and attention to a/r/tography is a process that is fragile, partial, and precarious. Madeline Grumet (1988) suggests that "the gaps, the contradictions, the leaks and explosions in the text are invitations" (p.67) to educators to enter into "complicated conversations" (Pinar, 2004) and relational encounters.

In thinking about dissonance, we turn to curriculum scholar Ted T. Aoki, who reminds us that art making, researching, and teaching should not be rendered universal, immobile, or harmonious—the diversity, multiplicity, and layers of voices and texts often conceal and obscure the unknowable and the unsaid. Sometimes on the surface it appears as if we are moving forward in a progressive stance, but underneath this wave are other currents, other images/sounds that require examination, critical reflection, and attention.

> In our busy world of education, we are surrounded by layers of voices, some loud and shrill, that claim to know what teaching is. Awed perhaps by the cacophony of voices, certain voices became silent and, hesitating to reveal themselves, conceal themselves. Let us beckon these voices to speak to us, particularly the silent ones, so that we might awaken to the truer sense of teaching that likely stirs within each of us. (Aoki, 2005, p.188)

The chapters in this section take up this call to question what it means to do a/r/tographical work ethically and relationally, but so too they amplify the gaps, the openings, and the undoings that must become a part of our future work, inquiry, and questioning.

Sylvia Kind's chapter examines the hopeful generativity of teaching. Drawing on the work of Emmanuel Levinas, particularly his perception that teaching is receiving from the other more than the self already holds, she explores how the foundations of teaching can be learning, process, change, and becoming: foundations that are constituted in ethical relation to others. In this sense, encounters, relationships, and conversations are the basis of pedagogy, knowledge and identities are co-constructed in the midst of dissymmetric relations where "teaching" is shared. It is teaching that thinks through alterity, dependency, vulnerability and receptivity. Kind develops her arguments for ethical relations of learning to listen through a reflective and autobiographical journey through memories of loss, grief, and coming to know in the context of a teacher preparation course at the University of British Columbia.

STEPHANIE SPRINGGAY

Dalene Swanson's narrative chapter explores the construction of difference and disadvantage in school mathematics in post-apartheid South Africa. Swanson draws on her doctoral study, which was situated in a range of schooling contexts with socio-economic and cultural differences, including contexts of extreme poverty, to navigate the in-between spaces of ever-shifting textual meaning and lived inquiry. She sets this against the slipping places of identity and agency and argues that a methodology of a/r/tography can be brought to bear on the ethical tensions of inquiry as it relates to purposeful action as well as personal and collective activism.

The third chapter, by Veronica Gaylie, illuminates how poetry engages urban students in cultural, material and social critique through language that is relevant to them. The project, set in a grade ten class at a large, inner city high school, involved engaging students in the processes of poetry—in talking, writing and reading poetry aloud. Student poetry and interview responses are juxtaposed to reveal both critical and creative interpretations of poetry, and of students' place in the world as inner city learners. Doing so invites the reader to consider the first hand experiences of marginalized students negotiating various language and social frameworks, where poetry offers "a place to begin".

The final chapter in this section describes a/r/tographical inquiry as a methodology of situations grounded in a collaborative project undertaken by a group of artists, educators, and researchers working with intergenerational families in Richmond, British Columbia. The project, "The City of Richgate", examines issues related to migration, place, and community through an artistically oriented inquiry. This investigation into "The City of Richgate" provides a way of elaborating upon a/r/tography as a methodology that provokes the creation of situations through inquiry, that responds to the evocative nature of situations found within data, and that provides a reflective and reflexive stance to situational inquiries. These situations are often found, created or ruptured within the rhizomatic nature of a/r/tography.

NOTES

[1] See http://www.belkin-gallery.ubc.ca/belmore/main.htm for a video clip.
[2] For essays on the theoretical framework of a/r/tography see Springgay, 2004a, Springgay, Irwin, & Kind, 2005; Springgay, Irwin, & Kind, in press; Springgay & Irwin, forthcoming. For exemplars of a/r/tographical research see Bickel, 2004; de Cosson, 2003, 2002, 2001; Irwin, 2003; Irwin & de Cosson, 2004; Springgay, 2005a, 2005b, 2004b.
[3] Un/folding is where perception is doubled, embodied, and tangled. A fold is both exterior and interior. In a fold inside and outside remain distinct, but not separate, rather they are doubled. Un/folding is not the reverse of a fold, but may result in additional folds. Thus, the fold appears interconnected, embracing touch and intercorporeality. The condition of the fold is the premise that it is not a void or an absence in the sense of nothing. Rather the fold is being as turned back on itself—touching. Deleuze (1993) translates the fold as sensuous vibrations, a world made up of divergent series, an infinity of pleats and creases. Un/folding divides endlessly, folds within folds

touching one another. "Matter thus offers an infinitely porous, spongy, or cavernous texture without emptiness, caverns endlessly contained in other caverns" (p.5). Challenging Descartes, Deleuze is mindful of the fold as matter that cannot be divided into separable parts. A fold is not divisible into independent points, but rather any un/folding results in additional folds, it is the movement or operation of one fold to another. "The division of the continuous must not be taken as sand dividing into grains, but as that of a sheet of paper or of a tunic in fold, in such a way that an infinite number of folds can be produced...without the body ever dissolving into point or minima. A fold is always folded within a fold" (p.6). Perception is not a question then of part to whole but a singular totality "where the totality can be as imperceptible as the parts" (p.87). Perception is not embodied in perceiving the sum of all parts, rather it is distinguished by and within the fold.

SYLVIA KIND

LEARNING TO LISTEN: TRACES OF LOSS, VULNERABILITY, AND SUSCEPTIBILITY IN ART/TEACHING

I wake in the morning with a vague heaviness weighing over me as I have done most days since my parents died and slip on a pair of soft felted boots before going downstairs to put on a pot of tea. The boots keep my feet warm on this chilly winter morning as the cold air creeps in from under the gap at the front door. I had knit the boots out of bulky white Icelandic wool while my mother was dying, her hands reaching out to help mine as I struggled with turning the heels and later had felted them with repeated washings in the washing machine. I had intended to embroider them with brightly coloured yarn, covering them with flowers and cheery motifs to carry her into the next world. Not that her death was a happy event—far from it—but she was at peace with her dying and with spring coming it had seemed like a fitting gesture. I knew she would never wear them with her feet so swollen from the effects of cancer but I had knit them for her anyhow and had tried to felt them as stiffly as the ones she had worn as a child during the long winters in Lithuania.

I never knew much about her early life in Lithuania, or about the war years that followed. My mother didn't talk much about those years and most of what I knew was pieced together from fragments of conversations, bits and pieces dropped in amongst a day's work, scattered comments, and from things not said. Yet in the months before she had died, knitting and felting had worked its way into several of our conversations. Her stories about wool and socks and knitting told me many things about her life before the war and I began to see her life through hands that knit and through memories of wool, yarn and needles. And I found myself learning in indirect ways.

On this particular winter morning I try to shake the cloud that hangs over me but it won't budge. My restlessness grows and finally I sit to write again and I pick up the threads of my art/teaching. While I had found the first weeks back in the classroom after each of my parents' deaths extremely difficult I had also known the hopeful generativity of teaching. I had known teaching as a generous, living, creative practice and what I believed about teaching was closely related to how I understood art and art making: both were emergent, living engagements and processes needing difficulty to provoke creative change and transformation. Shaun McNiff (1998) encourages artists to trust the process, enter the unknown, stay in uncertainty long enough for something new to emerge, and remain in the difficulty or aporia space (see also de Cosson, 2004; Derrida, 1993) in order to find one's way through. This, along with Alex de Cosson's (2004) statement that "an artist knows that a point of disjuncture is a point of learning" (p.xiv) prompted me to

S. Springgay et al. (eds.), Being with A/r/tography, 167–178.

inquiry and participating with the flow of creative thought (Csikszentmihalyi, 1990) and trusting artistic processes to help negotiate life's passages. And so I was provoked to stay inside the difficulty of teaching and to wait and trust that something new would emerge.

A/r/tographic teaching *is* artistic as the art, research, and teaching arise in relation to each other. Teaching, and particularly art/teaching, is informed by artistic ways of thinking, creating and being and takes shape (or ideally *should* take shape) as living relational artistic practice. A/r/tographic inquiry and artistic practices are also inherently pedagogical as the art/inquiry teaches, questions, and opens up conversations and understandings. In addition, a/r/tographic teaching thinks *through* teaching and understands teaching as instances of inquiry as well.

Over the past several years, as I have thought and worked through Emmanuel Levinas' views, particularly his perception that teaching is receiving from the other more than the self already holds (see Todd, 2003a). I have begun to appreciate how the foundations of teaching can be learning, process, change, and becoming: foundations that are constituted in ethical relation to others (Dahlberg, Moss, & Pence, 1999). In this sense, encounters, relationships, and conversations are the basis of pedagogy, knowledge and identities are co-constructed in the midst of dissymmetric relations, and "teaching" is shared. It is teaching that thinks through alterity, dependency, vulnerability and receptivity.

One of the closest examples I have come across so far that would help illustrate this can be found in the pedagogical practices of the Reggio Emilia schools in Italy. In these early childhood contexts young children use the arts as a central and vital source of inquiry. The children are engaged in a/r/tographic practice—that is they use artistic means (or musical, artistic, performative, and other languages) to test emergent theories and inquire about the world.

The classroom studio space, or *atelier*, is considered at once an idea and a place (Gandini, Hill, Cadwell, & Schwall, 2005). As a place it is an actual room or area aesthetically set up with materials and invitations for inquiry. As an idea it is a commitment to the arts as processes of meaning making and inquiry, to relational educational practices, and to an artistic, living pedagogy that is always kept open to new encounters and change. As Lella Gandini (Gandini et al., 2005) explains, the true atelier is a mind-set. It is a way of organizing spaces, observing children, documenting and communicating, and understanding education as an ongoing creative process of discovery and learning—for children *and* teachers. Children's art making is not viewed as individual self-expression, as if ideas are held inside of children and then expressed in paint, clay, or other media. Nor is art making delivered through teacher directed projects. Rather it is constructed in collaboration and community, and in engagements with the materials and with others.

Teaching in these contexts is conceived of as an art and as an ever changing, ongoing, creative, relational act (Hill, Stremmel, & Fu, 2005). It is founded on principles of collaborative research, ongoing inquiry, and openness to continual discovery and learning. The teachers learn from, through, and alongside the children, working together on emergent ideas and inquiries. In addition, research is not something added to one's teaching, rather it is essential to the processes and practices of teaching/being a teacher. For example a teacher spends an extended time listening to and learning from the children, documenting children's actions, speech, and processes of thinking and creating. This documentation is an "act of love" (Rinaldi in Hill, Stremmel, & Fu, 2005, p.178) and an integral part of fostering learning and re-imagining teacher-learner relationships (Rinaldi, 2001). The processes of documenting, researching, and questioning try to make visible the intangible and inarticulate elements of teaching and learning.

Reggio inspired practices, such as those described in the Stockholm Project in Sweden (see Dahlberg, Moss, & Pence, 1999), also draw on the work of Emmanuel Levinas (1969) and understand their learning communities in terms of ethical relationality and dependency relations rather than emancipation. Dependency is not understood as something to fix or to overcome and neither is it a sign of developmental immaturity. Rather, it is conceptualized as an ethical attention to otherness in a non-reciprocal relation. This is illustrated in Carla Rinaldi's (in Gandini et al., 2005) statement as she speaks about the responsibility teachers have for young children: "We should remember that there is no creativity in the child if there is no creativity in the adult. The competent and creative child exists if there is a competent and creative adult" (p.172). This statement also illustrates Levinas' pedagogical relation: that children's creativity is *dependent* on the creativity and openness of the teacher. This dependency presents itself as an obligation for the teacher to respond and in return become more that he or she contains (see Todd, 2003a).

As Bill Readings (1996) describes, dependency relations are not based on mutuality or exchange, as if our obligations to the other could be settled, instead the pedagogical relationship is compelled by an obligation to otherness and the responsibility one has *for* others. This means listening to and learning from others, and not just listening to the surface of what is said or to what can be said, imaged, voiced, or otherwise represented. Readings claims the "pedagogical relation is dissymmetrical and endless. The parties are caught in a dialogic web of obligations to thought... [and] thought appears as the voice of the other" (p.145). Pedagogy then is listening to thought; to that which cannot be said yet tries to be heard.

Therefore, entering, waiting, and listening amidst the difficult a/r/tographic spaces of teaching is not a passive waiting or distanced observation, rather it is an expectant, receptive attention and living engagement *with* the difficulties and processes. It is waiting that maintains an open, welcoming expectancy for something yet unknown to present itself (see Benso, 2000) and calls for the imaginative capacity to "look at things as if they could be otherwise" (Greene, 1995, p.19). It is to be still, to dwell with, to attend to, and to make time for the unexpected.

Questions Sent Out

I have a stack of cloth handkerchiefs sealed in a large zip lock bag on my desk. I had collected them when we had cleaned out my parents' home following their deaths. I had gathered these symbols of bodily excesses and tokens of grief and affection in the hopes of transforming them into something else. Some were my mother's with intricate hand stitched flowers and pink and white lace edgings, their delicacy so unlike her prudent and practical ways. Her handkerchiefs had rarely been used but were kept as they had been given as gifts from various relatives and friends. The rest were my father's, sensible pale coloured plaid bits of cloth with his odour still lingering, that he had used everyday. I found some stuffed in pants and jacket pockets as if expecting his return, others washed, pressed, folded, and laid out neatly in piles in his drawer alongside socks and undershirts. I carefully open the bag and touch their soft, faded fibres. In my mind I see them stitched, written on, cut open, and re-worked; hung on a line like clothes fluttering in the gentle breeze, releasing sorrows and sending out mournings, losses, and grievings. I feel the wind move through me, and the familiar smells within the fabric locates me back in moments of my childhood on the seaside bluffs on Southern Vancouver Island.

The air on the Island was always moving. Even on the hottest days of August there was always a light breeze coming off the ocean, gently echoing through the treetops, bringing the familiar smells of summer and pleasant sun filled memories. But there were other winds too. I remember storms and gale force winds that brought the waves crashing over the roads, spraying up over the breakwater, leaving the taste of salt water in my mouth. And I could feel the winds blowing through my centre, evoking memories of childhood fears that I would be carried up to the sky or thrown out to sea along with the storms that sprung up unexpectedly in the dark of night.

Typically in my artwork I let the materials speak. I start with questions not yet formed or issues that trouble me and see where the materials and images lead. At any other time I would take out the handkerchiefs, hang them up for a while, live with them, look at them, let them direct the process and I would follow. But when I open the bag the familiar familial odours will be released and I'm not sure I'm ready for it. It feels too important, too soon, and too risky—maybe this wind will be the one that actually carries me away and I'll be lost at sea. So I send out my uncertain questions and troubles in other ways.

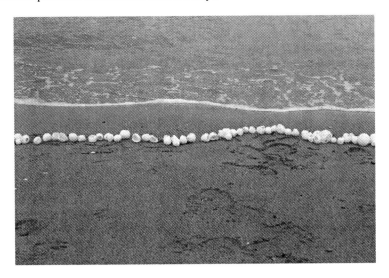

The Conditions of Learning

This term I'm teaching an art education course for pre-service and practicing teachers, which is shaped around an afternoon enrichment art program for children. We meet on Saturdays and for seven weeks of the term 30 children ages 5-11 from the community come for an art program. The teachers registered in the course collaboratively team-teach the art sessions and provide a focus and frame for the afternoon's art activities. Although they are expected to facilitate one of the weekly art sessions, the teachers' primary responsibilities are to work closely with one or two children, attend to their intentions and goals, offer support and hands-on help as needed, and to document in detail the children's work. When I first taught this course it was structured in fairly conventional ways; in an "application" model where students learned about art, teaching, and children, tried it out in "real" settings, then reflected on and made meaning of their learning—in effect, learned about teaching by talking about, engaging in, and reflecting on teaching. However, I've become convinced that what really matters can't be accessed directly.

My goal is for teacher's teaching to be transformed. I hope their art/teaching will know the joys and struggles of art making and will bring a life of creative and artistic inquiry to the students they will teach. Yet I don't directly focus on this.

Over the six years that I have taught this course my focus has gradually yet steadily shifted from emphasizing teaching (what the teachers do) to learning (how the teachers respond to what they are presented with through the children). And my primary concern has become how I might best facilitate the *conditions* of learning. While each year I make alterations to the course readings, change the theme and art activities, adjust assignments and other aspects of the course, the most significant changes have been in the conversations that make sense of things. Thinking through the personal, working through my own grief and disruptions, has profoundly dis/oriented and opened up this course.

Throughout the course I make every effort to keep the classes open and flexible. It requires constant attention and effort to resist the closures and unravel the certainties so spaces can be made and teaching and learning can move and breathe. This is particularly the case at the beginning of the art program until students start to get a taste of the spontaneity and responsiveness that is needed to keep the curriculum living and emergent and begin to appreciate that like any conversation the outcomes can not be known in advance.

I want the teachers to think about identities beyond typical school art collages that fix children's selves into interests and activities that can be named and glued; to explore identity as relational, constructed in response to others, and open— thinking into the unknown as well as the known. And I find my own questions and thoughts sent out as if asking the children what they think so I can write my own response. Teachers can be directors, artists, and creators, as they shape the curriculum that is taught and experienced in the classroom (Olsen, 2000) yet often the focus in creating is on the tangible elements of curriculum. But I'm far more curious about the intangible and invisible: The not so evident *personal* questions that are sent out in teaching.

Without Grasping

One of the greatest struggles in art programs is for teachers to take an attitude of waiting and listening to the children without knowing exactly what they are waiting and listening for; to not know and give attention to the not knowing and to wait for something to present itself. It seems to undermine the very essence of what they understand teaching to be. Unless they have some certainty of what it is they are listening for and tangible evidence in a list, an outline, or a set of criteria, they tend to approach the listening and receptivity with great anxiety. Of course I worry about this too. In different ways and for different reasons as I wonder if I will always carry this sadness. All I can say to my students is trust me. It will happen.

I ask the teachers to wait and take a listening and receptive attitude in several different ways. The primary one is that of attending to and learning *from* the children. While the art program is in session, after an initial large group instruction and focus time, teachers and children work in small informal groupings, sometimes one teacher with two children, and other times larger groups of three or four teachers to five or six mixed age, mixed gender groupings, all the while watching out for and attending to the one or two children that are their responsibility. I encourage the teachers to honour the children's ideas and intentions and follow their lead rather than setting the direction or controlling the outcomes. For novice teachers who are used to planning lessons in detail in advance this can be an adjustment. Yet it allows for a more responsive and receptive relation where the children are supported as strong protagonists of their own work. It also engages the teachers with the difficult task of figuring out how to support *this* child's intentions and processes. While it may be possible to find out what children in general need, the kinds of things boys or girls tend to create, or how children of certain ages are more likely to approach drawing, the teachers don't know *this* child that they are responsible for and thus are required to listen and attend closely in order to support this particular child's intentions.

Zygmunt Bauman (1993), in his book *Postmodern Ethics*, insists that taking responsibility for the other means not treating him or her as the same as us, rather the other must be recognized as being unique and unexchangeable, that is the relationship cannot be to a general other, but must be to a concrete, specific, and particular other. John Caputo (2000) also claims that in an ethical situation it is the singularity of the other that obligates me to respond. One cannot be responsible for children in general, but in the face-to-face with a particular child one cannot escape his or her uniqueness, "unclassifiability" and "unrepeatability" (p.179). Thus, "when I am in a singular situation, faced with something singular, I do not have it, rather it has me" (p.180). In this sense children do not belong to the teachers as properties to manage or control, rather we belong to them.

David Smith (1999) writes that the ability to attend to our students depends primarily on "a form of stopping, and the creation of a space in which we can truly listen" (p.98). And I encourage teachers to do this; to slow to the pace of the children, follow their lead, and respond to their purposes rather than imposing their own. This means teachers must listen carefully to children's meanings and intentions and take a receptive attitude of not knowing. Yet listening, as Bill Readings (1996) notes, is much more than attending to speech. It is careful attention to actions, silences, and thoughts—to that which is said and also unsaid and unknowable. Working alongside on the same art projects under the children's direction with the teacher assisting opens up embodied understandings and non-verbal interactions and helps teachers "think beside" (Readings, 1996, p.165) rather than about the children.

Nevertheless, this does not always work as smoothly as I would like. Teachers come to class already knowing about children. It is not uncommon for teachers to hold certain generalizations and assumptions and in this intimate setting there is the potential to do children great violence by teachers thinking they know beforehand what is best or right to do. I continuously find myself gently provoking openings, returning the teachers' own questions back to them, and carefully prompting them to take an attitude of receptivity, openness, and listening. For "it is the self's susceptibility to the Other, not knowledge about the other, to which education must address itself if it is not to inflict violence" (Todd, 2001, p.68). I encourage the teachers to record their own questions and responses, to attend to their own attending" (Simon, 2000) through visual journals and other reflective responses, to question and interrogate their own listening and learning processes, to recursively question their own understandings of their observations, and to look for places of interruption so that learning is always in some sense provoked and unsettled. At the same time I try to be very careful with the twists and turns and stay responsive to their understandings, anxieties and unsettlings.

Teachers are also positioned so they need to listen and attend to each other as well as to the children. As I continue to explore how teaching can loosen its hold on self-reliance and individual competencies, and begin to embrace a greater dependency on others (or responsibility *for* others), I have shifted the emphasis away from lessons that can be contained by objectives, procedures, and closures, towards more responsive and open engagements. For example, groups of teachers take turns planning and facilitating the weekly activities, with one lesson building on the last and leading into the next so that the whole of the art program takes shape as an emergent collaborative effort. Each group has some control over a part of the program so that the outcomes are left uncertain and emergent. To make this work the teachers need to listen for meaning, build on the previous lesson, and leave their own open so the activities can be interpreted and carried on by others. Again there can be a great deal of anxiety in having to give up the certainty of knowing where the lessons are leading. Every year I hear students protest that they could do it better on their own. Yet as a conversation, like "good improvisational jazz" (Smith, 1999, p.39), the teachers must be "committed to staying "with" each other, constantly listening to subtle nuances of tempo and melody, with one person never stealing the show for the entire session...in a spirit of self-forgetfulness, a forgetfulness which is also a form of finding oneself in relation to others" (ibid).

The teachers are pressed at the same time by their obligations to particular children and a desire to help and not harm, to be tender and act carefully, and to act with love—and it is this that makes things come together so beautifully. This presses in and summons the teachers to respond. It reveals their own lack, that they do not really know these children, their intentions in art making, or how they might best respond as teachers yet calls them to become more than they are, to be more than they contain. Their responsibility for and obligation to particular children and their growing awareness of their "unrepeatability" calls them to step into the uncertainty and the impossibility of knowing for sure. At some point in the program we all begin to relax into the impossibility of grasping and controlling the outcomes and the curricular conversation takes on a life of its own.

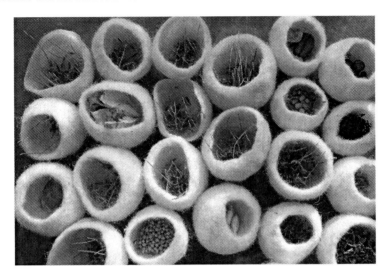

Risking Failure

We spent the afternoon drawing at the Museum of Anthropology. As I walk through the museum watching teachers and students drawing and talking about the works I catch bits of conversations, mostly life stories shared in small circles. Some groups are sitting in the dimly lit room near the Bill Reid sculpture. Others are seated around intricate carvings, on the floor in front of totem poles, and on benches with drawing pads and pencils on their laps. At the end of the class as we walk back to the education building one teacher guiltily remarked that he hadn't been much of a teacher that day as all he did was talk with the children. His "failure" seems to eat away at him, and he was obviously bothered by "not teaching" and not doing what he perceived he should be doing. We talked briefly about teaching and the meanings of being a teacher and I encouraged him to continue to listen to the children as I could see he was deeply troubled by the disjuncture of what he perceived teaching "should be" and what this moment with this child asked of him. Yet I also felt that no amount of talking about teaching or knowing the bounds and discourses of teaching would change how he felt or erase his discomfort at his perceived failure. His "agony" stayed with me as I turned it over and over trying to make something of it. These momentary pedagogical encounters stayed with me even years after. They stayed with me in my heart and in my thinking, my teaching taking shape as responses to them. Calvin Schrag (1997) writes that:

> The radical exteriority of the other as other needs to be acknowledged, attested, and assented to – and it is this acknowledging, attesting, and assenting that the genealogy of ethics finds its source. This constitutes the ethical moment, in which one understands oneself as a self-in-community, implicated in an acknowledgement of an other who is not of one's making, and to whose voice and action one is called upon to respond in a fitting manner. (p.100)

Yet this "responding in a fitting manner" is neither straightforward nor necessarily easy. It requires something of oneself, such as giving up certainty, stability and security and entering into the undoing and interrupting of the *said* (Levinas, 1969) of teaching. I would have liked to say that I recognized this at the time. But it wasn't until much later that I began to notice this particular teacher's distress that I heard things differently. At the moment of our conversation during the walk back from the museum I had seen him primarily as a beginning educator with preconceived notions of teaching. I had responded to what I thought he needed to know in light of who I thought he was, rather than hear the vulnerabilities and possibilities of the moment.

Levinas speaks of a "traumatism of astonishment" (in Todd, 2003b, p.36). Being traumatized is risking the security of one's identity and the possibility of its altering. According to Deborah Britzman (1998) this is not just an effect of education but central to it. "Learning to become", Sharon Todd (2003b, p.19) writes, is an inherently violent and traumatic activity. There is much at stake in becoming teachers and especially in the transformation of one's teaching particularly if that transformation means "failing" the given and the said of teaching. And I began to wonder how much room is made for failure in teacher education programs and in my own teaching. Do we work so hard to help education students succeed that we neglect to make room for the possibility of failure and for singular moments of failing the expected bounds of teaching? Amanda Berry (2004) for example, describes the hidden curriculum of teacher education as the tacit messages throughout the structures of a program that tenaciously reinforce traditional notions of teachers, teaching and education. Beginning teachers are caught between an allegiance to a program, institution, and the discourses of teaching and the invitation for newness that one child extends. Yet they must allow the given of teaching to be interrupted in order to re-imagine other possibilities. And it is encountering the otherness of others that "commands me to assume a responsibility beyond the care of my own self-preservation in being" (Trezise, 2004, p.1). Thus there is great risk in listening, responding, and attending to particular others.

As I encountered and tried to understand this one teacher's perceived failure I found my own difficulties of teaching in the midst of loss resonating with his. My experiences were certainly not the same as if understanding should be based in empathy or similarity of experience. Rather, it was based in an understanding that the concepts of disruption, opening and wounding are necessary conditions for change and transformation. This means not only focusing on behaviours or structures for optimal interaction, for example providing more time or opportunity for informal teacher-student conversations (although this *is* important) rather being attentive to the undoings, woundings, vulnerabilities, and risks teachers face in their relationships and interactions with children (and others). It means acknowledging and being sensitive to novice teachers' uncertain and vulnerable identities as they develop meaning in becoming teachers *and* acknowledging that it is their relation to otherness that provokes such vulnerability in the first place (see Britzman, 2003b). It also means attending to the contradictions and tensions inherent in taking up the obligation of the other. In a desire to comfort, repair, and end suffering it is too easy to try to remove the discomfort or to focus on how one "should" be as a teacher and to mend the wound through knowledge. Yet I am beginning to think it is far more important to tenderly make evident the wound, to carefully learn from it, and to attend to one's own learning and responding; to hold these grievings and failings for a while and let them speak. This makes teaching, and especially teaching teachers, a very delicate, profoundly risky, and ethical matter.

Release

I finally take the handkerchiefs out of the bag. I hold them close for a while, breathing in childhood and more recent memories of how my father smelled as he came home from work each evening, as he welcomed me with tight hugs after absences, how he was always happy to see me, how I had looked forward to his trip home after his last trip to Switzerland, how he was to be here visiting with me days after that trip, how he should have been at my brother's wedding, but instead we went over there to bring his remains home. I release the familiarity so that in the release it can become something else.

SYLVIA KIND

Tendering Other Things

And so we wait, listen, and enter another space of dwelling with and attending to. Silvia Benso (2000) explores the ethics of things and the tenderness (etymologically connected to a-tending-to) that is rooted in attention and the respectful attitude that waits for the other to make the first move. Benso also writes that the original meaning of ethos or ethics signifies a location or dwelling place. Ethics "opens up a space" (p.130) and a spaciousness "where distance is revealed, where difference is maintained" (p.131), where the remains, traces, in process and emergent presences cannot be grasped rather act as invitations for further responses: where knowledge cannot be possessed only inhabited.

To Love the Questions

The questions I started with at the beginning of the course weren't answered as I still don't know how long grieving takes. I expect I will miss both my parents for some time still. Yet something intangible was extended and I could see how, over the past several months, my teaching had begun to bear the traces of loss and bereavement and was finding its shape in dependencies and vulnerabilities. And I found other questions about who we are in relation to others and how our learning is dependent on otherness running as undersides in between encounters with students, children, and art works, prompting me to continue to inquire and to take other re-turns through art/teaching. These questions and inquiries shape the structure of teaching, and in particular shape the structures of a/r/tographic teaching. As Rebecca Martusewicz (1997) explains:

> To teach is to bring our questions to others, to share as teacher and as students in this process of thinking about who we are on this earth. But that means of course, facing the paradoxical space that circulates in our attempts to say or write or teach about this life and this earth, to face the constant and beautiful return of the question and our imperfection at answering. This means that teachers must learn to listen to and engage the questions posed by their students, even and perhaps especially when these questions are surprising or disconcerting...yes, teachers *with* their students must learn to love the questions. (p.112)

And as I see the end of another course and my students heading out to other teaching and learning encounters, the traces of their presence remains. The memory of momentary encounters—those described here as well as many others—provoke and prompt and incite other turnings and questionings. And learning continues.

DALENE M. SWANSON

SHADOWS BETWEEN US: AN A/R/TOGRAPHIC GAZE
ON ISSUES OF ETHICS AND ACTIVISM

There is a moon within a half circle of light.

Many choose not to see it.

They look upon the soft smooth arc,

the perfect curve,

and see its boldness.

But there are shadows between us,

and a moon behind the arc we fear to see,

for we have not yet learned the paths beyond the spaces we create,

the contours of the unimagined.[1]

Introduction

It is perhaps difficult to view despair, sorrow, or disadvantage as opportunity, but that is what it is, depending on how you choose to look at it. Depth gives impetus to height, dark gives emphasis to light. This is reminiscent of Charles Austin Beard's (1909) famous quote: "When it is dark enough, you can see the stars."

Sometimes the oppressiveness of a context makes us almost falter, to want to give in to the hopelessness as if this were an easier path for those who live it out. But, it is no easier path. It is only a perceived "easier path" for us, where we think we can escape from making moral choices. This way we avoid the weight on our consciences, by shrugging our shoulders and affirming that "it is out of our control." The 1913 version of the *English Webster Dictionary* speaks of morality as the "quality of intention," supported by the following quote: "The morality of an action is founded in the freedom of that principle, by virtue of which it is the agent's power, having all things ready and requisite to the performance of an action, either to perform or not perform it—South." Morality, then, is about personal and collective choice and is pivotal to it. Giving in to despair on behalf of others is a path of luxury. If we don't hold to the meaning of making choices, and continue to put ourselves in difficult places to contest the oppression, then

S. Springgay et al. (eds.), Being with A/r/tography, 179–185.

hope as lived, hope as embraced and experienced by those who choose to live it out as real despite their dire circumstances.

I have been overwhelmed by the spirit of hope and courage displayed by those who seem to have no cause for it. On my returning (from my doctoral fieldwork in South Africa in schooling community contexts of poverty and constructed disadvantage),[2] if there is one thing I carry with me as a gift of experience from my pedagogic/research journey, it is the spirit of kindness, generosity, overwhelming goodwill, openness, and reconciliation from the people whose lives touched my own. It is this spirit of the people, their wholesomeness and inner sanctum that holds me up and makes me intent on seeking more closely, empathetically, and collaboratively, for the most miniscule fissures of light within the vast gloom of situational despair. I know that it may take a gargantuan collective effort to prize it open, widen it, force it to new meanings that can be lived, so that the space of light becomes wide enough to be recognized, acknowledged, and legitimated. But, it has been done before, and it can be done again. In this intent lies a greater freedom of respect for all humanity, as well as oneself. Effort towards others' self-autonomy and empowerment gives back one's own self-integrity: dignity gained by giving dignity away.

These words begin the closing chapter of my doctoral dissertation, *Voices in the Silence: Narratives of Disadvantage, Social Context and School Mathematics in Post-Apartheid South Africa*. With this excerpt, I offer a textual moment of a/r/tographic inquiry. Intoned with "moments of articulation" (Swanson, 2004), a/r/tography brings the material and conceptual into a place of moral and aesthetic engagement, where the quotidian and the sublime are made to create relationships and (mis)alignments that are ever dynamic, as they are troubled, placated, sought, displaced, within a context of shifting identities and ways of knowing.

A/r/tography fosters an inquiry of breath, uncertainty, exposure, invention, and conceptual movement, performing itself through the interstitial frames of language, imagery, conscience and commitment. It is a métissage of hybrid possibilities that spill out and mix across the relational, social, political, cultural, and economic constitutions of daily life. It is, therefore, in the in-between spaces of ever-shifting textual meaning and lived inquiry set against the slipping places of identity and agency that a methodology of a/r/tography can be brought to bear on the ethical tensions of inquiry as it relates to purposeful action and personal and collective activism. It is this rhizomatic searching as a purposefully political and moral engagement in a process of eternally becoming that gathers ethical impetus and commitment. The ethical shift is an intertextual and intratextual movement. It asserts an unsettling even as it begins to loosen and tighten threads of resonance and resistance within the dilemmas, calling forth rather than repulsing the discomfort and dangers of the many contradictions, complicities and complications of being in community.

Through the intersections of art-making, researching, and teaching as sites of negotiated identities of self and other, a/r/tography opens spaces for dialectical relations that vibrate with power and possibility. These relations are always-ever dynamically shifting, seeking rootedness and meaning in the interstitial places between the bifurcations of dilemma or contradiction. These places of rupture and impossibility are embodied sites of struggle (Swanson, 2007) that are evoked and afforded presence through moments of articulation. These moments give rise to "lines of flight" (Deleuze & Guattari, 1983, p.107), offering possibilities of "micro-becomings" (Ibid., p.70) within the spaces of inquiry as we place "a greater emphasis on ethics and its relationship to the political" (Spivak, 1999, p.426). It is between the horns of dilemma that identities are constantly becoming reinscribed and negotiated in terms of choices, delimited or enabled, within a dialogue between ethics and activism. It is in this space, where practice and theory meet, that I continue this a/r/tographic journey here, living through the text the freedom to search, discover and (re)invent meanings of how we come to understand choice, moral commitment, ethical action, and above all the freedom to come to explore the nature of freedom itself underpinning these concepts.

Freedom and Contradiction

Hannah Arendt (1968) reminds us that it is a "logical impossibility" for us to know what freedom is, the difficulty of this coming to know lying in the "contradiction between our consciousness and conscience, telling us that we are free and hence responsible, and our everyday experience in the outer world, in which we orient ourselves according to the principle of causality" (p.143). Freedom is illusive, and the most "dangerous difficulty" for Arendt lies in how "thought itself, in its theoretical as well as its pre-theoretical form, makes freedom disappear". The contradiction coalesces around the Kantian notion of "practical reason" informed by "free will." It is ironic, for Arendt, that the very "faculty of will whose essential activity consists in dictate and command should be the harbourer of freedom". While political freedom cannot exist in the inner realm of thought, the distortion of the very idea of freedom lies in the transposing of freedom as conceived of "from its original field, the realm of politics and human affairs in general, to an inward domain, the will, where it would be open to self-inspection" (p.143). For one grappling with and coming to know through a radical unknowing of "the other" as "other," but as constitutive of self, freedom possesses many repeating challenges. When this grappling with the self-other relationship invests in ambiguities and ironies that highlight the multiple impossibilities of this enterprise of knowing, then setting this challenge to work to find a path towards justice and freedom in its broadest political sense, clears the way to the utopian. To attempt to internalize political freedom within the self is, for Arendt, a distortion of the idea of freedom itself, but the spilling out of the inner condition of freedom-seeking onto the world in the form of ethical action is equally complicated by the very fact that it is initiated by self. Here, the obscurity of our motives along with the unforseeability of the consequences of our actions, weaken our ability to effect change towards any sustained sense of political freedom more broadly defined. It is in the collective—not the self—that the possibility of freedom resides. Likewise, it is in the freedom of the relationship to the other that freedom of the self comes in to being. It is in the freedom of moral choice that defines how we engage with the

DALENE SWANSON

other that inner freedom becomes possible. Nelson Mandela (1994) hints at this freedom as he acknowledges the challenges for the post-apartheid nation:

> The truth is that we are not yet free; we have merely achieved the freedom to be free, the right not to be oppressed. We have not taken the final step of our journey, but the first step on a longer and even more difficult road. For to be free is not merely to cast off one's chains, but to live in a way that respects and enhances the freedom of others. The true test of our devotion to freedom is just beginning. (p.617)

This devotion to freedom to which Mandela refers is not a simple matter of inner freedom as much as it is a collective responsibility to mastering the freedom of the self in terms of the freedom in the relationship to the other in all the diverse contexts of such relationships. This inner freedom is derived from a self-consciousness of self in relation to other. Sartre (1937) posits that the self is not defined as existing through being an observer of an *a priori* world in which the self is situated. Rather, it is where the self becomes conscious of being an object of observation by others, where it comes to know itself as self through a "being-for-others." Here the self is one defined by the existence of the other and dependent on the other for its existence as human and as possessing human consciousness. Identity of self is shaped by the other in such a relationship. But Buber (1996) takes this a step further, out of the domain of the individual self as object, to a concept of reciprocity, where a greater spiritual freedom is achieved in the approximation of the *I-Thou* relationship. This is a dialogical relationship of encounter, a meeting of consciousnesses, a mutualism, initiated by the self, where consciousness is represented within the *I-Thou* conjunction as its own unity. The self is no longer a discreet conscious object represented by the physical self, but through the *I-Thou* relationship the self possesses an attitude to the other which defines the self's capacity for choice and freedom. It is in seeking this relationship of *I-Thou* through a continuous a/r/tographic process of self and situational questioning, repositioning oneself in terms of the shifting ethics of dynamic situations and multiple dilemmas, reflecting on and (re)inscribing one's self in relation to the other through political, cultural and positional lenses, that I offer another excerpt from my doctoral fieldwork that narrates this experience.

> When I left Visserman's Baai Hoër on the last day of my research there, I went to say goodbye to everyone I'd come to know and who had helped with my research. I knocked on the principal's door and was welcomed in. I think very highly of this man. He is so dedicated and determined, despite the constant academic "failure" at this school, the situational context of poverty, the gangs and family violence, the apathy of others about him or their dejection, the bullying by the education department. When everyone else had left the school for the day, you often walked past a classroom and saw him sitting there with students who had been given a detention. No one else wanted to take on this duty, but he would sit there trying to help these students with their homework. As a leader and role model, he was a very gentle man despite the harsh circumstances he had to work in, which I have no doubt, proliferated a multiple of daily dilemmas. But, he never shirked his

182

duty, and he had his spiritual faith which he held high like a torch. His demeanour, self-pride, and personal integrity, rose up from the murky quagmire of desperateness that reproduced itself daily.

In making light conversation after thanking the principal for everything he'd done for me during my stay, I made mention that it was often difficult to get permission from the Education department to do research in schools in South Africa, and that very many researchers had been turned away. He responded by saying: "No-one can stop you if you are sincere about trying to make a difference. They didn't stop you because they could see you are sincere." This was the greatest compliment I was given throughout my research travels. The principal of this purportedly "dysfunctional school," showed the wealth of his humanity to me, a pedagogic gift that could hardly be deemed unworthy, deficient, lacking. He transcended disadvantage with his heart. I realized then that *transformative* pedagogies, in the end, were really about *transcendence*—the capacity to rise above, to find goodness even in the slightest of things, to find the opportunity to turn deficit into human wealth, disadvantage into hope. Yes, it is about pedagogies of hope and the heart.

Here the mutual recognition of an *I-Thou* relationship that begins to diminish the power differential in the subjective gaze on the other, assists in a search for a mutual freedom; one that begins to transcend the limitations of an unequal situational context or the oppressions of an existing injustice. Here transcendence is found within the transformative moment of engagement when the *I-Thou* is strengthened. This is a transcendence which *rises above* situational limitations, but which also *spills out* from them with an excess of possibility and the potentialities of a freedom within the world. It is a freedom beyond the *I-Thou* through a capacity and transcendent depth in the I-Thou relationship, a relationship which is always-ever-becoming and never fully achieved. In this sense, the *I-Thou* as an ultimate attainment is utopian, and Buber recognized that within human relations it is not sacrosanct.

Moral Judgment and Humble Togetherness

It is in this complex space of always-ever searching for an *I-Thou* relationship, a relationship which I also discussed in my doctoral research in terms of the African indigenous epistemology of Ubuntu, that the difficulties of creating and maintaining mutualism in fieldwork inquiry, depending on positionality and situation, became forefronted. Similar to Buber's *I-Thou* relationship, Ubuntu is the African notion of brotherhood and sisterhood, a "humble togetherness" or "living in each other's spirits", emphasizing the collective over the individual. It is that which renders us human, where "I am because we are" (see Battle, 1997; Tutu, 2000). While Ubuntu *highlighted* the ambiguities, ethical dilemmas, and moral contradictions within narratizable research moments, even in their often ungraspable and irresolvable complexity, it also, ironically, provided a way *through*—of transcending the quagmires and sticking places of the research experiences and the disjunctions in the theoretical articulation within the empirical

DALENE SWANSON

moment. It is here that shadows are cast between the self and other, moments of experience that invoke ghosts, in the Derridean (1994) sense, between conversational voices and dialogical moments that slip into monologues with the self, the other being paradoxically present and not present at the same time. These eidolons, shadowy figures of missed possibility or rupture between the self and other, complicate our efforts and haunt our intentions towards ameliorating suffering, injustice and poverty. They shroud the motivations of our activism with doubtfulness, and raise the spectre of complicity. The struggle to seek an ethical path that accords with the commitment to activism is the shadow of the rupture between good intentions and the liberating moment. I offer an abbreviated moment of this struggle in my doctoral research as I seek to achieve Ubuntu with the principal of an impoverished school. Although I don't speak out about his practice of allowing teachers to stay off school for long periods of time, having meetings during class time, and other less accepted teaching practices, I become aware of my rising anger towards him, breaking a bond of respect and mutualism at that time.

At that moment...and it was not an epiphany...but a slow blurred form taking root...re-rooting in my mind. It was a slow re-realization of what I had done by wanting to "speak out" and to tell this principal that I thought it was "just not good enough"...It was a recognition of my *own* voice of violence...of what brutality I had done in feeding into the deficit discourse, on "disadvantage", I realized that my thoughts, framed within the discursive roots of my socialization, had established that "disadvantage" as "plain to see".

I began to realize that in my initial thought-words of anger, I had been taking on the colonizing voice that produces the deficit, and that creates, validates and establishes "the problem" from outside...from a place out there that can speak unmonitored by its own surveillance...I was ensuring its reproduction...albeit a silent language of thoughts.

My realization came only when I could begin to understand-feel with a *deeper listening*—the kind of deeper listening that renders one human...And so this had become my route...Instead of trying to find the "root *of* the problem" and trying to "root *out* the problem," like a cancer from living tissue, instead I was beginning to move towards searching for "*the source.*" The source of the problem lay silently *behind* the construction of "the problem" itself and threaded its way, like a tributary, to my very doorstep...I too was complicit, a collaborator of deficit discourse, a root of "the problem's" routedness. Now I became responsible as well, through acknowledging that responsibility.

The I-you dichotomy had been broken by the emergence of a new bond of responsibility...a *humbling togetherness, a sense of Ubuntu!* I needed to *listen* collaboratively to that "source" in collectively finding a way together of "re-sourcing" towards non-impoverishment, other possibilities and mutual healing. With the sense of responsibility and humility came the opportunity for transformation and transcendence, both political and spiritual. It was the kind of calling in which one could recognize oneself in the image of the other as an organic relationship of "humble togetherness."

In Closing: Shadows and Ghosts

Just as Derrida (1994) reminds us that we need to seek out the phantoms of the other that haunt us, and that a passion for justice means interlocuting with ghosts, so we need to search the shadowy places between our activism, ethics and motivations that deny us freedom—freedom of spirit and freedom of humanity. How we choose to engage in research, our frames of reference, our ways of being in the world, the acknowledgement of our complicity while seeking meaning and possibility of transformation and transcendence in the interstices of artist, teacher and researcher, are critical to the nature and form of the research itself as well as our relationship to it. A/r/tography, as a living inquiry, offers freedom in the search for shadows that collapse, even as they mark out, the self-other binary, and grants us opportunities to speak with the ghosts that haunt our ethical commitments and good intentions defined by the personal activism in our research. It also casts light—as it casts shadows—on what we need to attend to in our research in which our identities, our very souls, are infused.

NOTES

[1] This is a stanza from poetry I wrote into my doctoral dissertation
[2] My doctoral research was an exploration of the construction of difference and disadvantage in school mathematics in social context in post-apartheid South Africa. Fieldwork was undertaken in a range of schooling contexts with socio-economic and cultural differences, including contexts of extreme poverty.

VERONICA GAYLIE

POETRY IN URBAN SCHOOLS

WINDOW POEMS 19

Within things

there is peace, and at the end

of things. It is the mind

turned away from the world

that turns against it.

—Wendell Berry (cited in Wirzba, 2002, p. viii)

Background

Poet, scholar and activist, June Jordan described the poetic voice as a "...useful dialogue between people who are not only unknown, but mute to each other" (Quizod, 1999). As a former inner city English teacher, I have witnessed how the mandate of mastering the standard essay prevents many students from reaching a starting point in language. I also know that poetry, like justice, does not arrive "naturally" in classrooms. Instead, poetry provides a place for students to enter a dialogue of learning, and the insistence on poetry in classrooms gives disengaged students an alternative to detachment, silence and a learning life surrounded by strangers.

For this research study I worked with a Creative Writing 10 class at a large, urban high school in Vancouver, Canada. The main goal of the study was to allow students' concerns to emerge through poetry in order to investigate how students identify with poetic language in ways that are important to them. What were the students uniquely facing in their lives as inner city learners? What language was available to them as an outlet for expression, both in the classroom and in popular culture? Was it fair to force students to succeed in a system that disadvantaged them in the first place? The study involved critical discussions of local and global events; students were encouraged to write poetry in their own, "everyday" voices. I dared the students to "say what they really thought" and to write as if they were talking to each other. Twelve students were interviewed about their views on poetry and the role of language in learning. During the interview students considered their daily encounters with language both in the classroom and with mainstream news and popular media.

S. Springgay et al. (eds.), Being with A/r/tography, 187–203.

VERONICA GAYLIE

A Critical/Creative Framework

The classroom study emerged both from my research and my experience teaching in urban schools, where students often spoke about their sense of disconnectedness from classroom curricula and language. The work thus emerged from an intersection of literacy, narrative and critical pedagogic theory related to the ways students are forced to interpret (print based) curricula and classroom language that ignores their cultural, personal or social concerns (Heath, 1983; hooks, 1994). Students are expected to succeed within a literacy model that is based on decontextualized notions of text that exclude the socio-cultural, oral, creative and process oriented aspects of language (Brandt, 1990; Probst, 1988). To address this tendency toward decontextualization, critical theorists urge educators to become agents of social change and encourage them to make classroom learning relevant by addressing the concerns and troubles students actually face (Freire, 1998). They further suggest that incorporating creative, arts-based techniques will allow marginalized students to express themselves on their own terms (Greene, 1995). Some language-based studies in U.S. inner city schools suggest that students widely create oral language-based "alternative literacies" that exist on the periphery of mainstream classroom language (Keiser, 2000). Such studies indicate that "alternative" or "oral literacies" warrant attention and further research.

At the study location, schools are annually ranked based on standardized literacy and math test scores, and schools with the lowest rankings are often those in low income areas (Cowley & Easton, 2002). Such rankings often spark a call for even more standardized language testing and have even led to an outcry against the rankings themselves, which some see as producing negative psycho-social effects in students from these low ranked urban schools (Froese-Germain, 2002). Others suggest that school rankings emerge from a flawed, authoritative framework that ignores other forms of student achievement (Shaker & Heileman, 2004). One of the aims of this project was to present an alternative vision of students typically characterized by their low ranking school.

The study itself provided a space where students could see and write for themselves, in the context of their own, immediate worlds. Class discussions were centred on poetry and were fuelled by critical pedagogy. As a former classroom teacher, and as a poet, I had witnessed how poetry moves students from literacies of entrapment to poetry of empowerment. Taking an activist position in this research allowed me to shift classroom discourse from a framework of disengagement to an environment of critical and creative expression.

During the poetry workshops, students were eager to burst out of the mainstream media script on local and world events, and they began writing poems on a range of personal and controversial topics. Out of the blue, one student wrote a social activist poem set in Argentina; another wrote a poem about WWII from her perspective as a Japanese Canadian. In presenting a sample of the students' work for this piece, I wanted to let the poems speak, and disrupt, for themselves within the context of the student interviews and my own research journal. This piece is thus presented as a portion of dialogue between myself and the students with whom I worked. While the study emerges from various critical frameworks related to politics and power, particularly the marginalization of students in low ranked schools in low income neighbourhoods, the piece is also represented as a creative process where critical pedagogic theory is put into creative practice. In placing the students' poems within our discussions of language and poetry as active occurrences within standard prose, I demonstrate the students' engagement with the entire poetic process.

How do I teach/research/create as a poet in this piece? I hope, inexplicitly. My presence as a poet in the classroom brings permission: such permission to write and to speak to one another in a way that cultivates a poetic presence. The significance of poetry, and poets, in research is often that presence itself. The results, the data of poetic research, like a poem, are never known in advance; in fact, "results" are typically never known. The story of a poet in the classroom is felt in the process of being a poet in the classroom, which alters the terms by which "results" can be measured. As a poet, I am revealed through that presence, and I hoped that as the students engaged in poetry, they would be similarly revealed. In this research, the students' poems speak as gestures, as an engagement with learning which was previously absent. As classroom teachers know, for the student who has never before stood up to read their own work, it is the standing up, the representing, that signifies. I invite the reader to consider the multiple, poetic literacies that emerge in the process of poetry in the classroom.

FIRST DAY: HALLWAY TO HEAVEN

The front door is covered in names, scratched out in green paint. The hallways are so long, ceilings so high, you can't see people standing at the end, where the earth curves. Something about these halls, so long, I wonder if students or teachers dream of them years after they've left. The halls are so long, so full of students past and present, I know that some were never heard or known. In the office, the secretary is tired. She takes out a list of all the teachers in the school. There are over a hundred names. The principal pokes his head out of his principal's door and waves. Teaching and learning in high school is a time you never forget. It is only 10:15...

We walk up four flights of wide stairs, and down another long, dimly lit hallway. All the rooms are crammed with kids spilling out. There is more movement than sound; there are far too many people for this space. And, given the size of the space, the number of people, the amount of movement, the bus station-like acoustics, it is not very loud at all. But the hallway is full of candy wrappers that are shuffled from one of the hallway to the other, every time a class ends, and every time a new one begins.

VERONICA GAYLIE

Urban Learners Speak

SWISH AND SOAR

swish and soar

soar and swish

swish and soar some more

swishing is boring

wishing for soaring—

a goldfish in a bowl.

—Jack

The students say they enjoyed writing poetry; now, they all carry notebooks. Students perceived me as a notebook-carrying poet, and like the idea of being school poet-reporters. Throughout the interviews, the students emphasized language as a social process, a way of being "let in" or "left out" of both classroom work and in peer interaction. For them, it was all about audience and permission. Being a "poet" in the classroom presented an alternative where they could explore the world creatively, joyfully, angrily, but, most importantly, as themselves.

> Taylor: When a poet comes in we don't do what we usually do...it gets us out of that shell.

> Mical: I've always just written "poem poems" that rhyme, like you see in text books. When you showed us different ways of writing poetry and told us that...there was more than one way, it really inspired me.

The students say that poetry helps them clarify their own ideas and feelings in the early writing stages, when a topic is still "in their own minds". They use the terms "ideas" and "feelings" interchangeably. Poetry is a place for a heart *and* mind.

> Lynley: With poetry you don't have to be restrained...Poetry lets you not just write, but say what you want.

The students report that classroom writing is a rigid form of expression that does not permit alternative ideas and feelings, while...

> Jenny: ...in poetry you can be angry right away.

One student remarks, "(poetry) gets your mind going. It helps to know what you're feeling so you can later express it to other people". Another says, "in poetry you can get creative with your thoughts...like *really* creative. You can go overboard and it's still really, really good". Poetry is a place where ideas *are* feelings, where anger is fine, even encouraged. Poetry is a place for trying things out; poetry is a body, it listens...

Taylor: [Poetry is like] always having a friend to talk to. There are so many problems in society...it builds up and you try to reduce it because you could go crazy...with poetry, you put it in a format that you want...and you can write it out and read it again and again. You actually put something of yourself there. You can solve your problems with poetry...the paper does not judge.

BROKEN THOUGHTS

Broken eyes can't cry

Broken thoughts can't lie

Tattoo without purpose

For the rest of our lives

These are the broken thoughts.

—Taylor James

STRESS HAIKU

Stress and frustration

Looking for information

Project due Monday.

—Tanya Cortez

Mical: Poetry is a relief that permits freedom: "School is a popularity contest...you just don't know if they're gonna accept it or not. So you just kind of write a poem about it".

Alice: Poetry does not restrict...anyone can pick up a pen and write whatever they want and it's like you're talking. Okay, there's DJs...but who has money to spend on clothes and turntables...When you want poetry, you already have what you need. You can go to the sandbox and write your poem with a twig in the sand. It's rebellious, not corporate. Plus you don't have to go to The Gap to get your writing materials. You can just...start doing it.

NEVER WEAR A POPPY

They did nothing but serve and appreciate their freedom.

The men left first.

My great-grandpa was the spokesperson,

VERONICA GAYLIE

the voice for those rendered voiceless.

—Eddy

The students note how poetry is portable, personalized and adaptable:

Taylor: It is not just about certain people and certain places. It's about speaking up and saying things because you're not going to be in the same room all your life. You change from place to place.

Hamish: In grade eight you have opinions. You got rhythm and language. But you go through high school and....

Lynley: ...you realize you just gotta get it done.

The students say that spoken classroom expression is tightly controlled; the popular kids make sure others do not have a voice. Group discussion is seen as just another language obstacle because "only certain thoughts are permitted orally" when "you cannot choose who you share discussions with". In a crowded, pressure filled, inner city classroom, oral language is sometimes a privileged and deflating space:

Mical: Sometimes when your writing poetry you'll have some kind of beat in your head and you'll just kind of go into a beat, kind of like a rap song: "do, do-do, do-do," and then when you're reading it out loud you don't want to sound stupid by doing your own beat...so you just drone and read it without personality or rhythm, like normal. So they won't know. It's totally disappointing. Sometimes. It depends who's listening.

SUNDAY

...the gravel is cold and wet

our goalie, ready in the net

the whistle goes

everybody on their toes

watching, running, straining

yelling, kicking, sweating

...shake it off

I cough

I can't feel a thing...

we lost.

—Hamish O'Callaghan

JUNE

She runs for help with no voice to reach out.

The stranger from behind chases June...

June screams,

But not one spare hand approaches her.

—Kevin Tsang[1]

Language and Urban/Pop Culture

CNN NEWS AT SIX

The sky fell in Iraq

but according to Henny Penny

the Atlantic froze over

and fish with feet

have colonized France.

...Scientists believe

terrorists caused the menace.

—Jenny Lew

The students say media and advertising speaks *for* them, shaping their daily lives. They suggest that being "alternative" is really just being "themselves," however, they see little room left to be "themselves." The students are eager to take part in critical discussion, and to figure out the difference between "corporate music" and "real music." Real music has "a good rhythmic beat" while corporate music is "rap that is supposed to be different but is really demeaning to girls." Some appreciate the influence of rap music because of its "originality" and "willingness to talk about real things" even "simple stuff about a bad childhood." They especially like rap music from the 1980s that is not about "clothes and money and girlfriends". The students consider the corporate influence in pop music as media manipulation, a "cliché" that shapes listeners. Students discuss their lack of empowerment in the midst of corporate control, recognizing their role as "followers" in a "routine" that goes on "generation after generation."

Kevin: The songs are cliché but they're also about our lives....maybe our lives are cliché.

Alice: Corporations…want to herd us and make us conform…like cattle. You don't have to. That's what we've been conformed to think. It's a whole [George Orwell's] *1984* world.

When I ask if hip hop music expresses any of their current feelings, one student is firm:

Alice: It does not speak to me. We're afraid of repeating the same cliché and yet…we follow it. If you look at advertising and song lyrics and even the news it's all sort of the same thing.

Students discuss American media influences in their lives:

Jenny: I think we should be able to keep our culture, you know. You can like music that's not your heritage but it doesn't mean you have to abandon your culture completely.

Alice: We face some of the same problems as American people. Being poor does not restrict itself to one small market.

ON THE NUMBER 19

I get off

beer breath charges

into my nose

saying "spare some change"?

Following behind a big toothless grin

smiling I shake my head

"god bless"

"you too"

I smell dead chickens

I hear the feathers rustle inside

keep going

cars racing by my sides

dirty old men go back to your wives

I sit at the stop

wait

sardine can here I come

out the window

a young woman

wrinkles, dark circles, shouldn't be there

she's crouching

she's concentrating on her arm

I look away

and think,

what is this?

—Hamish O'Callaghan

The students want to name their worlds in their own words.

Jack: Do you know the Downtown East Side? Apparently that's Vancouver's ghetto. Me and Alice live right there, beside each other. It's not a ghetto.

ON A MOLDY SOFA

On my moldy sofa

In my dirty ally

A young girl lays

Slouched in an uncomfortable lump

…

I call the ambulance

They can't make a difference,

But she can't stay here.

And besides, it's my turn for the sofa.

—Jack

Kevin: What they're doing to us works…they don't even need to advertise.

Jack: The media and ads are like drugs. We know they're bad for us but we take them anyway.

I can still hear their words when I leave the school that day: *Depends who's listening.*

VERONICA GAYLIE

Interpreting Current Events

A LIFE WORTH LIVING

Forecast says: "There'll be no sun

Today or tomorrow"

You'd better borrow

An umbrella and disposition

to cover the frustration

Caused by all the precipitation

And the grey

Time to pray

To our silent gods so far away,

Maybe all too busy watching Survivor: Thailand.

—Eddy Garcia

The students want to be able to use language in ways that makes them "feel a part of the world." They say that having their voice heard in high school is practice "for older life" where "you'll be able to...express an opinion." One student says, "We always have a voice but can choose not to use it" while another insists, "No. Others choose not to hear it."

One student says that their school has been labelled seismically unsafe during earthquakes. They organized a rally to raise public awareness; the local TV station was there, but the school shut down the rally. They were troubled that they could not critically express themselves and they felt that they met the public's expectations of East side teenagers: "We just looked like a bunch of kids jumping up and down in front of a TV camera." They felt serious about the issue and some felt exploited by the news camera.[2] They critically comment on pop culture and fashion, but feel that they have little knowledge of important issues in their own school. Even knowing that their school could collapse around them in an earthquake, they feel powerless to change anything or to comment in a way that would incite change.

CRUSHED

...In the event of an earthquake

Don't duck and cover your head.

What is the point,

If we're already dead?

—Tanya Cortez

The students read the word and the world, naming their powerlessness:

Kevin: Some people still don't have voice…they're too shy or they wanna say something and they can't because they're scared. In one of my classes other voices overpower my voice.

TODO EL MUNDO DEBE IRSE

People clustered in parks voting.

Voting on what laws to make

voting on what buildings to

convert into housing.

Voting to help everyone.

People taking over broken down warehouses.

Making sweaters, hats and blankets

working without making money.

Working to help everyone.

People re-open abandoned hospitals.

Nursing the sick everyday

Nursing without making money.

Nursing to help everyone.

This is democracy.

Not the product "democracy"

For sale in the global market

People united:

Voting, nursing, working,

Helping everyone.

Everyone shouting

"Todo el mundo debe irse!"

—Sally Tucker

And when a large event takes place in the world,

> Jack: When September 11 first happened… I said (racist) things and I didn't know what I was talking about. Just repeating stuff I heard on TV. I didn't even know what the Middle East or the world was about.

they were without words.

> Kevin: Even though people express themselves… they're not being heard. I can tell you something, my feelings…but that's just where it goes…to whoever is listening or if no one is listening…if it's political…it just stays there. Your words just stay where you say them.

Most still experience events in ordinary ways:

CAMPING

Old hammock hangs in a corner

lopsidedly

a constant reminder of

Bears

Night

My feet hanging out in the bitter cold.

—Cindy Smith

One student says that words will only be meaningful when: "You change it so that your voice is actually useful".

A LIFE WORTH LIVING?

Here a camp

  there

A camp, everywhere a war camp

No more buffer zones

None of us immune

Doesn't matter what you know

But who you're close to...

—Eddy Garcia

Poetry offers a way to begin:

HOLLOW

New day

Same pain

Nothing new

Feeling hollow

empty,

unwanted.

Tears fall, a running tap.

No food to eat.

Nothing to spare.

Only wanting help

No pity please

Looking around

Seeing helpless eyes

Everywhere

They too feel

Hollow,

empty,

unwanted.

—Sam Quyen

Mical reads the first line from *Poem to Osama* for the audio recording.

VERONICA GAYLIE

What da ya have against us, eh?

She apologizes, says she "wishes it was better". One student raises their hand and says:

At least it sounds like you.

Afterwards

During this study, the students wrote, they stood up and read to each other and were made known to each other. With permission to explore alternative language, the students themselves decided the subject, the terms and, at times, the edges of that framework. Including critical pedagogic theory in poetry lessons opened students to an understanding of their class circumstances while offering an outlet for expressing such circumstances. Where critical theory offered them a way to enter discussions about school rankings, class, and their own positions as learners, poetry offered a way out, a path toward transformation.

The students often turned the conversation towards "survival" in both social and academic terms. Poetry was a tool that aided survival. As Leon Botstein (1998) states: "...in a classroom full of racial, gender, class, ideological and economic strife, hostility, suspicion, and everything else, the arts create something that forces some conversation that cannot be totally reduced into the pre-existing label and categories of expected discourse" (p.67). Offering students a creative outlet in poetry, an outlet that is not predefined, similarly honours the unplanned elements of their lives. The students immediately respected a creative framework that made room for them.

When students are permitted to express themselves creatively they will explore their lives and language with empowerment and critical depth. This study illustrates how poetry, as an oral language, provides a much needed starting point for urban students learning within a complex network of curricular, social and world pressures. Once they began speaking like themselves, others began listening. They did not have to wait to be strong, cool, perfect, standard or unemotional; in the process of writing they, and their words, became powerful. As we discussed and wrote poems, students slowly began to cut through the expectations of language in standard essays, television, the media and music. Poetry was the alarm clock that awoke people, groggy and blinking at first, to one another and to their local surroundings. Poetry in the classroom made language about speaking and listening; the students responded by speaking and listening.

It began with permission, with poetry and with awareness of the smallest goings on in the classroom. Speaking on the motivation behind his own work, First Nations rap artist Smallboy of (Alberta's "War Party") states that what stands out for him at concerts is not necessarily the voicing of his own concerns, but the ways in which his music opens a much needed outlet for others to express themselves (Pacienza, 2002). He also speaks about the importance of noticing the smallest details, explaining how many in the young audience approach him after a concert, sometimes talking for a long time:

There are so many things, personal issues such as...things concerning their own home, domestic disputes, as well, a young girl recently troubled over acne approached me....It's just verifying the need for people like us, people that are willing to stay an extra hour to chill and get the real story behind everything. (p.5)

A willingness to stay, and to get the "real" story is an important lesson for teachers, writers and researchers. For students, "staying" is the entry point for talking, listening, writing and reading, for meaningful, creative interaction with language. Poetry offers a reason to stay, and a way to begin.

swish and soar

soar and swish

swish and soar some more...

—Jack

After Words

The Five Obstructions, a film directed by Lars Von Trier and Jørgen Leth (2003), is about a director and an actor re-creating the same short film five times, each time with a new set of "rules." The film within a film is entitled "The Perfect Human." In the beginning, the director and the actor excitedly discuss how to solve problems posed by such a scenario, which includes limits like filming the entire film in twelve takes, or, entirely in animation. The film is set in Cuba, then Bombay, and as each film is completed, the idea of "the perfect human" also changes. First the human is symbolized as civilized and detached, able to utilize the (artificially applied) rules to represent the problem of "the perfect human". Over time, though, the words "perfect" and "human" disassemble as director and actor face the impossibility of reconciling the two terms. The final segment does not contain any rules, yet it is easily the most memorable of all the segments as principal players engage in the messy, humorous and, in some ways, perfectly human, representation of "the perfect human."

As a poet and educator, the film makes me wonder. Do humans, students, artists, educators communicate more profoundly without limits? As artists, as teachers, as educators and teacher educators, how do we represent our work as process, in ways that allow us to become human, even as we are expected to produce products within a set of (largely unspoken) rules? What work represents such complexity of becoming (if it is at all possible) to readers and viewers? What works allow us to become "perfect humans?"

This chapter is intended as an exemplar of a/r/tographical research, both in the way the students responded to their locations through poetry, and in the way the researcher engaged in the messy process of shaping a written product. I discovered difficulties, perhaps impossibilities, encountering this product/process dilemma. As a poet and teacher with interests in urban research and social theory, I found a constant in-between awareness of creating such work, which does not sit easily in one genre, nor with one set of rules. As a poet, and as a teacher, I want the work to show what it is. As an academic, I have to know what it is; and I am compelled to describe what it was.

Near the beginning of writing this piece someone said: "poetry and politics do not sit in the same room." And yet, there I was, a political poet and educator. Performing research in inner city schools involves allowing students to express the complexity of their sidewalks, and their local events, within their classrooms. I knew it was not "simply teaching," but research. I knew it was "something" but didn't know "what." It was in the process of discovery, of writing and recording the students' voices, of going to and coming from the school, of walking up and down the long hallways, that it became what it was. Poetry interrupted political awareness, and vice versa, on a daily basis. With permission to engage in the process, students previously left out of the process due to their social class, those constantly tasked with proving themselves through standardized academic tests, proved that—yes—poetry and politics could sit in the same room.

This chapter is just one piece in the process of becoming what it "perfectly" is. In the difficulty of writing, for myself and for my students, we were transformed. Not by rules, or by lack of rules, but by that process. In the finished piece, such awareness is represented in the way that student poetry interrupts. In writing this after the project ended, I am closer to knowing that this process was something. I also know the hybrid awareness of representing art, and teaching, as a process in a milieu defined by artistic proof, and academic products.

> It depends upon creation and invention, preferably among others who are also in quest, who recognize us for what we are striving to be and who win our recognition for what they are not yet. Risks, yes, and relativism, and an ongoing conversation. (Greene, 1994, p.218)

In this chapter, understandings of a/r/tographic theory and practice are explored as literate learning events from the perspective of a hybrid poet-researcher, where responses can lead students to, and beyond, standardized interpretation of curricula. In Jardine's (1992) words, "hermeneutical sites of learning are based on ambiguities and discomforts responsive to the urgent question: what needs to be said?" Jardine describes such conceptualizations of curricula as "a theorizing that erupts out of our lives" (1998, p.8).

This chapter then resides in the ongoing "eruption" of bringing theory into practice. From the value of incorporating poetry (and protests) in research products to including poetry in the design of new research, students and poets ultimately discover and transform artistic and pedagogical practice in teaching and learning. This writing thus brings poetic teaching and research processes to light, while remaining responsive to the communities that surround, and are potentially transformed, through such work.

NOTES

[1] The poem is about the Missing Women serial murder case in Vancouver. The trial involves the unexplained disappearances of over sixty women from Vancouver's downtown Eastside. Many of the students lived in or near the area where the women went missing.

[2] One year after this study, students organized to raise public awareness of seismic upgrading at the school. As a result of their lobbying efforts, the provincial government made seismic upgrading at this school a priority.

RITA IRWIN, RUTH BEER, STEPHANIE SPRINGGAY, KIT GRAUER,
GU XIONG AND BARBARA BICKEL

THE RHIZOMATIC RELATIONS OF A/R/TOGRAPHY[1]

A/r/tography is an arts and education practice-based research methodology
dedicated to acts of inquiry through the arts and writing (see Irwin & de Cosson,
2004; Irwin & Springgay, in press; Springgay, Irwin & Wilson Kind, 2005; Irwin,
Springgay & Kind, in press).[2] The name itself exemplifies these features by setting
art and graphy, and the identities of artist, researcher, and teacher (a/r/t), in
contiguous relations.[3] None of these features is privileged over another as they
occur simultaneously in and through time and space. Moreover, the acts of inquiry
and the three identities resist modernist categorizations and instead exist as poststructural conceptualizations of practice (for example Bickel, 2004; de Cosson,
2002, 2003). By emphasizing practice, a shift occurs from questioning *who* an
artist, researcher or educator might be, or *what* art, research or education is, to
when is a person an artist, researcher or educator and *when* is an experience art,
research or education (see Kingwell, 2005). These are important distinctions for
they reside in the rhizomatic relations of inquiry.[4]

In this article, we wish to describe a/r/tographical inquiry as a methodology of
situations and to do this, we share the journey of a collaborative project undertaken
by a group of artist, educator, researchers working with a number of families in a
nearby city. The project is entitled "The City of Richgate" and examines issues
related to immigration, place, and community within an artistically oriented
inquiry. Although the project itself would be of interest to the field of art
education, this article is dedicated to the elaboration of a/r/tography as a
methodology of situations. The project provides a way of elaborating upon
a/r/tography as a methodology that provokes the creation of situations through
inquiry, that responds to the evocative nature of situations found within data, and
that provides a reflective and reflexive stance to situational inquiries. These
situations are often found, created or ruptured within the rhizomatic nature of
a/r/tography. It is on this basis that the article is premised: rhizomatic relationality
is essential to a/r/tography as a methodology of situations.

Gilles Deleuze and Felix Guattari (1987) describe rhizomes metaphorically
through the image of crabgrass that "connects any point to any other point" (p.21)
by growing in all directions. Through this image they stress the importance of the
"middle" by disrupting the linearity of beginnings and endings. After all, one fails
to pursue a tangent if a particular line of thought is subscribed. Rhizomes resist
taxonomies and create interconnected networks with multiple entry points (see
Wilson, 2003). The metaphor of a map is another image they use to describe
rhizomes for maps only have middles, with no beginnings and endings: they are
always becoming. Deleuze and Guattari also suggest that once a map is grasped,

S. Springgay et al. (eds.), Being with A/r/tography, 205–218.

inspecting the breaks and ruptures that become invisible when the more stable tracing is laid upon the always becoming map, we are in a position to construct new knowledge, rather than merely propagate the old" (Alverman, 2000, p.117). In this way, maps *and* tracings work together to make connections that may not have been noticed through the phenomenon itself and/or the theoretical tangents. Rhizomes are interstitial spaces between thinking and materiality (see Meskimmon, 2003) where identities and in-between identities are open to transformations (see Grosz, 2001) and people, locations and objects are always in the process of creation (see Hasebe-Ludt & Hurren, 2003).

Rhizomatic relationality affects how we understand theory and practice, product and process. Theory is no longer an abstract concept but rather an embodied living inquiry, an interstitial relational space for creating, teaching, learning, and researching in a constant state of becoming (see also Britzman, 2003a). For a/r/tographers this means theorizing through inquiry, a process that involves an evolution of questions. This active stance to knowledge creation informs a/r/tographers' practices making their inquiries emergent, generative, reflexive and responsive (de Cosson et. al., in press; 2003; Sinner, 2004). Moreover, products and processes are conceived as relational. Process is an act of invention rather than interpretation where concepts emerge from social engagements and encounters (Darts, 2004; Dias & Sinkinson, 2005; Springgay, 2003, 2004a, 2004b, 2005). Theorizing and practicing are verbs that emphasize the need for being in the process of producing (Irwin, 2003, 2004b, 2006; Springgay & Irwin, 2004). This move toward destabilizing concepts, objects, and identities is also found in contemporary art discourse where "site" as a fixed geographical concept has moved to a relational concept re-imagined as a "situation" within political, economic, cultural and social processes. In contemporary educational discourse "sites of learning" are re-imagined as "places in process" (see Lai & Ball, 2002) or "pedagogies of place" set within political, economic, cultural, ecological and social processes (Gruenewald, 2003). For a/r/tographers, situations are related to pedagogies of place through a commitment to disrupting binaries (e.g. private and public or neither) by complicating understandings as relational, singular and rhizomatic. Situated practices emphasize "experience as a state of flux which acknowledges place as a shifting and fragmented entity" (Doherty, 2004, p.10). Moreover, relational aesthetics works to erode marginalization as the role of artist is shifted to become a facilitator, mediator and/or creative contributor within a community.

In the following accounts we share with you our rhizomatic journey through an a/r/tographical project entitled *The City of Richgate*.[5] We begin with a prelude (a way of imagining situations) that offers insights into how we first conceptualized the project. We then introduce an interlude on a/r/tographical praxis that reaches throughout the project before introducing an interlude on a/r/tography as a methodology of situations. Though the prelude shares the conceptualizations that occurred in order to receive funding, the interludes and situations are not written in any chronological order. Situations may seem to occur chronologically but they are rhizomatic. Learning/creating/inquiring in, from, through, and with situations occurs in the in-between spaces: those spaces that make connections that are often unanticipated. As a result, their timing cannot be planned. Situations are complex spatial and temporal processes that reach beyond linear and binary ways of understanding the world. The tentative postlude reinforces the importance of situations to a/r/tography by summarizing the politically informed nature of collective artistic and educational praxis. While our work is written in a linear fashion here, out of publishing necessity, we encourage the reader to engage with the work as a rhizome by moving in and out, and around the work, making connections in a personal way.

A/R/TOGRAPHY: A METHODOLOGY OF SITUATIONS

Prelude to a Situation: The City of Richgate

The "City of Rich Gate" comes from the translated Chinese and Japanese names for the City of Richmond.[6] For Chinese immigrants, the City of Rich Gate represents an ideological dream of a better place than their own homeland. The idea of wealth is an integral part of the early history of Chinese in Canada. During the "Gold Rush", Chinese immigrants arrived in North America to find a "Gold Mountain", however, this was only a dream. What awaited the Chinese railway workers in the Rocky Mountains was hard labour and often death. By 2003, the Chinese immigrant population in Richmond rose to 46% of the total population. Under globalization, Richmond is the gate to the Pacific region. Migrating individuals pass through its airport everyday: new immigrants from Hong Kong, Taiwan and mainland China arrive searching for an opportunity to gain wealth and lead a better life. In turn, they've built Richmond as a new "Chinatown"—a geographically and culturally hybrid place. Yet Richmond is more than a new Chinatown. It has a rich history of immigration from many other countries in the world, most notably, those in the Pacific Rim, India, Europe, Scandinavia, and the USA. Each brings their cultural traditions with them and each has contributed to the city in important ways.

The City of Richmond is still considered a frontier town in many ways, replete with unresolved confrontations, on the edge of the continent, on the verge of a new beginning, separated psychologically from the rest of Canada by the Rocky Mountains, bordering on the American northwest, and poised on the Pacific Rim. The City of Richmond is situated in the delta of the Fraser River and is comprised of two main islands and 15 other islands built up and shaped by the river. The city's history is rooted in fishing, agriculture, shipping and aviation with the airport forming an important gateway to the Pacific Rim. In the constantly shifting definition of this place, the displacement of the native people, the history of settlement by Europeans, and the immigration of people from non-European cultures play key roles. In the past two decades, the source of immigration of people to British Columbia has shifted from Europe to Asia. Immigrants from these countries and elsewhere offer the Canadian economy and culture another rich layer to its diversity.

In British Columbia society and elsewhere, "the language of diaspora is increasingly invoked by displaced peoples who feel [maintain/revive/invent] a connection with a prior home" (Clifford, 1997, p.255). Safran (1991) describes the main features of diasporic collective experiences: "a history of dispersal, myths or memories of the homeland, alienation in the host country, desire for eventual return, on going support of the homeland, and a collective identity importantly defined by this relationship" (cited in Clifford, 1997, p.247). Broadly interpreted, elements of this description apply to many residents of British Columbia, who have in common a history of dispersal and displacement: their connection with a prior home is strong enough "to resist erasure through the normalizing processes of forgetting, assimilating and distancing" (p.255). For these individuals, experiences of "loss, marginality and exile reinforced by systematic exploitation and blocked advancement" coexist "with the skills of survival...strength in adaptive distinction, discrepant cosmopolitanism, and stubborn visions of renewal" (p.256). Diasporic consciousness is thus constituted both negatively "by experiences of discrimination and exclusion" and positively "through identification with world-historical, cultural, or political forces" (p.256). Considered from an upbeat or assured perspective, diaspora culture can be seen to celebrate the good fortune of being [Canadian] differently, of feeling global, of being able to shuttle between worlds/cultures/locations (Sontag & Dugger, 1998). Diaspora consciousness affects an increasing number of people in British Columbia and elsewhere, bringing with it new definitions of nationhood and nationality. In fact, as Clifford (1997) claims, being unfixed in geography and in static cultures is the experience of most people. Site, home, location, can be more than one place, and more likely somewhere in between.

Detouring from notions of consensus and generalization, we examine the contingencies of individual and community experience from particular situated and located points of view. We do so by moving away from finite visions of a fixed map or portrait to a way of seeing through pedagogical visual experiences that are interactive and dynamic while nurturing an understanding of relationships between people, objects or places (Ellsworth, 2005). These ways of seeing are best described as journeys rather than static ideas isolated from their world (Clifford, 1997; Kwon, 2002).

We began our a/r/tographical study by posing two introductory questions: What artistic products might be created through a community-engaged process examining the Chinese-Canadian experience in the City of Richmond, a geographically and culturally hybrid place? What is brought forward from a prior place in immigrant or diasporic culture (see Beer 1999) and how is that culture and memory transformed and maintained through identity, place and community? As will become evident in the interludes and situations below, these questions evolved into new yet related questions. This is an important distinction between a/r/tographic work and many other forms of research. Whereas traditional forms of research formulate specific questions to be answered, a/r/tographic inquiry emphasizes the process of inquiry and therefore questions evolve as the shifting relationality found within the project informs the direction of the inquiry. In addition to this, a/r/tography encourages all those involved to become a/r/tographers (the extent to which suits their practices) and begins with the intention to create art and write for dissemination. Art making and writing are closely linked to the process of inquiry and continuous questioning. Thus questioning through inquiry is set in motion and the rhizomatic conditions for a methodology of situations emerges.

An Interlude about A/r/tographic Praxis

Although each of us knew of one another before this project began, we had never worked together. Through a sequence of events, inspired by the newly instituted Research Creation grants through the Social Sciences and Humanities Research Council of Canada, we came together to imagine a project that brought forward our mutual interests and strengths. In choosing a focus we explored ideas in cultural studies, visual culture, a/r/tography, adolescent culture, educational change, community-engaged practices, and other ideas before arriving at the project briefly outlined in the prelude. All of us were artists and educators interested in collaborative inquiry and we felt we had a focus for our deliberations. Yet, it wasn't as simple as that. Upon receipt of the funding, challenges began to emerge. Some of these challenges were resolved while others have persisted. Throughout this interlude we describe the process of the project and interject with the challenges we faced. These challenges are inevitable in an a/r/tographic inquiry for a/r/tographers recognize the need to pay attention to tangents, to interruptions, and to unsettling conversations. Furthermore, it was through rhizomatic challenges that we were forced to face our underlying assumptions and beliefs before redirecting the inquiry in ways we hadn't anticipated. We were beginning to learn that the rhizomatic nature of a/r/tography offers a methodology of situations.

The title of our project came when Gu Xiong, a Chinese Canadian, shared with us that the translation for Richmond into Chinese was "The City of Richgate." Given the demographics of Richmond, we felt Chinese families should be emphasized in our project but we appreciated how other cultural groups should also be represented. Our first challenge was to locate immigrant families who would consider joining our project. We contacted the Richmond Art Gallery and worked with them to offer a community symposium entitled "The Lay of the Land: Looking at a Changing Land through Geography, Immigration and the Creative Impulse".[7] This event was advertised in local English and Chinese newspapers. The symposium addressed issues of demographics, geography, history, immigration and art as they are related to landscape and changing cities. Two members of our research team gave presentations on their artworks at the symposium. At the end of this event, we introduced the project to those in attendance and invited them to contact the gallery if they were interested in working with us. Gallery staff, acting as our interlocutor, provided the participants with the ethical review forms required by our University. This event and its related publicity brought forward four families who were interested in working on the project. Though we knew we wanted to work with intergenerational immigrant families, we also knew that as a/r/tographers we needed to position ourselves within the project. We needed to examine our relationships with the City of Richmond, our stories of immigration, and our relationships with our families. We challenged ourselves to question the apparent lack of a representative sampling of ethnicities among the participants and our relationship with the participants. The four families that came forward represented three Chinese families and one Estonian family and though they did not represent the range of ethnicities in the city, we agreed that their self-nomination defined our research community.

While these challenges were being met, we also questioned our positioning in the project. As a/r/tographers, we knew we needed to pursue our own artistic and pedagogical inquiry within the project. Each of us began to imagine how our relationships with the City of Richmond could offer rhizomatic connections for our project. We soon realized that two members of the research team had very strong connections with the City of Richmond even though neither currently lived in the city. It was decided that we would include these two families in our research community. We hoped this would strengthen our connections with the other families. Although this decision proved successful in developing rapport, it also caused some confusion as to the focus of the project and it encouraged us to think about power relations. How could we ensure all families felt equally included in the decisions? Was this even possible? As a/r/tographers, we came to the project with a facility in education and art. Only one of the other family members had a background in art and education. What power could the families have in the project? These questions would cause us to be more reflective and reflexive as the project progressed since the complexity of the project demanded this level of awareness.

We believed that one benefit of the project was the chance to be represented as a member of the Richmond community and as a Canadian. We hoped the families would be interested in having their stories and their project artifacts kept in the city archives. Although most city archives maintain a library of the most important events and people in the community, they are open to collecting other materials from the community. We believed that sharing the stories (interview transcripts and other materials collected and created during the project) of immigrant families was a valuable contribution to the archives. This turned out to be important to each of the families.

We now had six families[8] (representing several generations) to work with us on our a/r/tographic inquiry. Over the next six months, we interviewed each family several times and collected images they believed represented their journeys. These interviews could be characterized as conversational interviews as the focus was intentionally broad and allowed for an emergence of ideas. Though we first envisioned one or two interviews (about 2 hours in length), the result depended upon the family. Some wanted to share more with us than could be covered in two sittings (and thus three or four were needed) while others pre-selected what they wanted to share and two visits were enough. While visiting the families, we took our own photographs of their homes and family members and kept our own field notes reflecting upon our observations and engagements, yet we also collected many photographs and memorabilia the families wished to share. We also held large group gatherings for all of the families every two to three months. At these gatherings, the families were able to meet one another and through dialogue began to form community linkages. Meanwhile, as the university-based researchers, we discussed what we were learning, started to create collaborative artworks, and read theoretical work related to the project. If the families wanted to pursue these lines of inquiry with us they were encouraged to do so, and in fact, two of the families became very involved in our collaborative art project. Initially we had hoped the families would become a/r/tographers in ways that suited their interests. This turned out to be a challenge. One could claim that some family members worked a/r/tographically alongside the university-based a/r/tographers as they collaborated on the creation of art, told their stories and examined some difficult issues but the commitment to a/r/tography remained with those times in which they were engaged with the university-based researchers.

In keeping with the intention of the Research Creation grant program, we wanted to create works of art coming from our a/r/tographic inquiry. With Gu Xiong's connections to China, and with some of our families having extended family in China, we decided to create an exhibition that would first travel to China before being shown in Canada. Furthermore, one Chinese university (where Gu Xiong had worked before immigrating to Canada) was hosting a "Canada month" and invited us to show our work. Knowing we would be exhibiting the work at one university, we pursued personal connections at another university that lead to another opportunity to exhibit our work. More importantly, however, was the fact that both sites were close to extended family members (two families in Chongqing and two families in Beijing). This allowed us an opportunity to engage with the extended families as a way of learning about their families, their understandings of immigration, and their reactions to the visual stories of their family members.

Conceptualizing The City of Richgate exhibition inspired many rhizomatic possibilities as the university-based researchers reviewed the data and imagined possibilities for creating art. One metaphor stood out: the metaphor of gates representing each family with a collection of gates describing a flow of immigration, a marking of place, identity and transformation, and a city of (rich) *gates*. As the university researchers we may have chosen the symbol of gates, but the families supported it. In a gathering of all of the families, the exhibition plan was presented and discussed. Families were willing to work with us even if they were not confident as artists themselves. As the process unfolded, large image-based gates (outside scale: 12' wide x 12' high with each individual banner being 3' wide) were created for each family. Each gate portrays one family's experiences of immigration or profound change. Each tells a visual narrative of a family's struggles to understand an adopted homeland, and, in a broader sense, the implications of dual/multiple cultures and past/present dimensions on identity, place and community. Creating the gates as a collaborative effort was often challenging. Being careful not to expect more of the families than they wished to provide, we attempted to balance time commitments with decision-making. Working together, families and artists made decisions on the images to be portrayed on each gate based on the story to be told and the aesthetic features to be emphasized. When families could not be involved, the decision rested with the artists though the families were consulted.

As the university-based researchers, we came together on a regular basis throughout the inquiry to engage in collaborative discussions. This often meant reading and analysing interview transcripts, as well as literary or theoretical texts. Whenever possible, it included an engagement with current art exhibitions or contemporary artists and their works. It also meant a collaborative interdependent engagement around the development of ideas. In this project, art had a social purpose and education was about social understanding. A/r/tography is based in relational aesthetics, relational learning, and relational inquiring. Relationships are not free of tension. Together we planned, changed plans, learned and relearned. It was often in these dialogical collaborative spaces that surprisingly rich connections and ruptures happened.

When we first conceptualized this project, we envisioned a community of families very engaged in our collective efforts. Yet as the project evolved, it became apparent that most of the families wanted some involvement while others preferred less. Typically one member of the family had more energy for the project than others. Where we once envisioned a community-engaged project we realized the project evolved into a "working with a community" project. While we were determined to establish rapport with the families, we also needed to recognize our own illusions. We questioned our complicity, that is, how our assumptions, actions, beliefs, and practices could have created this different orientation (see also David & Rogoff, 2004; Doherty, 2004). We also began to realize the significance of situations to the rhizomatic relationality of a/r/tography. In a "working with a community" project, when is a person an artist, researcher and/or educator? In other words, how can a/r/tographers work with others who are not a/r/tographers as they pursue their inquiries?

These questions brought us to the work of Kwon (2002, p.154) who talks about the impossibility of community, that is, the impossibility of total coherence within a social grouping or institution. Many community-based art projects are "understood as a *descriptive* practice in which the community functions as a referential social entity...In contrast, collective artistic praxis...is a *projective* enterprise" (italics in original; p.154). A collective artistic praxis resonates with our work for it begins in special circumstances created by a group of artist-educators aware of the social conditions and allowing for the "coming together and coming apart as a necessarily incomplete modelling or working-out of a collective social process. Here, a coherent representation of the group's identity is always out of grasp" (p.154). We could only be a community if we questioned our legitimacy as a community. For Kwon, this necessitates a "redefining [of] community-based art as collective artistic praxis" (p.155). Working with the families, we were working with an invented community through a collective artistic and educational praxis known as a/r/tography. Our coming together and coming apart marked situational turning points in our methodology and lead us to seeing a/r/tography as a methodology of situations.

An Interlude about A/r/tography as a Methodology of Situations

A/r/tography is a living inquiry of unfolding artforms[9] and text that intentionally unsettles perception and complicates understandings through its rhizomatic relationality. In so doing, space and time are understood in different ways. In the visual arts, rhizomatic relations can be seen in shifting relations between artists, art productions and their locations, and audience involvement. For several decades many artists have been interested in site-specific work and more recently have become concerned with adaptations to this idea through site-determined, site-oriented, site-referenced, site-responsive, and site related works (Kwon, 2002). Each of these conceptualizations is concerned with a relationship between the artwork and its site, that is, how the creation, presentation, and reception of an artwork is situated in the physical conditions of a particular location.

Yet, as Miwon Kwon (2002) argues, the term "site" needs to be re/imagined beyond a particular location if we are to understand the complexity of the unstable relationship between location and identity. In this sense, "sites" are not geographically bound, but informed by context, where "context [is] an impetus, hindrance, inspiration and research subject for the process of making art" (Doherty, 2004, p.8). This relational understanding is constituted through social, economic, cultural and political processes in what Nicholas Bourriaud (2001, 2002, 2004) calls *relational aesthetics*. Like Kwon and Bourriaud, Clare Doherty (2004) contends that "site-specific" art or "situations" encourage processes and outcomes marked by social engagements that effectively change conventional relationships between artists, artworks, and audiences. As Bourriaud (2004) states: "The forms that [the artist] presents to the public [does] not constitute an artwork until they are actually used and occupied by people" (p.46). Rather than simply interpreting art, audience members become analysers or interlocutors. In many instances, audiences are actually called to a specific time and place where they become active participants in the artwork and thus, argues Bourriaud (2004), alternative modes of sociality are created.

The City of Richgate installation was exhibited at two universities in China: Southwest Normal University (SNU in Chonqging)[10] and Beijing Normal University (BNU).[11] Though all of the gates were exhibited at each site, they were not designed for either site nor were they exhibited in similar ways. We were aware of the circular format for the first gallery but unaware of what was possible in the latter site. As each exhibition was installed, decisions were made based upon aesthetics, institutional concerns, and professional relationships. Fortunately, extended family members of two families represented by our gates visited the exhibition.

At Southwest Normal University (see images below) hundreds of people attended the exhibit and asked questions related to Canadian lifestyles, economics, and cultural representation. Those in the arts were interested in the use of photography, our interest in the everyday lives of family members, and the format of the gates. People passed through, around, between, and by the gates. People lingered with each pondering their meanings. The reverse side of each gate, softened by the whitened veils of the transparent images, evoked other reactions to the strong photographic images on the other side.

Richgate Exhibition. Art Gallery of Southwest Normal University, Chongqing, China. 5-9 July 2005. Courtesy of the artists.

Richgate Exhibition. Art Gallery of Southwest Normal University, Chongqing, China. 5-9 July 2005. Courtesy of the artists.

What was taken for granted at Southwest Normal University was tested at Beijing Normal University. With our first location being inadequate at BNU, we set out to find another location. We found another site in the senior administrative building which allowed us to suspend the gates from a fourth floor walkway into a large open concourse (see image below). The result was an exhibition structure that gave the illusion of an even larger gate-like structure. This was further exemplified in the architecture of the building itself being reminiscent of an imposing gate. Individuals witnessing the exhibit passed under the gates while looking up through the gates, around the gates and past the gates. Those in attendance asked about our families, Canada as a country, and our standard of living in Canada, immigration, and perhaps most importantly, they wanted to practice their English language.

Richgate Exhibition. Beijing Normal University, Beijing, China. 17-23 July 2005. Courtesy of the artists.

The circumstances around the BNU exhibition were politically fraught with administrative concern while the SNU exhibition, in a university gallery, was free of such concerns. At BNU every level of university governance was called upon to secure permission for the exhibition and in the end, we were allowed to exhibit the show for three days over a weekend when few people could see the show.[12] At SNU the exhibit was up for a week, with hundreds of visitors, and could have stayed much longer had our schedule permitted. Alternative modes of sociality were created at each site and each site created its own complex situation. As a/r/tographers we came to understand these complexities as situations for inquiry. One art exhibition taken to two places in one country brought about completely different engagements and reactions. Other questions in our inquiry emerged: Was the result an art/education exhibition, a political statement about immigrating to Canada, and/or an invitation to consider the lives of extended families in two countries? How did the exhibition influence the thinking of those in attendance?

To some, our work at BNU was seen as politically charged. For others, it was an opportunity to meet English-speaking individuals with whom one could practice their English. At SNU, many people were engaged with the images in thoughtful and often pedagogical ways, while others questioned the installation as art. And almost certainly, these dichotomous descriptions are overly simplified for there were some similar reactions at each site. As a/r/tographers, we realized the exhibitions created methodological situations for inquiry.

Upon our return to Canada, we attempted to map out our a/r/tographic journey. As mentioned at the beginning of this article, maps are a good metaphor for rhizomes for they only have middles with no beginnings or endings. In mapping our process, we could see how relational inquiry was important to the project whether it was represented in the chronological history of the project, the networking of individuals within and outside the project, the story telling of times past, present or envisioned for the future, and the sharing of images as a way of understanding experience. As we traced some of these pathways, we came upon visible and invisible ruptures and connections. The interruptions formed important situational turning points. For instance, one situational turning point occurred in the conversational interviews. Each immigrant family came to Canada for different reasons: education for their children or themselves; economics; a better quality of life; the clean air and beautiful country; political reasons; the western culture. Common themes did not emerge[13] with the exception that the political affects the personal and both the personal and political are important.

This was a situational turning point because many of the reasons surprised us. We needed to shift our understandings of individual immigrants. We had to face our stereotypical views. It was also a turning point because we began to recognize the transnational identities some of the Chinese immigrants held. Several lived in Richmond and Beijing, and although several others lived in both countries they belonged to neither for they were transnationals. They belonged to a new identity that surpassed borders: "a sense of belonging that is not bound to any specific location but to a 'system of movement'" (Kwon, 2004b, p.38). Furthermore, we had to recognize that families were reticent to share some experiences or difficult issues. Because project members were not anonymous, some difficult issues could not be broached. Yet, in spite of this, much was shared. This was especially evident when we shared our experiences in China upon our return to Canada. The families were curious as to the reactions of their extended families and the general public, as well as the institutions and didn't question our interpretation of the events.

While our Chinese families were proud to have their gates on display in their country of birth they were also proud to be represented as both Canadians and Chinese. They interpreted the gates to metaphorically represent openings and closings, transitions and transformations. Members of their extended families were less interested in the gates as objects and more interested in their visual stories. The gates became invitations to witness their relative's new lives, their standard of living, their prosperity and their accomplishments. The gates represented storied lives lived elsewhere. Yet not all family members were interested in the image or idea of gates. Those adults who immigrated to Canada appreciated the metaphor of the gate but their children (adolescents and early twenties) envisioned different metaphors such as virtual spaces (the web or the internet). We hope to pursue the children's perspectives in future inquiries, for recognizing the intergenerational differences has caused another situational turning point, another rhizome.

Working through a collective artistic and educational praxis, we have come to appreciate the interruptions and surprises that have led to situational turning points. A/r/tography as a methodology of situations is steeped in divergent rhizomatic relationalities that questions assumptions and invites new understandings of collaboration. The City of Richgate project continues. We have moved into the next phase. We've added families of different ethnicities and are finalizing their gates. We have also collected stories and images of significant sites in Richmond for each family and we are planning several collective artistic and educational praxis events that could occur a year from now. The situations derived from the rhizomatic relationalities discussed in this article have caused us to challenge our assumptions and directions, and each time emergent understandings have taken us to another level of awareness.

A Tentative Postlude within an Ongoing Inquiry

For educators Terrance Carson and Dennis Sumara (1997), the meaning of images and texts is contingent upon the relationships between and among artist, art work, text, and audience as well as the social, cultural, economic, and political contexts, and the ways these relations are altered by what Derrida (1978) calls the "as yet unnameable which begins to proclaim itself" (p.293). Thus, relationality is more than the contexts in which situations occur but rather the potentialities that constantly evolve and provoke meaning (Springgay, 2004).

By pausing for a tentative postlude within our ongoing a/r/tographic project, we are recognizing the rhizomatic nature of our inquiry. With rhizomatic form, this article becomes another situation in the journey. It is an event or an encounter with multiplicities that dislodges fixed ways of perceiving the world and offers us emergent ideas and perceptions that re/creates multiplicities. Though a preferred rhizomatic composition would have offered simultaneous admittance to the prelude, interlude and each situation, what remains possible now is a re/visiting in rhizomatic fashion. A re/consideration of this article may then echo the kinds of dialogic and rhizomatic connections or ruptures found among those involved in the project as well as the ideas that have emerged. Instead of preconceived coherence, the emphasis becomes a methodology of situations.

What does this teach us about a/r/tography? While much has been written in a/r/tography about the need for autobiographical inquiry (Irwin, 2003; 2004a; Irwin & de Cosson, 2004) more needs to be written about the challenges and insights gained through collective artistic and educational praxis. The City of Richgate project has underscored the political nature of a/r/tography as a methodology of situations created through rhizomatic relations. These situations are challenges to the power relations between and among a/r/tographers, all those involved in the project and the contexts in which the projects are shared. These situations acknowledge the difficulties in sharing that which has not yet been revealed. And, these situations enable the political to occur. For without a/r/tographical inquiry, some of these situations may never have occurred. A/r/tography is, after all, a methodology that inspires situational inquiry through rhizomatic relations.

NOTES

[1] Reprinted with permission of the National Art Education Association: Irwin, Rita L., Beer, Ruth, Springgay, Stephanie, Grauer, Kit, Gu, Xiong, & Bickel, Barbara. (2006). The Rhizomatic relations of a/r/tography. *Studies in Art Education, 48*(1), 70-88.

[2] We are indebted to other arts and education practitioners who are exploring and creating new forms of inquiry (Cole & Knowles, 2001; Barone 2000, 2001b, 2003; Blumenfeld, 1995; Denzin, 1998; Donmoyer & Yennie-Donmoyer, 1995; Dunlop, 1999; Eisner, 1997; Eisner & Barone, 1997; Emme, 1999; Fels, 1999; Finley & Knowles, 1995; Gouzouasis & Lee, 2002; Leggo, 2005; Richardson, 2000; Sanders-Bustle, 2003; Slattery 2001; Sullivan 2004; Weber & Mitchell, 1996).

[3] The slashes in a/r/tography (and other related words) purposefully illustrate a doubling of identities and concepts rather than a separation/bifurcation of ideas.

[4] We wish to thank the reviewers for their thoughtful and insightful comments. They provoked us to write a stronger article and to consider other rhizomatic directions as we imagine the future of the project.

[5] We wish to thank the Social Sciences and Humanities Research Council of Canada for their generous support of our research program entitled "The City of Richgate: Research and Creation into Community-Engaged Arts Practices" (2004-2008).

[6] Richmond is a suburb of Vancouver, British Columbia and is the site of the Vancouver International Airport Terminal.

[7] October 29, 2004.

[8] We wish to thank our families for their participation in this project. Their contributions have been incredibly important. The Chinese families include: 1) Mei Lin, Tam Wang and Crane Wang; 2) Bob Duan, Linda Gu and Ying Duan; 3) Yuzhang Wang, Hong Yang and Steven Wang; 4) Gu Xiong, Ge Ni and Gu Ye. The Estonian family is: 5) Gabriele and Brian Ailey. The German family is: 6) Kit Grauer and Carl Grauer. Recently we have added the Gill family and Sameshima family.

[9] Though any artform may be performed or produced in a/r/tography, for the purpose of this paper, visual forms are emphasized.

[10] Southwest Normal University has been renamed since our exhibition. It is now Chonqging Normal University.

[11] Both exhibitions took place in June 2005.

[12] Gu Xiong and a Chinese administrator on site explained this situation to us.

[13] The constant comparative method was used for analysis.

PART IV

FURTHER OPENINGS

PETER GOUZOUASIS

TOCCATA ON ASSESSMENT, VALIDITY & INTERPRETATION

Andante[1]

"I don't feel comfortable with presenting my poetry and music as research," says Marc.

"Yeah, I feel like my performances are research, more than just in a round about way, but after all the courses I've taken so far, I still don't feel confident enough talking about my performing as inquiry when I'm talking with colleagues in the music faculty. I just don't have the literature down," Cathy remarks.

We're planning our research project at Marc's school, but the going is slow. Both Marc and Cathy are extremely talented musicians and teachers. They've been in graduate school for two years now. I'd been involved with them in a course over a year ago, and am presently their instructor in another research course in music education that has moved in some very interesting directions over the past 8 weeks.

"Hey, you're both more than capable musicians, excellent teachers, and your writing is really coming along. A/r/tography is a frame of mind. It's a process—an artistic teaching, learning, and research process—and we're involved in this process together. As process, it's ongoing—a becoming. So what is it that makes you feel insecure and uncertain about our projects?"

"It just doesn't seem 'valid' that we can do our music and our teaching and reflect on it and write about it and pull it together in such a way that we can call it research," says Marc. "It's way too natural and way too much fun."

"Yeah, you're doing all this work, Peter—some of it's even quantitative—all that numerical analysis that impresses the media and policy makers. Don't you feel that some of your research is more valid than other projects you're working on?"

I pause and reach for a stack of articles I've downloaded over the past 4 months, as well as some portions of book chapters. In honesty, I've been searching for answers to those questions and have developed even more questions over the two year long process. In one sense, if I pause on the wheel of becoming and take a snapshot of my being, where I am now is thinking reflexively about the culmination of my music studies, music teaching, and learning over the past 25 years. When in doubt, start from the beginning. Try to recall the basics and start a story from there.

S. Springgay et al. (eds.), Being with A/r/tography, 221–232.

"For me it all started in intense reflections on Kuhn (1962) and Pepper (1942). Notions that all data has some theory in it, that there is no such thing as pure data. That empirical data is data that is rooted in experience. Remember, experience can be numerical and highly technical, but it can be even more powerful when rooted in human experience. And our stories about lived experiences—experiences in all aspects of music—are the most powerful 'data' we can use in our research. It's all rooted in lived experience, and identifying the extraordinary in the ordinary as a form of 'pre-research,' so why not think of all lived inquiry as story telling?"

"All research is story telling?" they both speak out simultaneously.

It's a mantra I'd like to share with everyone I know.

"Sure. And think of the stories we share as being on a research continuum. A journey. Some researchers are mired in writing what they would consider purely scientific stories, and others think that by reporting ethnographic research in the third person, they're being more 'objective' about the 'subjective' so they take a realist, post-positivist stance in writing their stories. Researchers who continue in that mode do so dutifully and follow conventions and get published in the 'right' journals, and act as if they've got the answers to all the research questions nicely packaged in the conclusions of their studies."

"Little boxes on the hillside, little boxes made of ticky tacky, little boxes, little boxes, little boxes all the same."

Marc sings the old Malvina Reynolds song and we giggle and smile. He provides a needed respite from my somewhat sombre tone.

"We can never totally extract ourselves from the data. If you're a quantitative researcher, you're always trying to find different ways of massaging the numbers to find some significance to the differences or relationships you're investigating. And the interpretations of the findings, especially unexpected findings, are frequently stories based on purely theoretical assumptions, even so-called 'educated guesses' that are couched in theoretical babble. If you're a qualitative researcher, it's nearly impossible to work with data—interviews, videotape, music, visual art, stories—on an abstract, detached level. Researchers can't possibly be as objective and treat data as antiseptically as they pretend to do, hiding behind their tidy little theories and carefully 'culled facts' as Van Maanen (1988) calls them, to establish authority, rigor, and power in their texts. The bottom line is that we're all writing fictions— invented, crafted, made, created, constructed—pick your theory-laden term. And some of us write 'factions,' a combination of fact and fiction that Alex Haley (2007) coined and others write what I call 'frictions.' Just because they're written in one style or another, a scientific or literary style, shouldn't define or establish their validity as serious research. People like Strathern (1987) and Atkinson (1992) talk about these issues in these two pieces."

I hand the articles over to my students.

"And Richardson's (2000) ideas of writing as a way of knowing, 'a method of discovery and analysis,' emphasizing how 'form and content are inseparable.' That all ties in with how we as a/r/tographers can think about how the form of our art informs our research and vice versa. Like Eisner (2001) said, 'form matters, that content and form cannot be separated, how one says something is part and parcel of what is said.' And as we've shared in our research meetings, the form informs the research and the research informs the form."

"Do you mean that when we use a music form such as fugue, like you did with Karen Lee (2002), that our interpretations are influenced by the form of the representation? That different music forms and styles can help us express different meanings about the same thing?"

Cathy's questions illuminate her face.

Marc chimes in, "Yeah. That was dense reading. It was very fugue-like—especially the stretto section where the ideas that'd been introduced as subjects and countersubjects all piled up on top of one another. That was very powerful for me, but it seemed like something was missing at one point in the story."

"Yeah," I reply, "you're not the first person to notice. The editor made us remove two portions of the fugue. And not only was the form distorted by that, I also felt that the data—you know, the story itself—had been disrupted by the edit. But on an even bigger level, what's the 'real' difference between using a design structure such as a two by two ANOVA to organize numerical data and using a fugue to organize narrative data?"

I can't help but ask that question even though I don't expect it to be discussed right away.

Cathy looks irritated.

"Well, there's something else, even more basic, that kind of confuses me about a/r/tography."

The tone of her voice becomes more serious.

"It seems that the fugal composition has more than one type of research going on at the same time. There's a fictional quality about it, it also has some poetry, some autobiographical segments in it, and there are some confessional qualities to some sections. If you and Karen read it at a conference, there would be a dramatic element to it too."

"Absolutely. A/r/tography, as a way of doing research, a living inquiry, is all about process. We can use all the literary tools that are available to us—poetry, autoethnography, ethnodrama, fiction, creative non-fiction, action research, as well as numerous performing and visual art forms—to conduct our inquiries. There's no one way, no one form, to compose a/r/tography."

"In olden days, a hint of stocking was looked on as something shocking, now heaven knows, anything goes. Good authors to who once knew better words now only use four-letter words—writing prose. Anything goes." Marc sings, gleefully showing off his knowledge of show tunes and years of doing musicals at the high school level.

Was Cole Porter an a/r/tographer?

"Well, yes, there's a broad set of epistemological, metaphysical, and methodological assumptions that we can use to base our stories upon. But now we get into the can of worms, the black box, that no one seems to want to open. And it's full of questions. What is good a/r/tographic research? What criteria do we use to assess our inquiries? Do we assess the research and writing separately? Can we? Why would we? Is it all relative? Is any of it both relative and relational? What does good a/r/tography look like, read like, sound like, feel like? What is validity, reliability, and dare I say it, 'truth' in a/r/tographic research?"

"Etcetera, etcetera, etcetera" Marc adds in his best Yul Brenner imitation.

We all chuckle. It's much needed comical relief in the midst of what has turned out to be a messy conversation. I wonder to myself if we'll ever get to talk about the research project today or if that's just an afterthought to the questions I've just posed. Another thought crosses my mind.

"I don't believe we can use Stanley and Campbell's (1963) traditional criteria for validity because those criteria were invented for positivist, scientific story tellers. And Gordon's (1986) purposive split of subjective and objective validity is contradictory. Similarly, we can't even use the criteria of those who in the early days of qualitative research wrote realist stories in an attempt to make their writing seem more objective, academic, and scholarly. We need to look at a/r/tography on its own terms, not using the values and judgments made of older forms of research, but values based on the new work in arts-based educational research that has emerged over the past 15 years."

"Like what?" Cathy says with a hint of disbelief to her voice.

"Yeah, like what?" Marc adds, notably without a tune to his latest entry into the conversation.

I hear the skepticism in their voices and that's a good thing.

"Look, we can read anything by any leading author and find fault with it on numerous levels, especially if we don't use criteria by which they crafted the research in the first place. And especially in music education research, people are going to feel threatened not only by the kind of research that we're doing, but also by the fact that we're radically breaking from traditions. You know how rooted in traditions musicians can be—it's the greatest flaw in music research. We're our own greatest enemy. In attempting to make music more 'scientific,' we've been seduced into objectifying our art—music learning, music teaching, music itself—when it is really quite loaded with subjectivity. And here we are bringing this subjective, arguably unquantifiable thing into a marriage with an emerging approach to social science research— a/r/tography—to make a/r/tography even more progressive, more radical than standard literary forms of arts-based educational research."

"Yeah, but you're not answering the question."

"Well, I think I've begun to answer the question and, more importantly, have revealed even more questions. We all come to do research with our own sets of presuppositions and predispositions based on various epistemological and ontological positions. Those positions form a part of what we do in the research and how we do it, as well as what, why, and how we write in ways that we write. Since we don't have a unified way of looking at teaching and learning in music, why should we expect a set of unified criteria to assess and validate all music research? The fundamental, philosophical positions that have evolved in music education research over the past 100 years are incommensurable on their own, so why should we think about validity any differently? And you've learned that we can dismiss a piece of research based on our belief systems alone—concepts like content validity, face validity, and construct validity—when we look at scientific and realist tales, let alone other aspects of validity. So there's no question that we need to use different criteria for different forms of inquiry. The criteria need to be organic and changeable, not realist and stilted."

I'm thinking fast to keep them in tune with this line of thought. But where are those criteria, where can we find them, where do I get my hands on a textbook full of them? Where is my thesaurus of assessment terms for a/r/tographic research? I think I have some answers. But it's risky and I'm afraid I'm going to be more than obtuse unless they read some preliminary pieces to prepare them for my epiphany.

Allegretto

Another day, another research meeting, but I'm looking forward to what Marc and Cathy think about the readings I've shared. We begin with light banter about the music that's rattling about our brains and bodies, Marc's ensemble music and show preparations, Cathy's solo and ensemble performance music.

"Do you remember how Kuhn (1962) and Laudan (1977) challenged and displaced Popper's notions of falsification theory? They argued that we can't disprove theories, but we can look at things like epistemic threats and the quality of the threats to how the theory fits with reality—with what's 'out there'—to determine whether we need to abandon a theory or merely make modifications to it."

"So we can't disprove the, I guess we'd say, 'validity' of a/r/tographic research?" Marc asks.

He's getting warmed up and has the look in his eyes that he gets when he's in a great improvisational groove.

"If you're a realist, hard core positivist like Karl Popper, you may take the position that theories and research traditions can be disproved and dismantled by finding single flaws. But thinkers like Kuhn and Laudan left those archaic notions in ruins years ago. In educational research, Atkinson (1992) said "reliability and validity are not necessarily the appropriate evaluative standards for a life history interview," and Riessman (1993) hits this note clearly with her position that we cannot "rely on realist assumptions and consequently are irrelevant to narrative studies" (p.43). We can think along those same lines and talk about it in terms of the incommensurability of terminologies across research traditions—we can't just keep throwing terms related to the assessment of scientific and realist tales over the wall hoping that people doing a/r/tography can adapt them to their own research."

"So what can we do?" Marc and Cathy chime in unison.

"Well, even though some qualitative researchers, like Patti Lather (1986), have tried to work with adaptations of traditional notions of validity, other people – Bruner, Eisner, Ellis, Guba, Lincoln, Pelias, Richardson, Sandelowski, Schwandt, Tierney, Wolcott – have invented new notions of assessment that allow us to let go of traditional boundaries. Ideas like verisimilitude (Eisner, 1991; Schwandt, 1997), width, coherence, insightfulness, parsimony (Lieblich et al., 1998), various kinds and forms of truth (Sandelowwski, 1994), authenticity criteria like fairness, ontological and educative authenticity, catalytic and tactical authenticity (Lincoln & Guba, 2000), comprehensiveness of accounts (Taylor, 2002), substantive contribution, aesthetic merit, reflexivity, impact, expression of a reality (Richardson, 2000), believability, plausibility, the author's role, interpretations, reflectivity (Tierney, 1997), coherence, plausibility, imaginative aesthetic transaction, empathy (Pelias, 1999), and authenticity (Lincoln, 1993). When you read all of those researchers, as well as the final segment of Sparkes' text (2002), I think you'll come to the notion that validity is 'not valid' in the assessment of a/r/tography."

Marc adds an afterthought.

"It seems we use similar kinds of criteria to assess and evaluate music performances and compositions."

"And because of the complexity of a/r/tographic research, we can use those criteria on the artistic, research, and teaching aspects of the topics we research."

Cathy sings with the glee of discovery, continuing Marc's thought as if she were anticipating the melody of a familiar tune.

I pause for a moment and think. Just as some music compositions challenge us to take multiple improvisatory choruses of the same chord progression, with its various tritone and minor third substitutions on two-five (ii-V) changes, a/r/tography challenges us to ask more questions rather than come to finite conclusions.

"How about if we blow on the changes of 'All the things you are' for a half hour and call it a day?"

"You mean 'All the things you could be by now if Sigmund Freud's wife was your mother'," Cathy says in reference to a Charles Mingus version of the same classic tune.

We all smile as we reach for our axes, each of us knowing that, hours after we leave each other, our minds will reverberate with the research ideas we've been discussing. And our hearts, minds, and fingers will embody the changes to that tune. And all of these ideas will haunt us for a lifetime of learning.

Adagietto

A *toccata* sounds like a highly improvisatory composition. Literally a "touch piece" in the Renaissance period, it was used by organists to warm up to the feel, form, and function of an organ. It was an introductory piece of music, and featured imitation, virtuosic arpeggios, and intricate ascending and descending melodic passages. Tempos may suddenly vary within the same composition. One may metaphorically compare the ornate, extravagant, filigree of Baroque architecture, furniture, and painting with textural features of the Baroque toccata. The lute and guitar equivalent of the toccata was called the *ricercar*. Ricercar by Francesco da Milano are highly imitative and contrapuntal. Historically speaking, by the Baroque period the ricercar had developed into the fugue. In J.S. Bach's *Musicalisches Opfer* (*Musical Offering*, BWV 1079, 1747), the first letter of each word of his personal inscription to King Frederick II—*Regis Iussu Cantio Et Reliqua Arte Resoluta*—spell the word ricercar (Goble, 1985, p.35-36).

For me, the preceding narrative was also a warm-up—an attempt to "feel around" for some of the answers to difficult questions. A journey on a path where I am still learning to play, finding my way around the music instrument we call a/r/tography. As any guitarist knows, because of the complexity of the instrument and diverse variety of stylistic possibilities, playing guitar is a lifelong endeavour with layer upon layer of ideas, techniques, and theoretical foundations that challenge understanding. Also, there are many great players, and mature guitarists learn and develop an understanding of numerous music ideas from each other. They listen with ears wide open. For me, on a metaphorical level a/r/tography is no different, and the preceding dialogue amplifies some of the issues I believe we need to consider in discussing validity, assessment, and interpretation.

Much of how we come to understand research paradigms, models, world views, research programs, and metatheories, as well as interpret the research conducted within and from those perspectives, depends on one's personal epistemological and ontological understandings. Researchers have described modernism as an objectivist stance and post-modernism as a relativist stance. Also, it is reasonable to suggest that post-modernism is an extension of and dependent upon the basic tenants of modernism. Amodernism (Latour, 1993, 1999; Overton, 1997a, 1997b,

1998) may be interpreted as a denial of both modernism and post-modernism, and I position my work in this emerging research metatheory.

Amodernism is considered as a related and relative (i.e., relative-relativist) stance. Latour's ontological relationality abolishes boundaries and hierarchies of categories between traditional binaries established through modernist and post-modernist thought, e.g., subject-object, stability-change, reason-emotion, interpretation-observation, nature-nurture, arts-sciences, curriculum-psychology. Another way to interpret his work is that it demolishes the split, competing dichotomies that have troubled modernist and post-modernist thought in the 20th century. This is important to arts researchers because if one considers both relatedness and relativity in the development of their research program, one may consider issues such as the integral, holistic role (i.e., fusion) of the arts/artist/arts researcher/arts teacher in a broad variety of inquiries. Thus, as embodiment is a synthesis of biological-cultural-personal (Overton, 2003), it is also a synthesis of artistresearcherteacher in a/r/tographical inquiry. Overton (pp.24-25) uses M.C. Escher's *Drawing Hands* to redefine the relationship between dichotomous binaries that function as competing alternatives in modernist and post-modernist thought; binaries are transformed and reconceptualized as complimentary, supportive partners in inquiry through relational metatheory.

It is possible to consider these fused, relational alloys on a number of related levels. Traditionally speaking, from an ontological perspective and with regard to studying the acquisition of knowledge, metaphilosophers and researchers were concerned with the relationship between concepts and percepts – i.e., do percepts (i.e., that which is sensation, material, experiential, cultural) generate concepts (i.e., that which is thought, innate, inbuilt biological structures, genetic), do concepts generate percepts, or do we need both concepts and percepts in developing our understandings of "what is"? Overton (1984) extended those three considerations in examining the relationship between theory and data—i.e., 1) do data generate theory, 2) does theory generate data, or 3) do we need both theory and data in our explanation of nomena—the "world of understanding" as it is, in and of itself—and phenomena—the "world of appearances" as it appears to our senses?

When conducting a/r/tographic inquiry, we may take those perspectives one step further in posing the questions: 1) do the arts inform the inquiries we conduct, 2) do our inquiries inform the arts/the way we do our art making, or 3) do we need both inquiry (i.e., research) and arts to form and inform one and the other in our understandings of teaching and learning others and ourselves? The later position is where artists/researchers/teachers may reside with their inquiries, where research and art define and refine each other, where we recognize a/r/tography as neither subject nor object but as a project (Langer, 1989, pp.23-26) in an ongoing process of living inquiry.

John Searle (1992) postulated, "the fact that a feature is mental does not imply that it is not physical; the fact that a feature is physical does not imply that it is not mental" (p.15). Similarly, the fact that a feature is research does not suggest that it cannot be artistic; the fact that a feature is artistic does not suggest that it cannot be research. Like musicians who are able to bring music meaning to a score, we bring understanding to the creation and recreation of our inquiries and our selves. As expert musicians who learn new music, rather than merely take meaning from an experience (e.g., the music on the page), we breathe meanings into our artist/researcher/teacher inquiries (i.e., our performances and newly composed works of arts-based educational research).

By the very nature of research design—i.e., identifying the general purpose and problem, selecting a distinct segment of research literature, choosing a methodology, setting up research procedures, analysing the data, reporting and interpreting the results, and posing conclusions, suggestions, or considerations for further research—one may posit that there is no such thing as pure data. Researchers, human beings who by their very nature and nurture possess numerous biases, are involved in every aspect of the research process. Gadamer posited, "unacknowledged presuppositions are always at work in our understanding" (1981, p.111). The personal perspectives of a researcher are inseparable from the research process. In a/r/tographic works, rather than posing problems to the process of inquiry, we revel and rejoice in the interconnectedness of our mind, body, spirit, and heart through and in our inquiries. That is because inquiry without being in tune with one's self in relation to the worlds we live in is meaningless.

Some researchers would like to lead readers to believe that their works are a presentation, or representation, of cold, hard, indifferent fact(s). However, one may question, "which aspect of fact? Are they not different aspects of the same whole?" Gadamer (1981) posited, "There is no such thing as a fully transparent text" (p.106). Acknowledging the turmoil surrounding data, fact, and error demolishes notions of absolute certainty and reveals our deeply rooted, sincere doubts about an ultimate Reality and about traditional ways of knowing (Overton, 2002). For a/r/tographers, this enables a new beginning – an opening and invitation to revealing understanding (*Verstehen*) as epistemology, and interpretation as the procedure that leads us to understanding. It enables us to begin to understand why we are always becoming in our lives and invites an interpretive, hermeneutic approach to our inquiries. And it opens possibilities to new ways of thinking about interpretation as the key to understanding how we may speak of assessment and validity in a/r/tographic inquiry. As Gadamer (1994) suggested, "The important thing is to be aware of one's own bias, so that the text can present itself in all its otherness and thus assert its own truth against one's own meaning" (p.269).

Traditionally speaking, interpretation may come from either top-down (e.g., researcher to reader; this approach is more common in, though not exclusive to, quantitative research) or bottom-up (e.g., readers bringing their interpretation to the research to seemingly make the research more meaningful; this approach is more common in, though not exclusive to, qualitative research). On a parallel level, one may also consider this as either an inside-out (e.g., insider reaching out, as in a researcher/writer relating to reader) or outside-in (e.g., an outsider looking in, reader relating to an inquiry) relationship. Moreover, the interpretation of data—in the form of interviews, stories (i.e., narratives, autobiographies, autoethnographies), poetry, music, and visual art forms—may happen between both the researcher and participant(s) (i.e., side-by-side) to reveal an even richer texture of understandings of events or outcomes (see Beattie, 1995, 2004).

PETER GOUZOUASIS

Many researchers, not just a/r/tographers, share concerns over the slippery, messy, conflicting, strident, restrictive aspects of traditional assessment, validity, and interpretation of research. That raises important considerations in terms of who is best equipped to assess a work of a/r/tography. Obviously, there are a variety of entry points in this discussion; however, it seems reasonable to suggest that communities of informed creators, readers, and participants are best able to attend to that task. After all, while we can describe the pitfalls, pratfalls, and negative aspects of positivist research projects and programs, what is the point? Why should falsification—a negative approach to understanding research, theories, and research programs—be the fundamental aspect of the assessment of research?

Like Elliot Eisner (1991), I believe that corroboration is one of our most powerful evaluative tools. Corroboration is a way of making things more certain; for Stephen Pepper (1942), the work of legitimate criticism is corroboration. Pepper is credited with slaying the "dragon of logical positivism" (Hare, 1982) and the notion of structural corroboration may be traced to Pepper. Structural corroboration involves the correlation of hypothesis with hypothesis, which Pepper calls "fact with fact." The product of this approach is called danda, and danda are data loaded with interpretations. It is a coherence theory of truth, where one considers truth as a logical relationship among things. Whereas positivists and conventionalists maintain that theories and models are ultimately reducible to some hard, fixed data and that they are not even necessary, from a structural corroborational view, theories matter and theorizing is important. Theories change the ways we come to understand what we are concerned with, what we are thinking about in our inquiries. They are like lenses that transform the world, rather than a window that we merely look through. Furthermore, if we take the lenses off, all we see is a blur.

Structural corroboration allows us to consider the shifting ground and uncertainty of common sense, and the notion that we will never find absolute answers to specific research questions and entire projects of inquiry. From that starting point, we can consider starting our research from what Pepper calls dubitanda—that which can be doubted, that which is dubitable. It enables us to think of all data as theory laden, that concepts are rules for ordering human experiences, and that the rules themselves are constructed by our active mind, heart, and spirit. From this perspective, interpretation is necessary and inquiries are not merely about observation. On a continuum, rough data—video data, photographs, poetry, music—falls between dubitanda and danda (data), so rough data is actually rough danda—it is all theory laden. On the other hand, multiplicative corroboration—which is based solely on repeated observations of the same phenomenon (i.e., repeated observations and empirical tests)—merely allows us to affirm or deny the validity of data. It is so rigid, dogmatic, and dictatorial that positivists and post-positivists who use multiplicative corroboration believe that it is self-evident and the sole aspect of evidence—that we just observe and the data will stand alone in that fashion with no interpretation. But we cannot reduce all interpretation to data and only data. I believe that we need to go back and read Pepper, Laudan, Overton and many more of the metaphilosophers who enabled us to arrive at these understandings, and more, over the last 60 years.

230

Some researchers use terms such as reliability, validity, precision, and statistical power to describe the impact and importance of their work. We may not be able to use Cureton's (1951) and Campbell and Stanley's (1963) criteria for validity because those criteria were invented for positivist, scientific storytellers. Those terms are insufficient and inappropriate to arts-based educational research contexts. They are criteria of those who in the early days of qualitative research wrote realist stories in an attempt to make their writing seem more objective, academic, and scholarly. We need to look, hear, feel, and conceptualize a/r/tography on its own terms, and not use the values and judgments made of older forms of research. Rather, our values need be based on new work in various forms of arts-based educational inquiry that has emerged over the past 15 years.

That is because to a great extent, the inquiries of a/r/tographers are highly interpretive. The richness, breadth, and depth of the interpretations that may come from the researcher, from reader(s), and collaboration of researcher-participant(s) may be considered an indication of the impact of a piece of arts-based educational research. We acknowledge the interpretive nature and nurture of our work, and revel in its strength, durability, malleability, tensility, reflectivity, reflexivity, applicability, imaginativity, and tangibility, as well as its verisimilitude, width, coherence, insightfulness, parsimony, various kinds and forms of truth, fairness, ontological and educative authenticity, catalytic and tactical authenticity, comprehensiveness, substantive contribution, aesthetic merit, impact, expression of a reality, coherence, plausibility, imaginative aesthetic transaction, empathy, and authenticity mentioned in the opening narrative. Those are all criteria by which we may assess a/r/tography in a contemporary, meaningful manner. Those aspects of a/r/tographic work define what is unique about the ways that we think about a/r/tography. Moreover, they promote creative, illustrative terminology that we may use to consider various aspects of a/r/tographic inquiry. That is because the fecundity and limitlessness of artistic creativity, expressivity, and imagination are embodied (*Lebensform;* Merleau-Ponty, 1963) in a/r/tography. The more questions we unearth from fertile s/p/laces (de Cosson, 2004) of inquiry and the more we describe and understand the qualities of our work in new, imaginative ways, the less finite, reckless, fleeting, and self-absorbed our work may become.

That our research is as much about process as it is about product, more about progress than a particular point in time or finality (i.e., telos), leads us to understand that we are ever becoming as our a/r/tographic works develop, change, evoke, provoke, and evolve. A/r/tography invites change and challenge, play and imagination, creativity and imagination. A/r/tographers seek transformational change that leads to the unfolding of something new, substantially different, and novel. As such, it involves imaginative, novel approaches to interpretation, assessment, and validity. That our inquiries involve the whole person—the artistresearcherteacher—in holistic endeavours, positions the work we call a/r/tography as integral and inseparable with the arts, arts-research, arts-based educational research, and arts researchers.

PETER GOUZOUASIS

NOTES

[1] The tempo markings at the beginning of each section are interpretational, and suggest to the reader to engage with the composition at a particular pace. Before tempo markings proliferated in the 19th century, tempo was usually interpreted based on the form (e.g., minuet, rondo) of a piece of music, as well as the movement of melody, harmony and rhythm in space, with articulation, accents, and dynamics taken into consideration. *Andante* is a walking tempo, *Allegretto* is rather fast, and *Adagietto* is a slow walking tempo.

GRAEME SULLIVAN

AFTERWORD: CONTINUING CONVERSATIONS OUTSIDE THE CIRCLE

Reading *Being With A/r/tography* is very much like 'listening in' to a series of conversations among a circle of colleagues sitting around an academic dinner table discussing perceptions, problems, and surprises surrounding the progress of their most recent research projects. This is a small but growing community of inquirers who are provoked by common desires that are sharpened by the intensity of their practice as artists, researchers and teachers. They have taken up a challenge to develop critical and creative methods to respond to pressing problems facing education today. These are not conference papers or research reports committed to print, because few of the common conventions for 'talking at' an audience are used. Instead, the editors and the authors contributing to this anthology prefer to 'talk with' those who will join them at their table. These are episodes that are responsive to personal and public interests in the experiences they reveal and the issues they cover. Consequently the chapters represent a different approach to reporting and reflecting on what it is to design and carry out research that investigates ways of negotiating human understanding. There is no less attention given to the rigor and scrupulous attention to detail required to draw connections, confirmations, conclusions or confusions, for these are the outcomes of all forms of effective research. The difference here is that data, in whatever form it is realized, is not an inert passenger on these research journeys. As the editors explain and the authors enact, a/r/tographic research is "living inquiry." By this they mean that research is located within and between the values, needs, interests and actions of communities, and where the issues have local resonance and global relevance.

As I continue the conversation I should introduce myself and the situation that shapes my response because 'talking with' someone also involves 'talking back' because communication is multivocal. Talking back is inclusive as position is negotiated, interpretations grounded, and perspectives acknowledged. The narrative journeys that are characteristic of the chapters in *Being with A/r/tography* invite a response for they open up the possibility of a parallel performance that is enlivened by the public issues debated and the personal passions invoked. This afterword, therefore, continues to expand the rhizomatic geography of discussion as ideas are acknowledged, additional themes are explored, some issues looked at differently. This is undertaken within the spirit of the text where the authors achieve an elegant energy in their quest to understand the simple complexity of what it is to know and question at the same time. For this is what is at the heart of inquiry that is artistic in form and content because critical intelligence is necessary to see possibility within what is not obvious, and creative insight is crucial to move from the unknown to the known. This is a research trajectory that is not like those

S. Springgay et al. (eds.), Being with A/r/tography, 233–244.

GRAEME SULLIVAN

outcomes, or those that look to discover plausible interpretations deep within the analysis of constructed realities. Rather, the stakes are much higher here because the collective practices of the artist, researcher and teacher have the potential to open up different opportunities for inquiry and the possibility of new conceptions of understanding. This is the art that is at the heart of the matter. It is provoked by my reaction to the conversations begun by the authors and it is enlivened by the situation informing my response.

Beyond the Circle and the Grid

I often construct commentaries that are framed by a range of academic structures and institutional conditions from my vantage point amid the urban corridors of New York. I purposefully use these conventional systems to advantage so as to point out differences between and among theories and practices that inform what we do as researchers and teachers working within arts educational communities. Knowing the parameters that close around the conceptions and methods used by many researchers in the social sciences and education is important because there is a need to be able to persuade and counter argue in language that has common meaning. Difference is intensified when seen from the perspective of what it is *not*. For some, however, the canons of conventional educational research can also be a restriction that then blinds them to other possibilities. This is unfortunate because the means should not define the ends. At issue is the need to create and construct new knowledge that helps to better understand and explain how we live and learn as individuals and communities. This is a complex quest as the authors in *Being with A/r/tography* attest, and cannot readily be reduced to convenient metrics or matrices. Therefore the boundaries that circumscribe approaches to research can be seen as bridges and links to many other ways of being and ways of seeing. Grids and circles of influence in this sense need to be offset by more organic systems that allow for movement back and forth so that new geographies of possibility may be charted, and transdisciplinary processes enacted. The rhizome is the preferred metaphor of the authors in this text and the themes explored give rise to a multiplicity of approaches and a multitude of insights. It seems appropriate that my part of the conversation takes its metaphor from a different kind of grid to that which I usually deploy. Consequently, formal structural parameters are relinquished in favour of a more flexible shaping process–in this instance, a grid made of water.

From my position in a small apartment overlooking the canals of Venice I'm reminded how much this city works as a metaphor for A/r/tography. The physical layout of Venice depicts two interlocked islands. Overall the shape of Venice is like a large fish amid others dispersed around the wider lagoon. But closer scrutiny shows Venice itself to be two smaller fish linked together by locked jaws, which is outlined by the Grand Canal as a contiguous line between the two interlocked islands (see Figure 1). This is not your usual image of the fish food chain where larger fish always consume smaller ones in a quintessential hierarchy of size and power. The image of the twin islands of Venice suggests that survival is best achieved by supporting each other. Similarly, the watery lines that allow Venice to

234

'work' have to be respected rather than regulated. The ebb and flow conforms to a time and space that is quite different to the institutionally driven pulse that I know. But the cultural customs surrounding art, community and commerce resonate. Ritual, of course, brings its own sense of comfort as the conditions that shape the comings and goings of everyday life need to be adhered to. However, accepted practice in one setting can be different to habituated actions in another and herein lies an opportunity to re-think possibilities. Annina Suominen Guyas, in her chapter on self-study and autobiography captures this image well when she talks about the need for teachers as researchers to be conscious of the contexts and framing mechanisms that influence their pedagogical practice. Her image of keeping a journal that has lined pages is instructive given that the pervasive tendency is to stay between the lines in accounting for what is done. Yet "filling lined pages" needs to be balanced by a sense of anticipation that is open to questions and intuitions, much like the processes that inform her art practice. Here Suominen Guyas talks about how she likes to "follow the flow of water." This has both rhetorical and conceptual appeal and her *Water Series* of artworks show forms that are partially abstracted from the source, yet this indexical meaning retains a freedom by not being framed as a formalist composition because the images are edgeless and have the potential to move in any direction. From my temporary perspective in Venice, data as 'water' sounds about right, especially if the vessels carrying the water have the capacity to take on alternative forms.

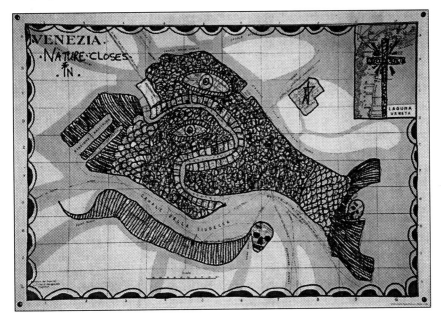

Damian Le Bas. Gypsyland (Venice). Pen on printed map, one of 21 maps.. Dimensions variable.

GRAEME SULLIVAN

Artwork included in *Paradise Lost: The First Roma Pavilion,* Venice Biennale, June 10 – Nov 21, 2007, curated by Timea Junghaus. Reproduced courtesy of the artist.

Alternative Spaces and Shifting Sites

Alternative spaces framed less by grids and circles, and shaped more by the shifting sands of perspective is a central tenet of A/r/tography. These spaces not only refer to the places where research is carried out but those arenas of exchange and transaction that are not bound by physical properties such as the sites and settings of everyday activity. These are the liminal spaces the editors describe as the interstices in and between phenomenon that warrant study for it is within these places where the focus of desires and dilemmas, ideas and actions, and wants and needs reside. This is a messy, inchoate world that resists the freeze-framing of conventional research methods where the usual means of constructing theories and conceptual networks offer inadequate abstractions at best. If the premise holds that effective theories help explain and predict things then the variability of the realities and subjectivities that shape our experiences are far too complex to be reduced to elemental axioms. Although the modernist triumph of rationalist practice added enormously to our understanding of the physical determinants shaping human nature, the more complex components of the human condition remained elusive. Yet the questioning continues. And artists these days as much as social scientists are making headway in re-fashioning ways of envisioning who we are and what we do. This is the line of inquiry taken by the authors in the text who advocate that an outcome of research is the production of knowledge as "difference" and that as users of research individuals and communities ought to be given the option to see things differently.

For instance, the a/r/tographic inquiries of Stephanie Springgay seek to understand the world through a form of embodied knowing that is related to our sense of touch and what is experienced in an incorporeal way. Here there is an active involvement with subject matter and material, rather than feigned objective distancing. As an outcome of research, meaning is not merely a consequence of iterative analysis or thematic synthesis. Rather, effective research increases the opportunity to raise better questions that not only seek to add information to our store of knowledge by helping come to understand what we don't know, but simultaneously requires us to problematize what we do know. Alternatives are sought to the conventional classification of phenomena which uses empirically based conceptual frameworks to categorize things. Instead, an interconnectedness is envisioned; similar to the way some researchers describe Indigenous epistemologies where criteria are used to identify relationships among entities of interest, rather than a tendency to disaggregate things into typologies and hierarchies.[1] Research activity can therefore be seen as an enlivened understanding of a complex array of potential and possibility that resides within a subjective engagement with ways and forms of knowing. The guiding assumption is that there are circumstances, settings and situations that cannot be accessed though conventional methods of language, logic and rationality typically associated with the social sciences. As the editors acknowledge, "a/r/tography is a methodology of embodiment, of continuous engagement with the world: one that interrogates yet celebrates meaning" (p. xxiii).

An instructive example of the inability of conventional conceptual structures to accommodate the complexity of what the authors of *Being with A/r/tography* know to be real is to be found in a satellite exhibition of the 2007 Venice Biennale. Titled "Paradise Lost," the exhibition is housed in the Palazzo Pisani Santa Marina, a 16th century Venetian palace in the city's Cannaregio district. It is significant that this group exhibition is being held at a venue separate from the mainstream sites of the Giardini and Arsenale where the conventional pavilions and thematic exhibitions representing the various participating countries are located. Paradise Lost is an exhibition of participants from eight European countries who share a common heritage and who have been brought together to comprise the first Roma[2] pavilion. Damian Le Bas, whose artwork is shown in Figure 1, resides in Great Britain. What these participating artists share is that they are part of a transnational minority population that is characterized as much by differences as similarities, yet without the presumed comfort of residing within a nation state. What is common is a passionate belief in self-identity and cultural presence; what is different is the diasporic discontinuity of Roma communities dispersed across Europe. In creating responses to Roma identity, the artists in Paradise Lost deal with the discourse of location, of origin, and raise questions about the ethics and ideologies of constructing concepts of how to define what a 'nation' is.

An important issue raised in the artworks in Paradise Lost is that the fifteen contributing artists are clearly identified and acknowledged Roma individuals of emerging reputation who resist the tendency to be lumped together in anonymous categories such as outsider artists or folklorists.[3] The parallel emergence of Roma cultural theorists and researchers is helping position the histories, legacies and identities within infrastructures that support an educational agenda necessary to resist the tendency to create a 'cultural ghetto' of Roma art. There is a palpable presence in the work of the artists in Paradise Lost that takes up this challenge as they interpret for themselves what it is to be Roma. The curator of Paradise Lost, Timea Junghaus, explains: "These artists embrace and transform, deny and deconstruct, oppose and analyse, challenge and overwrite the existing stereotypes in a confident and intellectual manner, reinventing the Roma tradition and its elements as contemporary culture" (2007, p. 21).

Views from Across the Way

The renderings that comprise the chapters in *Being with A/r/tography* profile individual voices and each translates in a different way many of the "points of location" described by the editors that inform these studies. A common characteristic is the various ways that the researchers give form to their inquiries through their art practice and writing–which is the genesis of 'art'/'graphy.' Several themes are broached that cut across the research content covered in the chapters. These include explorations focused on autobiographical accounts and the central role of making art forms as an agency in individual and community inquiry;

the significance of metaphor and other figurative forms of arts language that assist in conceptualizing and realizing forms of research; the collaborative character of research that invests in the creative capital and critical acuity of communities; and the continual questioning that takes place among researchers who seek new ways to define and design research approaches that are truly driven by the issues at hand. These positions are briefly discussed as I add my voice to the circle of conversation opened up by the editors and authors of *Being with A/r/tography*.

Self in the Making

For Carl Leggo it is poetry that helps him to recount and re-visit the past in order to find the sense-of-self necessary to respond with critical clarity to the present. However, Leggo's notion of finding voice is also about the need to sample other voices and to search out alternatives because it is through a multiplicity of voices that forms and images can be brought into sharper focus—and here he uses poetic forms to verbally sketch out positions and possibilities. Leggo uses another distinctive image in considering how autobiographical writing is mostly about dealing with fragments from the past and the way story telling is about dealing with holes and gaps along with the fragments. Here he invokes the image of 'fractals' and says that "perhaps our autobiographical writing is numerous fragments that, like fractals, hold the possibilities of the wholes" (p. 20). This is an important image because it not only helps to see the relationships among the parts and the wholes, but also allows us to consider the similar relational scale between things from the past and the present. In fractal language, this 'self-similarity' suggests that there is no underlying core structure upon which events and stories build, rather these are similar patterns to the factual and fictional accounts we render and these reverberate across time and space. The notion of 'reverberate' is also important because it not only forces a shift in perspective as it shakes up complacent and convenient assumptions, but as Gaston Bachelard (1964) reminds us, reverberation can be considered the opposite to causality. In this sense, it is futile to look to discover the 'causes' of, say, the poetic impulse; rather there is more merit in coming to understand how poetry echoes and reverberates with the insights it offers. Again, the distinctive difference in the purposes and methods of research advocated by A/r/tographers is apparent.

The need to make physical forms by creating visual or verbal images has the benefit of making concrete many of the a/r/tographic principles described by Rita Irwin and Stephanie Springgay in the introduction to the text. Renee Norman is an inquirer who integrates the roles of the teacher-practitioner who responds to everyday opportunities for learning by "doing and making" events that critically reflect on concerns she sees to be important in the learning life of herself and her students. She refers to the way she often creates a "contrapuntal melody" that builds an integrated rhythm of learning activities that lead to knowing and understanding. For me this dialectic is best appreciated if I consider contrapuntal images to be those segmented forms placed on an accordion fold so that when viewed from each side you see quite different scenes, yet when viewed from in front, there is a seamless integration of images. Teaching to this artful rhythm has an elegant appeal. The shards and fragments Pauline Sameshima uses to piece together mosaics of meaning allow her to "learn in my head what my body already recognizes" (pp. 49). For Sean Wiebe the art form takes control because "writing becomes the teacher" (p. 99). For Veronica Gaylie, privileging the process of writing opens up an alternative vision of students typically characterized by the collateral damage of a low ranking school. Using criteria that honour the authenticity of alternative literacies where students are encouraged to write for themselves Gaylie ruptures the notion of a normalcy curve that skews and skewers the minority in relation to the majority.

For Dónal O Donoghue, it is the visual image that carries meaning in ways that other discursive forms cannot. In his chapter on communities of men who teach in elementary schools he takes many photos, and manipulates them in many ways. He creates visual texts that are written and re-written to capture emergent realizations and to disrupt misperceptions. As artworks are research artifacts they can be looked at, critiqued, and interrogated because "these artworks may serve to disrupt or rupture that which we think we know about what it means to be a male teacher at elementary level" (p. 115). He uses images to conceptualize notions of an 'in-between' conceptual space, which is a position his research indicates is readily understood by male teachers in elementary schools for masculinity is not a stable state easily defined as a social construct. Rather it is an open concept that is framed by changing circumstances and situations so it easily slips between the cracks of discussion. However, as O Donoghue acknowledges, the boundaries of discourse "hem these men in and keep them out" (p. 121), but as his photographic essays show, boundaries are also "sites of possibility" (p. 122).

Metaphor and Meaning

Research-centred art-making processes can also be richly metaphorical. For instance, the braided narratives of Erika Hasbe-Ludt, Cynthia Chambers, Antoinette Oberg and Carl Leggo build relational contexts as themes and issues, which are interwoven into narrative webs that are supportive and transformative because of their intersubjective strength. Barbara Bickel's visual journeys explore the intense aesthetic of seeing sisterhood as a collaborative process where sharing and individual ownership are mutually compatible constructs; where contradiction is given collective authority as an emblem of difference and identity. For Marcia McKenzie and Nora Timmerman, the virtual space of the Internet and the interactive opportunities of hypermedia open up creative new ways of re-defining community processes. Here, digital technology is not a 'thing' to be used as a means to an end, but a 'place' in which to reside where conventional parameters don't necessarily apply. This is not unlike the setting of Venice that currently surrounds me with its attendant simulacra of time and space, illusion and pastiche, where the digitally enhanced realities of the Venice Biennale coexist with the trashiest of trinkets and the hyperreal allegories of Titian or Tintoretto. In these complex relational spaces, linear and logical ways of seeing and doing seem remarkably one-dimensional.

239

The consciously creative and critical processes that render art forms as powerful and insightful accounts that can stop us in our tracks is precisely the kind of 'art as research' that Stephanie Springgay advocates. In her search for an ethical and activist practice she clearly distances herself from some arts-based researchers who tend to use the arts mostly as alternative modes of representation. The arts certainly give access to different ways of conceptualizing and communicating information, but this is only part of what the arts do, and if these expressive functions are all that is used then the research mostly amounts to clever forms of social science. As Springgay states, "while many forms of arts-based educational research focus on the creation of artistic products as representations of research, a/r/tographical inquiry is constituted through visual and textual *understandings* and *experiences* rather than visual and textual *representations*" (p. 185 italics in original). Her reference to the art of First Nations Canadian artist Rebecca Belmore gives powerful voice to the aspect of art practice that is distinctive and powerful that anyone who works in a studio space or is physically involved in a deep engaged way with art making in any form knows—creating with forms, intentions, drives, and ideas is a provocative and intensely unknowing process that engages the whole body as what is known comes face to face with what is not and this propels the inquiry.

Cultural Creativity and Community Critique

The centrality and power of the arts as agencies of human understanding and community processes is at the creative and critical core of a/r/tography. This is given full focus by Rita Irwin and the community colleagues involved in the Richgate project. What is being learned is not only about the significance of cultural hybridity and social understanding, but also about the difficult reality in developing research processes that seek to reconceptualize learning and inquiry through transformation. For instance, there are cautions to be considered concerning assumptions about interventions in communities. As experienced field researchers, those directing the Richgate project were mindful of their positionality and authority, yet they rightly realize that when artists and art practices become part of the language of research, then other concerns about perception, reification and power relations arise. Further, if the purpose is to move toward an informed state of new understanding then anything other than a critically engaged perspective will probably end up as an exercise in cultural reproduction. Irwin describes a/r/tography as living inquiry and an a/r/tographic community of practice as a "community of inquirers working as artists, researchers and pedagogues committed to personal engagement within a community of belonging who trouble and address difference" (p. 72).

In her compelling account of the construction of difference within school contexts in post apartheid South Africa Darlene Swanson modelled the process of a/r/tography as a form of living inquiry. For Swanson the emerging process of engagement and realization "offers freedom in the search for shadows that collapse, even as they mark out, the self-other binary, and grants us opportunities to speak with the ghosts that haunt our ethical commitments and good intentions defined by the personal activism in our research" (p. 185). Sylvia Kind, in her chapter on *Learning to Listen*, reminds us that learning to become a person, a teacher, or a researcher, is a traumatic process where 'failure' is a necessary element in coming to know oneself. She picks up on the philosophical notion that bears out ancient wisdom, which holds that teaching is more about self-learning rather than imparting knowledge. This is also true of doing research itself because there are continual reflective and reflexive processes at play as questions and queries are turned back onto the researcher as much as the research.

Ongoing Conversations about Research Practice

In their chapter on *Dialoguing Scripted Data*, David Beare and George Belliveau raise the intriguing issue of "fictional data" as they use information collected through their research and use that as the content for crafting composite factual and fictional accounts that are played out in scenarios in dramatic scripts. Beare and Belliveau prevaricate somewhat over the notion that they may be accused of fabricating data. This, however, is not really at issue. In fact, as researchers using artistic processes they not only have the right, but also the responsibility to 'push' the interpretation of the data into new forms. It is only through a creative interpretation that new ways of looking at existing phenomenon can be taken up–the important scholarly element for Beare and Belliveau to remember is that when they take back to the field the critical insights gained it is this new knowledge that needs to be qualified in relation to what is known and not known. This is what I mean when I describe the use of artmaking processes within contexts of inquiry that require researchers to create and critique phenomenon. This is the point I end with in *Art Practice as Research*, where I acknowledge "the messy resistance of new understanding relies on the rationality of intuition and the imagination of the intellect and these are the kind of mindful processes used in art practice as research" (2005, p. 226).

Overhearing the free-flowing conversations with Peter Gouzouasis and his research students is a reward and a reminder: I am rewarded by the insights revealed about the complex issues surrounding the efficacy of a/r/tographic research, and I am reminded of the realities of the political discourse surrounding research accountability. The dilemma of maintaining an improvisational agility that is responsive to the research contexts, and the need to be mindful of the flexibility of the arts in informing theory and practice, frames these discussions. A working conclusion is reached that perhaps there is little merit in adapting approaches to concerns such as validity that are based on scientific research because the reasoning is antithetical to the ways the arts are conceived and presented. Consequently it is not so much a falsificationist perspective that should be invoked, but rather a more consensual approach—and here an impressive array of strategies are rolled out that have been applied in various qualitative contexts. This line of argument rightly highlights the elusive process of dealing in doubly abstract forms if the units of variability in any inquiry are quantitative because in these cases one never really 'measures' the impact of any intervention–rather the strategy is to assess the probability that it was *not* error that influenced the change in what was observed. Peter Gouzouasis suggests there is more merit to be had if the effort is directed towards reaching consensus through corroboration and collective agreement. Given these different options I find inquiry in the arts still to be very much grounded in finding forms that emerge from the rhythm of oppositional tension as much as the improvisational response to find a common edge. I guess I am suspicious of the overall quest to find resolution through consensus among what may be competing artifacts of evidence, mostly because of the human tendency to find support for one's views, whether it is there or not. I like the messy ontological landscape that Gouzouasis and other a/r/tographers in this text are scouring over because the questioning and skeptical attitude speaks to a creative impulse and a critical attitude that not only disrupts and debates, but opens up the possibility to see things differently–and this is very much what the arts have to offer to human understanding.

Conclusion

If one of the purposes of the editors of *Being with A/r/tography* is to open up conversations and relationships through research, whereby an opening is not only seen as a rupture or incision, but also as an opportunity to creatively and critically explore new possibilities, then it has succeeded in provoking a response from outside their circle of discourse. The chapters in the text are not prescriptions of 'how to' undertake a/r/tography—they are incomplete gestures, thoughtfully compiled, that point to new possibilities–but it's up to readers and interpreters to add meaning of their own. This is not a textbook that is solely instructional–it's impressionistic and you need to fill in your own outlines. In listening in to these conversations about 'raw' material being collected in different contexts of inquiry and enlivened by being braided into new forms and perspectives, I was reminded of why I enjoy collecting things from the streets to be later turned into artworks in the studio, and later returning to install them in the streets.[45] There is something real about not knowing at the time why a decision was made, but having a felt need that an object or image may hold significance and meaning that may be revealed later. When artistic practice is used within the context of inquiry, there is an investment in the potential that insight may emerge as a reflexive action sparked by a creative impulse that can help to see things in a critically different way.

One of the joys of changing perspectives by physically re-locating to an alternative space for an extended period of time is the conceptual disruption it causes. Even as a temporary insider one's response to things seen and felt is inevitably changed. This is especially so when it is further disrupted by viewing artworks transported from around the globe that are re-sited within pavilions, former dockyard buildings, temporary white cubes, and historic palazzo spaces as happens during the Venice Biennale. Old and new, traditional and innovative, conventional and controversial, as all perspectives are invoked. Yet it is in the uncertainty and tension among these states of mind that are provoked and the realization that outcomes at best are imprecise but insightful glimpses into alternative visions that holds promise. Perhaps the critically important, if elusive goal, the writers in *Being with A/r/tography* set for themselves can be best captured by a Streetworks projection that was part of a series I installed while in Venice. This time it was images rather than and objects that were collected from the streets, or the Grand Canal in this case, as digital photographs of palaces were taken and then re-situated by being projected at night onto canals throughout Venice. Perhaps this image of the mutability of tradition and gentle intervention reflects the capacity of artful inquiry to disrupt assumptions so as to see things in new contexts.

Figure 2. Graeme Sullivan. Streetwork: Venetian Palazzo Projections, July, 2007, Venice, Italy. Reproduced courtesy of the artist.

NOTES

[1] See, for example, Linda Tuhiwai Smith, (1999), *Decolonizing methodologies: Research and indigenous peoples.*

[2] "Roma" is the consensus term used to denote Gypsy, however, Timea Junghaus notes, Roma may be the politically correct term, but it does not describe all the groups of Gypsies. He adds: "I consider it far less important to use a politically correct term than to clean the word "Gypsy" of prejudices and negative stereotypes, and to rehabilitate it by employing it in positive contexts" (2007, p. 23).

GRAEME SULLIVAN

[3] The fifteen participating artists in Paradise Lost include: Daniel Baker, Tibor Balogh, Mihaela Cimpeanu, Gabi Jiménez, András Kallai, Damian Le Bas, Delaine Le Bas, Kiba Lumberg, Omara, Marian Petre, Nihad Nino Pusija, Jenö André Raatzsch, Dusan Ristic, István Szentandrássy, Norbert Szirmai/János Révésv.

[4] See www.streetworksart.com

REFERENCES

Abalos, David. (1998). *La communidad in the United States*. Westport, CT: Praeger.

Agamben, G. (1993). *The coming community*. (M. Hardt, Trans.). Minneapolis, MN: University of Minnesota Press. (original work published 1990)

Ahmed, S. (2000). *Strange encounters: Embodied others in post-coloniality*. London, UK: Routledge.

Ahmed, S. (2002). This other and other others. *Economy and Society, 31*(4), 558-572.

Alexie, S. (2005). *The Lone Ranger and Tonto fistfight in heaven*. New York: Grove Press.

Allan, J. (1993). Male elementary school teachers: experiences and perspectives. In C. Williams (Ed.), *Doing women's work: Men in nontraditional occupations* (pp. 113-127). Newberry Park CA: Sage.

Alverman, D. E. (2000). Researching libraries, literacies, and lives: A rhizoanalysis. In E. A. St. Pierre & W. Pillow (Eds.), *Feminist poststructural theory and methods in education* (pp. 114-129). NY: Routledge.

Alvesson, M. (2002). *Postmodernism and social research*. Philadelphia, OH: Open University Press.

Amis, M. (2000). *Experience*. New York: Hyperion.

Anderson, K. T. (1999). Ethnographic hypermedia: Transcending thick descriptions. In *Sights: Visual Anthropology Forum*. Retrieved June 22, 2006, from http://cc.joensuu.fi/sights

Ang, I. (2001). *On not speaking Chinese: Living between Asia and the West*. New York: Routledge.

Aoki, T. T. (1992). In the midst of slippery theme-words: Living as designers of Japanese Canadian curriculum. An invited paper presented at Designing Japanese Canadian Curriculum Conference held on May 21-23, 1992, at the Novotel Hotel, North York, ON, Canada. In W. Pinar, & R. L. Irwin (Eds.). (2005). *Curriculum in a new key: The collected works of Ted T. Aoki.* (pp. 263-277) Mahwah, NJ: Lawrence Erlbaum.

Aoki, T. T., Low, M., & Palulis, P. (2001). *Re-reading metonymic moments with/in living pedagogy*. Paper presented at the American Educational Research Association Annual Meeting, Seattle, WA.

Arendt, H. (1958). *The human condition*. Chicago, IL: The University of Chicago Press.

Arendt, H. (1968). *Between past and future*. New York: Penguin Books..

Atkinson, P. (1992). *Understanding ethnographic texts*. London: Sage.

Atwood, M. (1995). Marsh languages. In M. Atwood (Ed.). (1995). *Morning in the burned house.* (p.54). Toronto, ON.: McClelland & Stewart.

Ayers, W. (1988). Fact or fancy: The knowledge base quest in teacher education. *Journal of Teacher Education, 39*(5), 24-31.

Bal, M. (2002). *Traveling concepts in the humanities*. Toronto, ON: University of Toronto Press.

Bachelard, G. (1964). The poetics of space. New York: The Orion Press.

Barone, T. (2000). *Aesthetics, politics, and educational inquiry: Essays and examples.* NY: Peter Lang.

Barone, T. (2001a). Science, art and the predispositions of educational researchers, *Educational Researcher, 30*(7), 24-28.

Barone, T. (2001b). *Touching eternity: The enduring outcomes of teaching.* New York, NY: Teachers College Press.

Barone, T. (2003). Challenging the educational imaginary: Issues of form, substance, and quality in film-based research. *Qualitative Inquiry, 9*(2), 202-217.

Bataille, G. (1985). *Visions of excess: Selected writings 1927-1939.* (A.Stoekl, Trans.). Minnesota, MN: The University of Minnesota Press.

Battle, M. (1997). *Reconciliation: The ubuntu theology of Desmond Tutu.* Cleveland: Pilgrim Press.

Bauman, Z. (1993). *Postmodern ethics.* Cambridge, MA: Blackwell Publishers.

Beare, D. (2002). *Therapeutic theatre: The weaving of self and theatre-A performative inquiry of the collaborative play-creating process and optimal adolescent development.* Unpublished master's thesis, University of British Columbia, Vancouver, Canada.

Beard, C.A. (1909). Tendencies affecting the size of the ballot. *Proceedings of the American Political Science Association,* Vol. 6 Sixth annual meeting, 93-99.

Beattie, M. (1995). The making of a music: The construction and reconstruction of teacher's personal practical knowledge during inquiry. *Curriculum Inquiry, 25* (2), 133-150.

Beattie, M. (2004). *Narratives in the making: Teaching and learning at Corktown community high school.* Toronto, ON: University of Toronto Press.

Becker, C. (2002). *Surpassing the spectacle: Global transformations and the changing politics of art.* Boulder, CO: Rowman & Littlefield.

Becker, H. (1982). *Artworlds.* Berkeley, CA: University of California Press.

Beer, R. (1999). *Landscape and identity: Three artist/teachers in British Columbia.* Unpublished doctoral dissertation, The University of British Columbia, Vancouver, Canada.

Beittel, K. R. (1985). Art for a new age. *Visual Arts Research, 11*(1), 90-104.

Beittel, K. R. (1989). *Zen and the art of pottery.* New York: Weatherhill.

Beittel, K. R., & Beittel, J. (1991). *A celebration of art and consciousness.* State College, PA: Happy Valley Healing Arts.

Bella, D., & Mason, B. (1998). Hypermedia and ethnography: Reflections on the construction of a research approach. *Sociological Research Online, 3*(3). Retrieved June 21, 2006, from www.socresonline.org.uk

Belliveau, G. (2004a). Pre-service teachers engage in collective drama. *English Quarterly,* 35(3), 1-6.

246

REFERENCES

Belliveau, G. (2004b). Struggle to success: Collective drama on anti-bullying. *Canadian Theatre Review*, 117, 42-44.

Belliveau, G. (2005). An arts-based approach to teach social justice: Drama as a way to address bullying in schools. *International Journal of Arts Education*, 3, 136-165.

Belliveau, G. (2006a) Collective playbuilding: Using arts-based research to understand a social justice drama process in teacher education. *International Journal of Education & the Arts*. (7)5. Retrieved March 26, 2007, from http://ijea.asu.edu/v7n5

Belliveau, G. (2006b). Using drama to achieve social justice: Anti-bullying project in elementary schools. *Universal Mosaic of Drama and Theatre - IDEA Publications*, 5, 325-336.

Benso, S. (2000). *The face of things: A different side of ethics.* New York: State University of New York Press.

Berry, A. (2004). Self-study in teaching about teaching. In J. J. Loughran, M. L.Hamilton, V. Kubler LaBoskey & T. Russell (Eds.), *International handbook of self-study of teaching and teacher education practices* (pp.1295-1332). Norwell, MA: Kluwer Academic Publishers.

Berry, W. (2002). *Window poems.* In N. Wirzba (Ed.). *The art of the commonplace: The agrarian essays of Wendell Berry.* (p.viii). Washington, DC: Shoemaker & Hoard.

Bhabha, H. K. (1994). *The location of culture.* London: Routledge.

Bhabha, H. K. (2004). *The location of culture.* (2nd ed.). New York: Routledge.

Bickel, B. (2004). *From artist to a/r/tographer: An autoethnographic ritual inquiry into writing on the body.* Unpublished master's thesis. The University of British Columbia, Vancouver, Canada.

Bickel, B. (2005). From artist to A/r/tographer: An autoethnographic ritual inquiry into writing on the body. *Journal of Curriculum & Pedagogy, 2*(2), 8-17.

Bickel, B., & Fisher, V. D. (2005). Awakening the divine feminine: A stepmother-daughter collaborative journey through art-making and ritual. *Journal of the Association for Research on Mothering, 7*(1), 52-67.

Bickel, B., & Sheppard, J. (1995). *The art and poetry of sisters.* Calgary, AB: In Search of Fearlessness Press.

Bickel, B. & Fisher, R. M. (2006). Presence and precedence: Staying close to ground zero in art/research/education. Manuscript submitted for publication.

Biella, P. (Ed.). (1997) *Yanomamö interactive: The ax fight CD-ROM.* With N. A. Chagnon and G. Seaman. Fort Worth: Harcourt Brace. Retrieved July 25, 2006, from www.anth.ucsb.edu/projects/axfight/updates/biellaintroduction.html

Bird, E. (2000). Research in art and design: The first decade. *Working Papers in Art and Design, 1.* Retrieved July 24, 2005 from http://www.herts.ac.uk/artdes1/research/papers/wpades/vol1/bird1.html

Blanchot, M. (1988). *The unavowable community.* (P. Joris, Trans.). Barrytown, NY: Station Hill.

Blumenfeld-Jones, D. S. (1995). Dance as a mode of research representation. *Qualitative Inquiry, 1*(4), 391-401.

Boler, M. (1999). *Feeling power: Emotions and education.* New York, NY: Routledge.

Bolter, J. D. (2001). *Writing space: Computers, hypertext, and the remediation of print* (2nd ed.). Mahwah, NJ: Lawrence Erlbaum.

Booth, D. (2005). *Story drama: Creating stories through role playing, improvising and reading aloud (2nd ed.).* Markham, ON: Houghton Mifflin.

Bourdieu P. (1996). *The rules of art: Genesis and structure of the literary field.* (S. Emanuel, Trans.). Cambridge: Polity.

Bourriaud, N. (2001). *Post production.* New York: Lukas & Sternberg.

Bourriaud, N. (2002). *Relational aesthetics.* (S. Pleasance & F. Woods with M. Copeland, Trans.). Paris: Les presses du réel. [Electronic version also available] Retrieved Nov. 15, 2005 from http://www.gairspace.org.uk/htm/bourr.htm

Bourriaud, N. (2004). *Berlin letter about relational aesthetics.* In C. Doherty (Ed). *Contemporary art: From studio to situation* (pp. 43-49). London: Black Dog Publishing.

Borradori, G. (2003). *Philosophy in a time of terror: Dialogues with Jürgen Habermas and Jacques Derrida.* Chicago: The University of Chicago Press.

Botstein, L. (1998). What role for the arts? In W.Ayers & J.L. Miller (Eds.), *A light in dark times: Maxine Green and the unfinished conversation* (pp. 62-70). New York: Teachers College Press.

Brandt, D. (1990). *Literacy as involvement: The acts of writers, readers and texts.* Carbondale, IL: Southern Illinois University Press.

Britzman, D. P. (1998). *Lost subjects, contested objects: Towards a psychoanalytic inquiry of learning.* Albany: SUNY Press.

Britzman, D. (2003a). *Practice makes practice: A critical study of learning to teach* (revised ed.). New York: SUNY Press. (Original work published 1990)

Britzman, D. (2003b). *After-education: Anna Freud, Melanie Klein, and psychoanalytic histories of learning.* Albany: SUNY Press.

Brown, N. (2000). The representation of practice. *Working Papers in Art and Design,* Vol. 1 . Retrieved July 24, 2005 from University of Hertfordshire Web site: http://www.herts.ac.uk/artdes1/research/papers/wpades/vol1/brown2full.html

Buber, M. (1996). *I and thou: A new translation, with a prologue and notes.* (W. Kaufmann, Trans.). NY, New York: Touchstone.

Bullock, A. (1990). *Hitler: A study in tyranny.* London: Penguin Books. (Original work published 1952)

Bullough, Jr., R. V. and S. Pinnegar. (2001). Guidelines for quality in autobiographical forms of self-study research. *Educational Researcher.* 30 (3), 13-21.

Bullough, Jr., R. V. Jr., Knowles, J. G., & Crow, N. A. (1991). *Emerging as a teacher.* London, UK: Routledge Kegan.

Burbules, N. C. (1998). Rhetorics of the web: Hyperreading and critical literacy. In I. Snyder (Ed.), *Page to screen: Taking literacy into the electronic era.* (pp. 102-122). New York, NY: Routledge.

Burbules, N. C., & Callister, T. (1996). Knowledge at the crossroads: Some alternative futures of hypertext learning environment, *Educational Theory, 46*(1), 23-50.

Burbules, N. C., & Lambeir, B. (2003). The importance of new technologies in promoting collaborative educational research. In P. Smeyers & M. Depaepe (Eds.), *Beyond empiricism: On criteria for educational research.* (pp. 41-52). Leuven, Belgium: University Press of Leuven.

Buss, H. M. (2005). Katie.com: My story: Memoir writing, the internet, and embodied discursive agency. In M. Kadar, L. Warley, J. Perreault, S. Egan (Eds.), *Tracing the autobiographical* (pp.9-23). Waterloo: Wilfred Laurier University Press.

Butler, J. (2006). Sexual difference as a question of ethics: Alterities of the flesh in Irigaray and Merleau-Ponty. In D. Olkowski & G. Weiss (Eds.). *Feminist interpretations of Maurice Merleau-Ponty* (pp. 107-125). University Park, PA: The Pennsylvania State University Press.

Campbell, J. (1972). *Myths to live by.* New York: Bantam Books.

Campbell, D. T. & Stanley, J. C. (1963). Experimental and quasi-experimental designs for research. Boston, MA: Houghton Mifflin Company.

Caputo, J. D. (2000). *More radical hermeneutics: On not knowing who we are.* Bloomington, IN: Indiana University Press.

Carrington, B. (2002). A quintessentially feminine domain? Constructions of primary teaching as a career. *Educational Studies, 28*(3), 287-303.

Carson, T. R., & Sumara, D. J. (Eds.). (1997). *Action research as a living practice.* New York: Peter Lang.

Chabon, M. (2000). The recipe for life. *Organ: Collecting the uncollected.* Retrieved April 1, 2006, from http://www.michaelchabon.com/archives/2005/03/the_recipe_for.html

Christians, C. (2003). Ethics and politics in qualitative research. In N. Denzin & Y. Lincoln (Eds.). *The landscape of qualitative research* (pp. 208-243). New York: Sage.

Clarke, A., Erickson, G., Collins, S., & Phelan, A. (2005). Complexity science and cohorts in teacher education. *Studying Teacher Education, 1*(2). 159-177.

Clifford, J. (1997). *Routes: Travel and translation in the late twentieth century.* Cambridge, MA: Harvard University Press.

Clifford, J., & Marcus, G. E. (Eds.). (1986). *Writing culture: The poetics and politics of ethnography.* Berkeley, CA: University of California Press.

Coffey, A., Holbrook, B., & Atkinson, P. (1996). Qualitative data analysis: Technologies and representations. *Sociological Research Online, 1*(1). Retrieved June 21, 2006, from www.socresonline.org.uk

Cole, A. L. (1990a). Personal theories of teaching: Development in the formative years. *Alberta Journal of Educational Research, 36*(3), 203-222.

Cole, A.L. (1990b, April) *Teachers' experienced knowledge: A continuing study.* Paper presented at the Annual Meeting of the American Educational Research Association, Boston, MA.

Cole, A.L. (2004). Provoked by art. In A. Cole, L. Neilsen, J.G. Knowles, & T. Luciani (Eds.) *Provoked by art: Theorizing arts-informed research.* (Vol. 2, Arts-informed research series). (pp. 11-17). Halifax, NS: Backalong Books & Centre for Arts-informed Research.

Cole, A. L., & Knowles, J. G. (2000). *Researching teaching: Exploring teacher development through reflexive inquiry.* New York: Alynn & Bacon.

Cole, A.L. & Knowles, J. G.(2001). *Lives in context: The art of life history research.* Walnut Creek, CA: Altamira Press

Collins, B. (2001). *Sailing alone around the room: New and selected poems.* New York: Random House.

Conklin, J. (1987). Hypertext: An introduction and survey. *IEEE Computer, 20*(9), 17-41.

Connell, R.W. (1995). *Masculinities.* Berkeley, CA: University of California Press.

Connell, R. W. (2000). *The men and the boys.* Berkeley, CA: University of California Press.

Conway, J. K. (1998). *When memory speaks: Exploring the art of autobiography.* New York: Random House.

Coover, R. (2004). Working with images, images of work: Using digital interface, photographs, and hypertext in ethnography. In S. Pink, L. Kurti, & A. I. Afonso (Eds.), *Working images: Visual research and representation in ethnography* (pp. 185-203). London: Routledge.

Coulter, R. P. & McNay, M. (1993). Exploring men's experiences as elementary school teachers. *Canadian Journal of Education, 18*(4), 398-413.

Cowley, P., & Easton, S.T. (2002). *Report card on British Columbia's secondary schools.* Vancouver: Fraser Institute.

Crane, D. (1989). Reward systems in avant-garde art: Social networks and stylistic change. In A. W. Foster & J.R. Blau (Eds.), *Art and society: readings in the sociology of the arts (*pp. 261-278*).* New York: State University of New York Press.

Creely, R. (1985). *Selected Poems,* New York: Charles Scribner's Sons.

Csikszentmihalyi, M. (1990). *Flow: The psychology of optimal experience.* New York: Harper & Row.

Cureton, E. E. (1951). Validity. In E. F. Lindquist (Ed.), *Educational measurement* (pp. 621-694). Washington, DC: American Council on Education.

Dahlberg, G., Moss, P. & Pence, A. (1999). *Beyond quality in early childhood education and care.* London: Falmer Press.

REFERENCES

Darts, D. (2004). *Visual culture jam: Art, pedagogy and creative resistance.* Unpublished doctoral dissertation, The University of British Columbia, Vancouver, Canada.

David, C. & Rogoff, I. (2004). In conversation. In C. Doherty (Ed.), *Contemporary art: From studio to situation* (pp. 81-89). London: Black Dog Publishing.

Davidson, A. E., Walton, P. L., & Andrews, J. (2003). *Border crossings: Thomas King's cultural inversions.* Toronto, ON: University of Toronto Press.

Davies, B. (2000). *A body of writing: 1990-1999.* Walnut Creek, CA: Alta Mira Press.

Davis, B. (2004). *Inventions of teaching: A genealogy.* Mahwah, NJ: Lawrence Erlbaum.

Davis, B., & Sumara, D. (2006). *Complexity and education: Inquiries into learning, teaching, and research.* Mahwah, NJ: Lawrence Erlbaum.

Davis, B., Sumara, D., & Luce-Kapler, R. (2000). *Engaging minds: Learning and teaching in a complex world.* Mahwah, NJ: Lawrence Erlbaum.

de Cosson, A. F. (2001). Anecdotal sculpting: Learning to learn, one from another. *JCT: Journal of Curriculum Theorizing, 17*(4), 173-183.

de Cosson, A. F..(2002). The hermeneutic dialogue: Finding patterns amid the aporia of the artist/researcher/teacher. *The Alberta Journal of Educational Research, XLVIII* (3), CD-ROM.

de Cosson, A.F. (2003). *(Re)searching sculpted a/r/tography: (Re)learning subverted-knowing through aporetic praxis.* Unpublished doctoral dissertation, The University of British Columbia, Vancouver, Canada.

de Cosson, A.F. (2004). The hermeneutic dialogic: Finding patterns amid the aporia of the Artist/Researcher/Teacher (Rewrite #10 in this context). In R. L. Irwin and A. de Cosson (Eds.), *A/r/tography: rendering self through arts-based living inquiry.* (pp. 127-152). Vancouver, BC: Pacific Educational Press.

de Cosson, A., Irwin, R. L., Grauer, K., & Wilson, S. (2003, July). Hanging identities: Artist's dancing interruptions into corridors of learning. A performance/paper presented at the *International Conference on Imagination and Education*, Vancouver, Canada. Retrieved January 1, 2006, from http://www.ierg.net/pub_conf2003.html

de Cosson, A., Irwin, R. L., Kind, S., & Springgay, S. (in press). Walking in wonder. In J.G. Knowles, A. Cole, & T. Luciani (Eds.). *The art of visual inquiry.* Halifax, NS: Backalong Books.

De Freitas, N. (2002). Towards a definition of studio documentation: Working tool and transparent method. *Selected working papers in art & design* (Vol. 2). Retrieved July 26, 2005, from University of Hertfordshire Web site: http://www.herts.ac.uk/artdes1/research/papers/wpades/vol2/freitas.html

Dean, T. & Millar, J. (2005). *Art works: Place.* New York: Thames and Hudson

Deleuze, G. (1993). *The Fold: Leibniz and the baroque.* Minneapolis, MN: University of Minnesota Press.

Deleuze, G. & Guattari, F. (1983). *On the line.* (J. Johnson, Trans.). New York: Semiotext(e).

Deleuze, G. & Guattari, F. (1987). *A Thousand plateaus: Capitalism and schizophrenia.* Minneapolis, MN: University of Minnesota Press.

Deleuze, G. & Guattari, F.. (1994). *What is philosophy?* New York: Columbia University Press.

Denzin, N. K. (1998). The art and politics of interpretation. In N. K. Denzin & Y. Lincoln (Eds.), *Collecting and interpreting qualitative materials* (pp. 313-344). Thousand Oaks, CA: Sage.

Denzin, N.K. (2005). Emancipatory discourses and the ethics and politics of interpretation. In N. K. Denzin & Y. S. Lincoln (Eds.), *The Sage handbook of qualitative research* (3rd ed., pp. 933-958). Thousand Oaks, CA: Sage.

Denzin, N.K., & Lincoln, Y.S. (2000). Introduction: The discipline and practice of qualitative research. In N. K Denzin & Y. S. Lincoln (Eds.), *Handbook of qualitative research* (2nd ed., pp. 1-29). Thousand Oaks, CA: Sage Publications.

Denzin, N.K. & Lincoln, Y.S.. (1998). *The landscape of qualitative research.* Thousand Oaks, CA: Sage.

Derrida, J. (1978). *Writing and difference.* Chicago, Il: University of Chicago Press.

Derrida, J. (1993). *Aporias: Dying-awaiting (one another at) the "limits of truth"* (T. Dutoit, Trans.). Stanford, CA: Stanford University Press.

Derrida, J. (1994). *Spectres of Marx.* London: Routledge.

Dewey, J. (1933). *How we think: A restatement of the relation of reflective thinking to the educative process.* Boston, MA: Heath.

Dias, B., & Sinkinson, S. (2005). Film spectatorship between queer theory and feminism: Transcultural readings. *International Journal of Education and the Arts, 1*(2), 143-152.

Dicks, B., & Mason, B. (1998). Hypermedia and ethnography: Reflections on the construction of a research approach. *Sociological Research Online, 3*(3). Retrieved June 21, 2006, from www.socresonline.org.uk/socresonline/3/3/3.html

Dicks, B., Mason, B., Coffey, A. & Atkinson, P. (2005) *Qualitative research and hypermedia: Ethnography in the digital age.* London: Sage.

Dietrich, M. (2001). *Marlene Dietrich: Mythos und legende* (Myth and legend) [CD]. London: EMI Records.

Disch, L. J. (1996). *Hannah Arendt and the limits of philosophy.* Ithaca, NY: Cornell University Press.

Doherty, C. (Ed.). (2004). *Contemporary art: From studio to situation.* London: Black Dog Publishing.

Doll Jr., W. E. (2005). The culture of method. In W. E. Doll Jr., M. J. Fleener, D. Trueit, & J. St. Julien (Eds.). *Chaos, complexity, curriculum and culture: A conversation* (pp. 21-76). New York: Peter Lang.

Donmoyer, R. & Yennie-Donmoyer, J. (1995). Data as drama: Reflections on the use of readers' theatre as a mode of qualitative data display. *Qualitative Inquiry, 1*(4), 402-428.

Driver, T. F. (1997). *Liberating Rites: Understanding the transformative power of ritual*. Boulder, CO: Westview Press.

Duncan, B. J. (1997). Hypertext and education: (Post?)structural transformations. *Philosophy of Education Society Yearbook*, Retrieved June 19, 2006 from University of Illinois at Urbana-Champaign website: www.ed.uiuc.edu/eps/PES-Yearbook/97

Dunlop, R. (1999). *Boundary bay: A novel as educational research*. Unpublished doctoral dissertation, The University of British Columbia, Vancouver, Canada.

Dunn, S. (1994). *New and Selected Poems* 1974-1994. New York: W.W. Norton & Company.

Eakin, J.P. (1999). *How our lives become stories*. Ithaca, NY: Cornell University Press.

Eisenhauer, J. (2006). Beyond bombardment: Subjectivity, visual culture, and art education. *Studies in Art Education, 47*(2), 155-169.

Eisner, E. W. (2001). Concerns and aspirations for qualitative research in the new millennium. *Qualitative research, 1*(2), 135-145.

Eisner, E. W. (1991). *The enlightened eye: Qualitative inquiry and the enhancement of educational practice*. New York: Macmillan.

Eisner, E. W. (1997). The promise and perils of alternative forms of data representation. *Educational Researcher, 26*(6), 4-10.

Eisner, E. W. & Barone, T. (1997). Arts-based educational research. In R. M. Jaeger (Ed.), *Complementary methods for research in education* (pp. 73-79). AERA. Washington, DC.

Ellis, C. & Bochner, A.P. (2000). Autoethnography, personal narrative, reflexivity: Researcher as subject. In N.K. Denzin & Y.S. Lincoln, (Eds.), *Handbook of qualitative research.(2nd ed.),* (pp. 733-768). Thousand Oaks, CA: Sage.

Ellsworth, E. (1997). *Teaching positions: Difference, pedagogy, and the power of address*. New York: Teachers College Press.

Ellsworth, E. (2005). *Place of learning: Media, architecture, pedagogy*. NY: Routledge/Farmer.

Emme, M. (1999). Unruly research: Visuality in the academy. *Canadian Review of Research in Art Education, 26*(1), 34-43.

Felman, S., & Laub, D. (1992). *Testimony: Crises of witnessing in literature, psychoanalysis, and history*. NY: Routledge.

Fels, L. (1999). *In the wind, clothes dance on a line: Performative inquiry, a (re)search methodology: Possibilities and absences within a space-moment of imagining a universe*. Unpublished doctoral dissertation, The University of British Columbia, Vancouver,Canada.

Fenman Orenstein, G. (1987). The reemergence of the archetype of the goddess in art by contemporary women. In H. Robinson (Ed.), *Visibly female feminism and art today: An anthology. (pp. 160-161)*. London: Camden.

Finley, S., & Knowles, J. G. (1995). Researcher as artist/ artist as researcher. *Qualitative Inquiry, 1(1),* 110-142.

Foster, H. (1996). *The return of the real: The avant-garde at the end of the century.* Cambridge, MA: MIT Press.

Foucault, M. (1980). *Power/knowledge: Selected interviews and other writings (1972-1977).* In C. Gordon (Ed.). New York, NY: Pantheon Books.

Fox, M. (1988). *The coming of the cosmic Christ.* NY: Harper & Row.

Freire, P. (1998). *Pedagogy of freedom: Ethics, democracy and civic courage.* Lanhman, MD: Rowman and Littlefield.

Freire, P. (1999). *Pedagogy of hope: Reliving pedagogy of the oppressed.* New York: Continuum. (Original work published 1992).

Freire, P. (2000). *Pedagogy of the oppressed (30th anniversary ed.).* New York: Continuum. (Original work published 1973)

Froese-Germaine, B. (2002, June). Coming to a school near you: Fraser institute rankings of Canadian high schools. *Canadian Teachers Federation.* http://www.ctffce.ca/e/WHAT/OTHER/ASSESSMENT/fraserinstitute-art.htm

Fulford, R. (1999). *The triumph of narrative: Storytelling in the age of mass culture.* Toronto: Anansi.

Fynsk, C. (1991/2004). Foreword: Experiences of finitude. In P.Connor (Ed). *The Inoperative Community.* (P.Connor, L. Garbus, M. Holland, S. Sawhney, Trans.). Minneapolis, MN: University of Minnesota Press.

Gadamer, H. G. (1981). *Reason in the age of science.* (F.G. Lawrence, Trans.). Cambridge, MA: MIT Press.

Gadamer, H.G. (2004). *Truth and method.* (D. Marshall & J. Weinsheimer, Trans.). (2nd revised ed.). London: Continuum (Original work published 1960; first published 1975; second edition 1989)

Galeano, E. (1991). *A book of embraces* (C. Belfrage with M. Schafer, Trans.). New York: W.W. Norton.

Gandini, L., Hill, L., Cadwell, L., & Schwall, C. Eds.). (2005). *In the spirit of the studio: Learning from the atelier of Reggio Emilia.* New York: Teachers College Press.

Garoian, C. & Gaudelius, Y. (2007). Performing embodiment: Pedagogical intersections of art, technology, and the body. In S. Springgay & D. Freedman (Eds.), *Curriculum and the cultural body* (pp. 3-20). NY: Peter Lang.

Gatens, M. (1996). *Imaginary bodies: Ethics, power and corporeality.* New York: Routledge.

Gebser, J. (1984). *The ever-present origin* (N. Barstad & A. Mickunas, Trans.). Athens, OH: Ohio University Press.

Geertz, C. (1980). Blurred genres. *American Scholar, 49,* 165-179.

REFERENCES

Giroux, H. (1994). *Disturbing pleasures: Learning popular culture.* New York: Routledge.

Giroux, H. (1995). Borderline artists, cultural workers, and the crisis of democracy. In C. Becker & A. Wiens (Eds.), *The artists in society: Rights, roles and responsibilities* (pp. 4-14). Chicago: New Art Examiner.

Giroux, H. (2000). *Impure acts: The practical politics of cultural studies.* New York: Routledge.

Goble, S. (1985). *Symbolism in Johann Sebastian Bach's Saint Matthew Passion.* Unpublished Master's thesis, University of Washington.

Goldstein, T. (2001). Hong Kong, Canada: Playwriting as critical ethnography. *Qualitative Inquiry* 7(3), 279-303.

Gonick, M. (2003). *Between femininities: Ambivalence, identity, and the education of girls.* New York: State University of New York Press.

Gonzalez, J.B. (2006). *Temporary stages.* Portsmouth, NH: Heinemann.

Gordon, E.E. (1986). *Designing objective research in music education.* Chicago: G.I.A.

Gough, N. (1993). Environmental education, narrative complexity and postmodern science/fiction. *International Journal of Science Education, 15*(5), 607-625.

Gouzouasis, P. (2002). *Music narratives: Developmental recapitulations in arts-based educational research.* Unpublished manuscript.

Gouzouasis, P. & Lee, K. V. (2002). Do you hear what I hear? Musicians composing the truth. *Teacher Education Quarterly. 29* (4), 125-141.

Gray, R. & C. Sinding. (2002). *Standing ovation: Performing social science research about cancer.* Walnut Creek, CA: AltaMira Press.

Greco, D. (1995). *Cyborg: Engineering the body electric.* Watertown, MA: Eastgate Systems.

Greene, M. (1995). *Releasing the imagination: Essays on education, the arts, and social change.* San Francisco, CA: Jossey-Bass.

Greene, M. (1994). Postmodernism and the crisis of representation. *English Education, 26*(4), 206-219.

Griffin, S. (1992). *A chorus of stones: The private life of war.* New York: Anchor Books.

Griffin, S. (1995). *The eros of everyday life: Essays on ecology, gender and society.* New York: Doubleday.

Grimes, R. L. (1995). *Beginnings in ritual studies.* Columbia, SC: University of South Carolina Press.

Grosz, E. (1994). *Volatile bodies.* Bloomington, IN: Indiana University Press.

Grosz, E. (2001). *Architecture from the outside: Essays on virtual and real space.* Cambridge, MA: MIT press.

Gruenewald, D. A. (2003). Foundations of place: A multi-disciplinary framework for place conscious education. *American Educational Research Journal, 40*(3), 619-654.

Grumet, M. (1988). *Bitter milk.* Amherst, MA:University of Massachusetts Press.

Haley, A. (2007) Haley describes writing Roots. *Antiquarian Booksellers Association of America.* Retrieved May 03, 2007, from http://search.abaa.org/dbp2/book337282528.html

Hall, J. (2000). Art education and spirituality. In R. Hickman (Ed.), *Art 11-18: Meaning, purpose and direction* (pp. 133-151). London: Continuum.

Hallward, P. (2001). *Absolutely postcolonial: Writing between the singular and the specific.* Manchester, UK: Manchester University Press.

Hand, S. (Ed.). (1998). *The Levinas reader.* Oxford, UK: Blackwell Publishing.

Hare, P. H. (1982). What Pepperian response to Rorty is possible? *Journal of Mind and Behavior, 3,* 217-220.

Hargittay, C. (2004). Within and beyond the wall: Berlin photographs 1957-2003. *Canadian Art, 21*(3), 156-157.

Harper, D. (2001). Online etymology dictionary. Retrieved March 27, 2007 from http://www.etymonline.com

Hasebe-Ludt, E. & Hurren, W. (2003). *Curriculum intertext: Place/language/pedagogy.* NY: Peter Lang.

Hass, R. (Ed. & Trans.). (1994). *The essential haiku: Versions of Basho, Buson & Issa.* Hopewell, NJ: Ecco Press.

Hayles, N. K. (1992). The materiality of informatics. *Configurations, 1*(1), 153-154.

Hayles, N.K. (1999). *How we became posthuman: Virtual bodies in cybernetics, literature, and informatics.* Chicago, IL: University of Chicago Press.

Heath, S.B. (1983). *Ways with words: Language, life, and work in communities and classrooms.* Cambridge, MA: Cambridge University Press:

Heilbrun, C. G. (1999). *Women's lives: The view from the threshold.* Toronto, ON: University of Toronto Press.

Heller, A. (1990). *A philosophy of morals.* Oxford: Blackwell.

Heron, J. (1981). Experiential research methodology. In P. Reason & J. Rowan (Eds.), *Human inquiry: A sourcebook of new paradigm research* (pp. 153-166). Chichester, UK: John Wiley & Sons.

Hesford, W. (1999). *Framing identities: Autobiography and the politics of pedagogy.* Minneapolis, MI: University of Minnesota Press

Hill, L. Stremmel, A. J., Fu, V. R. (2005). *Teaching as inquiry: Rethinking curriculum in early childhood education.* Boston: Pearson Education.

Hillman, J. (1987). *Puer papers*. Dallas, TX: Spring Publications.

hooks, b. (1994). *Teaching to transgress: Education as the practice of freedom*. New York: Routledge.

hooks, b. (1995). *Art on my mind: Visual politics*. New York: The New Press.

Hunt, D. E. (1987). *Beginning with ourselves*. Cambridge, MA: Borderline Books.

Hutchings, M. (2001, December). *Towards a representative teaching profession: Gender*. Paper presented at the Future of the Teaching Profession seminar at the Institute for Public Policy Research, London.

Hwu, W. (1993). *Toward understanding poststructuralism and curriculum*. Unpublished doctoral dissertation. Department of Curriculum and Instruction, Louisiana State University, Baton Rouge, Louisiana, U.S.A.

Irigaray, L. (1985). *When our lips speak together: This sex which is not one* (pp. 205-218). Ithaca, NY: Cornell University Press.

Irvine, K. (2006). *Anticipation* (March 18 - May 20, 2006), exhibition catalogue. Chicago, IL: Museum of Contemporary Photography.

Irwin, R. L. (2004a). A/r/tography: A metonymic métissage. In Irwin, R. L. & de Cosson, A. (Eds.). *A/r/tography: Rendering self through arts-based living inquiry* (pp. 27-38). Vancouver, BC: Pacific Educational Press.

Irwin, R. L. (2003). Towards an aesthetic of unfolding in/sights through curriculum. *Journal of the Canadian Association for Curriculum Studies, 1*(2), 63-78 Retrieved January 1, 2006 at: http://www.csse.ca/CACS/JCACS/PDF%20Content/07._Irwin.pdf

Irwin, R. L. (2004b). Unfolding aesthetic in/sights between curriculum and pedagogy. *Journal of Curriculum and Pedagogy 1*(2), 43-48.

Irwin, R. L. (2006). Walking to create an aesthetic and spiritual currere. *Visual Arts Research, 32*(1), 75-82.

Irwin, R. L. (2007). Plumbing the depths of being fully alive. In L. Bresler (Ed.), *The international handbook on research in arts education*. Dordecht, NL: Springer.

Irwin, R. L., Beer, R., Springgay, S., Grauer, K., Xiong, G., & Bickel, B. (2006). The rhizomatic relations of a/r/tography. *Studies in Art Education. 48*(1), 70-88.

Irwin, R. L., Crawford, N., Mastri, R., Neale, A., Robertson, H., & Stephenson, W. (1997). Collaborative action research: A journey of six women artist-pedagogues. *Collaborative Inquiry in a Postmodern Era: A Cat's Cradle, 2*(2), 21-40.

Irwin, R. L., & de Cosson, A. (Eds.). (2004). *A/r/tography: Rendering self through arts-based living inquiry*. Vancouver, BC: Pacific Educational Press.

Irwin, R. L. & Grauer, K. (Eds.). (2001). *Readings in Canadian art teacher education* (second edition). London, ON: Canadian Society for Education through Art.

Irwin, R. L., Mastri, R. & Robertson, H. (2000). Pausing to reflect: Moments in feminist collaborative action research. *The Journal of Gender Issues in Art and Education, 1*, 43-56.

Irwin, R. L. & Springgay, S. (in press). A/r/tography as practice-based research. In M. Cahnmann & R. Siegesmund (Eds.), *Arts-based inquiry in diverse learning communities: Foundations for practice.* Mahwah, NJ: Lawrence Erlbaum.

Irwin, R. L., Springgay, S., & Kind, S. (in press). Communities of a/r/tographers engaged in living inquiry. In G. Knowles & A. Cole (Eds.). *International Handbook of the Arts in Qualitative Social Science Research.* Thousand Oaks, CA: Sage.

Irwin, R. L., Stephenson, W., Neale, A., Robertson, H., Mastri, R., & Crawford, N. (1998). Quiltmaking as a metaphor: Creating feminist political consciousness for art pedagogues. In E. Sacca & E. Zimmerman (Eds.), *Women art educators IV: Herstories, our stories, future stories.* (pp. 100-111). Boucherville, QC: CSEA.

Irwin, R. L., Stephenson, W., Robertson, H., & Reynolds, J. K. (2001). Passionate creativity, compassionate community. *Canadian Review of Art Education, 28*(2), 15-34.

Jackson, A. (2005). The dialogic and the aesthetic: Some reflections on theatre as a learning medium. *Journal of Aesthetic Education* 39 (4), 104-118.

Jaggar, A. (1994). *Living with contradictions: Controversies in feminist social ethics.* San Francisco, CA: Westview.

Jaggar, A. (1992). Feminist ethics. In L. Becker & C. Becker (Eds.), *Encyclopedia of ethics.* (pp. 363-364). New York: Garland Press.

Jardine, D. W. (1992). Reflections on education, hermeneutics, and ambiguity: Hermeneutics as a restoring of life to its original difficulty. In W.F.Pinar & W.M. Reynolds (Eds.), *Understanding curriculum as phenomenological and deconstructed text.* (pp. 116-130). New York: Teachers College Press.

Jardine, D. W. (2003). The profession needs new blood. In D. W. Jardine, P. Clifford, S. Friesen (Eds.), *Back to the basics of teaching and learning: Thinking the world together* (pp. 55-71). Mahweh, NJ: Lawrence Erlbaum.

Jardine, D. W. (1998). *To dwell with a boundless heart: Essays in curriculum theory, hermeneutics, and the ecological imagination.* New York: Peter Lang.

Jardine, D., & Friesen, S. (2006, May). *The contemporary state of curriculum: What is happening to the disciplines?* Paper presented at the Canadian Society of the Study of Education (CSSE) for the Canadian Association of Curriculum Studies (CACS), York University, Toronto, ON.

Johnson, J., Mc Keown, E. & Mc Ewen, A. (1999). Choosing teaching as a career: The perspectives of males and females in training. *Journal of Education for Teaching, 25*(1), 55-64.

Jørgensen, M., & Phillips, L. (2002). *Discourse analysis as theory and method.* London: Sage.

Joyce, M. (1995). *Of two minds: Hypertext pedagogy and poetics.* Ann Arbor, MI: University of Michigan Press.

Joyce, M. (1996). *Afternoon: A story* [CD digital audio]. Watertown, MA: Eastgate Systems.

Junghaus, T. (2007). Paradise lost: The first Roma pavilion. In T. Junghaus & K. Szekely (Eds.), *Paradise Lost,* (pp. 16-23). Art and Culture Network Program: Open Society Institute.

Kadar, M., Warley, L., Perreault, J., & Egan, S., (Eds.). (2005). *Tracing the autobiographical.* Waterloo, ON: Wilfrid Laurier University Press.

Keiser, D. (2000). Battlin' nihilism at an urban high school. In K.A. McClafferty, C.A. Torres & T.R. Mitchell (Eds.), *Challenges of urban education: Sociological perspectives for the next century.* (pp. 271-198). Albany: SUNY.

Kelly, D. M., & Brandes, G. M. (2001). Shifting out of "neutral": Beginning teachers' struggles with teaching for social justice. *Canadian Journal of Education, 26*(4), 437-454.

Kelly, K. (1994). *Out of control: The new biology of machines, social systems, and the economic world.* Cambridge, MA: Perseus.

Kelly, U. A. (1997). *Schooling desire: Literacy, cultural politics, and pedagogy.* New York: Routledge.

Kimmel, M. S. (1994). Masculinity as homophobia: Fear, shame and silence in the construction of gender identity. In H. Brod & M. Kaufman (Eds.), *Theorizing masculinities* (pp. 119-141). Newbury Park, CA: Sage.

Kimmel, M. S. & Messner, M. A. (2001). *Men's lives. Fifth edition.* Boston: Allyn & Bacon.

King, J.R. (2000). The problem(s) of men in early education. In N. Lesko (Ed.), *Masculinities at school* (pp. 3-26). Thousand Oaks CA: Sage.

King, J.R. (1998). *Uncommon caring: Learning from men who teach young children.* New York: Teachers College Press.

King, T. (1990). (Ed.). *All my relations: An anthology of contemporary Native fiction.* Toronto, ON: McClleland & Stewart.

King, T. (2003). *The truth about stories: A native narrative.* Toronto, ON: House of Anansi.

Kingwell, M. (2005, Summer). Imaging the artist: Going to eleven. Canadian Art, 60-63.

Knowles, J. G. (1994, Winter). Metaphors as windows on a personal history: A beginning teacher's experience. Teacher Education Quarterly, 21(1), 37-66.

Knowles, J. G. (2004, July/August). Sense-of-place: Reflexive artful inquiry and ecological identity. Education course: EDCI 508, Section 951, Course Outline. University of British Columbia, Vancouver, Canada.

Knowles, J. G., Cole, A. & Luciani, T. (Eds.), (in press). The art of visual inquiry. Halifax, NS: Backalong Books

Koh, G. (2005). project > Shell. Retrieved September, 2005, from http://www.germainekoh.com/shell.html

Kolb, D. (1994). Socrates in the labyrinth: Hypertext, argument, philosophy. [CD-ROM] Watertown, MA: Eastgate Systems.

Kress, G. (1998). Visual and verbal modes of representation in electronically mediated communication: The potential of new forms of text. In I. Snyder (Ed.), *Page to screen: Taking Literacy into the electronic era.* New York, NY: Routledge.

Kristeva, J. (1991). *Strangers to ourselves.* New York: Columbia University Press.

Kuhn, A. (1995). *Family secrets: acts of memory and imagination.* London: Verso.

Kuhn, T. S. (1962). *The structure of scientific revolutions.* Chicago, IL: University of Chicago Press.

Kumashiro, K. K. (2001). "Posts" perspectives on anti-oppressive education in social studies, English, mathematics, and science classrooms. *Educational Researcher, 30*(3), 3-12.

Kumashiro, K. K. (2004). *Against common sense: Teaching and learning toward social justice.* New York, NY: Routledge-Falmer.

Kwon, M. (2002/ 2004a). *One place after another: Site-specific art and locational identity.* Cambridge, MA: MIT press. (Original work published 2002).

Kwon, M. (2004b). The wrong place. In C. Doherty. (Ed.). *Contemporary art: From studio to situation* (pp. 29-42). London: Black Dog Publishing.

Lahelma, E. (2000). Lack of male teachers: A problem for students or teachers? *Pedagogy, Culture and Society*, 8 (2), 173-186.

Lai, A. & Ball, E. L. (2002). Home is where the art is: Exploring the places people live through art education. *Studies in Art Education: A Journal of Issues and Research, 44*(1), 47-66.

Lakoff, G., & Johnson, M. (1980). *Metaphors we live by.* Chicago, IL: University Press.

Landow, G. P. (1997). *Hypertext 2.0: The convergence of contemporary critical theory and technology.* Baltimore, MD: John Hopkins University Press.

Lane, P. (2004). *There is a season: A Memoir.* Toronto, ON: McClelland & Stewart.

Langer, M. M. (1989). *Merleau-Ponty's phenomenology of perception: A guide and commentary.* Tallahassee, FL: The Florida State University Press.

Lather, P. (1986). Issues of validity in openly ideological research: Between a rock and soft place. *Interchange, 17* (4), 63-84.

Lather, P., & Smithies, C. (1997). *Troubling the angels: Women living with HIV/AIDS.* .Boulder, CO: Westview Press.

Latour, B. (1999). *Pandora's hope: Essays on the reality of science studies.* Cambridge, MA: Harvard University Press.

Latour, B. (1993). *We have never been modern.* Cambridge, MA: Harvard University Press.

Laudan, L. (1977). *Progress and its problems: Toward a theory of scientific growth.* Berkeley, CA: University of California Press.

REFERENCES

Lazarus, J. (2004). *Signs of change: New directions in secondary theatre education.* Portmouth, NH: Heinemann.

Leggo, C. (2005). Autobiography and identity: Six speculations. *Vitae scholasticae: The Journal of Educational Biography, 22*(1), 115-133.

Leggo, C. (2001). Research as poetic rumination: Twenty-six ways of listening to light. In Neilson, L. & Cole, A. L. & Knowles, J. G. (Eds.), *The art of writing inquiry* (pp. 173-195). Halifax, NS: Backalong Books.

Leggo, C. (2004a, August/September). The modern scholar. *University Affairs* .Retrieved July 21, 2006, from http://www.universityaffairs.ca/issues/2004/augsept/poetry_01.html

Leggo, C. (2004b). The poet's corpus: Nine speculations. *JCT: Journal of Curriculum Theorizing, 20*(2), 65-85.

Lesko, N. (2000). *Masculinities at school.* Thousand Oaks, CA: Sage.

Levinas, E. (1969). *Totality and infinity: An essay on exteriority.* (A. Lingis Trans.). Pittsburgh, PA: Duquesne University Press.

Lieblich, A., Zilber, T., & Tuval-Mashiach, R. (1998). *Narrative research: Reading, analysis, and interpretation.* Thousand Oaks, CA: Sage.

Lincoln, Y. S. (1993). I and thou: Method, voice and roles in research with the silenced. In D. McLaughlin & W. G. Tierney (Eds.), *Naming silenced lives* (pp. 29-47). New York: Routledge.

Lincoln, Y. & Denzin, N. K. (2005). Locating the field. In N. K. Denzin & Y.S. Lincoln (Eds.), *Handbook of Qualitative Research* (pp.33-41). Thousand Oaks, CA: Sage.

Lincoln, Y. S. & Guba, E. G. (2000). Paradigmatic controversies, contradictions, and emerging confluences. In N. K. Denzin & Y. S. Lincoln (Eds.), *Handbook of qualitative research.* (pp. 163-188). Thousand Oaks, CA, Sage.

Lionnet, F. (1989). *Autobiographical voices: Race, gender and self-portraiture.* Ithaca, NY: Cornell University.

Lippard, L. R. (1995). *The pink glass swan: Selected essays on feminist art.* NY: The New Press.

Mac an Ghaill, M. (1994). *The making of men: Masculinities, sexualities and schooling.* London: Open University Press.

Macel, C. (2003). The author issue in the work of Sophie Calle. In *Sophie Calle, M'as-tu-vue* (pp 17-28*).* New York: Prestel.

Mac Giolla Léith, C. (2002). Troubled memories. In C. Christov-Bakargiev, & C. Mac Giolla Léith (Eds.), *Willie Doherty: False memory* (pp. 19-25). London: Merrel, in association with Irish Museum of Modern Art Dublin.

MacLure, M. (2003). *Discourse in educational and social research.* Philadelphia, PA: Open University Press.

Mandela, N. R. (1994). *Long walk to freedom.* Randburg, South Africa: Macdonald Purnell.

261

Marks, L. (2000). *The skin of the film: Intercultural cinema, embodiment, and the senses.* London, UK: Duke University Press.

Marshall, J. (1998). Michel Foucault: Philosophy, education, and freedom as an exercise upon the self. In M. Peters (Ed.). *Naming the multiple: Poststructrualism and education* (pp. 67-83). Westport, CT: Bergin & Garvey.

Martin, L.A. (2005). The waters of Venice: Rebecca Belmore at the 51st biennale. *Canadian Art, 22(2), 48-53.*

Martino W., & Frank, B. (2006). The tyranny of surveillance: Male teachers and the policing of masculinities in a single sex school. *Gender and Education, 18*(1), 17-33.

Martino, W. & Pallotta-Chiarolli, M. (2003). *So what's a boy?* Buckingham, UK: Open University Press.

Martusewicz, R. A. (1997). Say me to me: Desire and education. In S. Todd (Ed.), *Learning desire: Perspectives on pedagogy, culture, and the unsaid* (pp. 97-113). New York: Routledge.

Mason, B., & Dicks, B. (1999). The digital ethnographer. Cybersociology Magazine, 6. Retrieved June 21, 2006 from, http://www.socio.demon.co.uk/magazine/6/dicksmason.html

Mason, B. & Dicks, B. (2001). Going beyond the code: The production of hypermedia ethnography, *Social Science Computer Review, 19*(4), 445-457.

Matthews, G. (2005, Fall). The arts as a metaphor for learning about self: Four stories in a teacher narrative. *Journal of the Canadian Association for Curriculum Studies, 3*(1), 75- 91.

May, Todd G. (1997). *Reconsidering difference.* University Park, PN: The Pennsylvania State University Press.

McKenzie, M. (2005, September). The "post-post period" and environmental education research. Special issue focus article. *Environmental Education Research, 11*(4), 401-412.

McKenzie, M. (2006). Three portraits of resistance: The (un)making of Canadian students. In M. Stack & D. Kelly (Eds.), The Popular Media, Education, and Resistance, *Canadian Journal of Education* [special issue], *29*(1), 199-222.

McNiff, S. (1998). *Trust the process: An artist's guide to letting go.* Boston, MA: Shambhala.

Merleau-Ponty, M. (1963). *The structure of behavior.* (Alden Fisher, Trans.). Boston, MA: Beacon Press.

Merleau-Ponty, M. (1964). *Signs.* Evanston, IL: Northwestern University Press.

Merleau-Ponty, M. (1968). *The visible and the invisible.* (A. Lingis, Trans.). Evanston, IL: Northwestern University Press.

Meskimmon, M. (2003). Corporeal theory with/in practice: Christine Borland's Winter Garden. *Art History, 26* (3), 442-455.

Messner, M. (1997). *Politics of masculinities: Men in movements.* Thousand Oakes, CA: Sage.

Mezirow, J. (2000). *Learning as transformation: Critical perspective on a theory in progress*. San Francisco, CA: Jossey-Bass.

Mienczakowski, J. (2001). Ethnodrama: Performed research–limitations and potential. In P. Atkinson, A. Coffey, S. Delamont, J. Lofland, & L. Lofland (Eds.), *Handbook of ethnography* (pp. 468-476). Thousand Oaks, CA: Sage.

Miller, S. I., & Fredericks, M. (1988). Uses of metaphors: A qualitative case study. *Qualitative Studies in Education, 1*(3), 263-276.

Mills, M., Martino, M., & Lingard, B. (2004). Attracting, recruiting and retaining male teachers: Policy issues in the male teacher debate. *British Journal of Sociology of Education, 25*(3), 355-369.

Minh-ha, T. (1989). *Woman, native, other: Writing postcoloniality and feminism*. Bloomington, IN: Indiana University Press

Minh-ha, T. (1999). *Cinema interval*. New York: Routledge.

Minh-ha, T. (2005). *The digital film event*. New York: Routledge.

Mirón, L., Darder, A, & Inda, J. X. (2005). Transnationalism, transcitizenship, and the implications for the "New World Order". In C. McCarthy, W. Crichlow, G. Dimitriadis, & N. Dolby (Eds.), *Race, identity and representation in education, 2nd ed.* (pp. 289-305). New York: Routledge.

Morgan, W. (2000). Electronic tools for dismantling the master's house: Poststructuralist feminist research and hypertext poetics. In E. St. Pierre, & W. Pillow (Eds.), *Working the ruins: Feminist poststructural theory and methods in education* (pp. 130-150). New York: Routledge.

Morrell, E. (2002). Toward a critical pedagogy of popular culture: Literacy development among urban youth. *Journal of Adolescent and Adult Literacy*. 46 (1), 72-77.

Moulthrop, S. (1995). *Victory garden* [CD digital audio]. Watertown, MA: Eastgate Systems.

Mulholland, J. (2001). *Meeting the demand for male primary teachers?* Paper presented at the Australian Teacher Education Association Conference. Retrieved June 19, 2006, from http://www.atea.schools.net.au/papers/mullohandjudith.pdf

Munby, H., & Russell, T. (1989, March). *Metaphor in the study of teachers' professional knowledge*. Paper presented at the Annual Meeting of the American Educational Research Association, San Francisco, California.

Mutua, K., & Swadener, B. B. (2004). Introduction. In K. Mutua, & B. B. Swadener (Eds.), *Decolonizing research in cross-cultural contexts: Critical personal narratives* (pp. 1-23). Albany, NY: SUNY Press.

Nancy, J. L. (2000). *Being singular plural*. (R.D. Richardson & A.D. O'Bryne, Trans.).Stanford, CA: Stanford University Press.

Nancy, J. L. (2004). *The Inoperative community* (P. Connor, Ed., P. Connor, L. Garbus, M. Holland, & S. Sawhney, Trans.). Minneapolis, MN: University of Minnesota Press. (Original work published in 1991)

Needlands, J. (2006). Re-imagining the reflective practitioner: Towards a philosophy of critical praxis. In J. Ackroyd (Ed.) *Research methodologies for drama education* (pp. 15-39). Stoke on Kent, UK: Trentham Books.

Neilsen, L. (1998). *Knowing her place*. San Francisco, CA: Caddo Gap Press

Neilsen, L. (2002). Learning from the liminal: Fiction as knowledge. *Alberta Journal of Educational Research*. Fall, *48*(3), 206-214.

Neilsen, L. (2003). Learning to listen: Data as poetry, poetry as data. *Journal of Critical Inquiry into Curriculum and Instruction.* Summer, 33-35.

Neilsen Glenn, L. (2004). Housecleaning. *Journal of Canadian Association of Curriculum Studies, 2*(1), 101-112. Retrieved on July 15, 2007 at: http://www.csse.ca/CACS/JCACS/V2N1/PDF%20Content/essay_neilsen_glenn.pdf

Nelson, T. H. (1992). *Literary Machines 93.1.* Sausalito, CA: Mindful Press.

Nemerov, H. (1991). Trying conclusions: New and selected poems of Howard Nemerov. Chicago: University of Chicago, Press.

Norman, R. (1984). A jungle drama. *Dance/drama 2d, 3*(2), 69-77.

Norman, R. (2001). *House of mirrors: Performing autobiograph(icall)y in language/education.* New York: Peter Lang.

Norman, R. (2002). Power as pedagogy: The potent possibilities in drama education. *English Quarterly, 34*(1-2), 69-74.

Norman, R. (2004). Elementary drama in British Columbia: Out of the ashes. In M. Burke (Ed.), *Canadian drama mosaic: A historical perspective of Canada's theatre-in-education.* (pp. 2-3).Vancouver, BC: Theatre Canada.

Norman, R. (2005). *True confessions.* Toronto, ON: Inanna Publications.

Northrup, L. A. (1997). *Ritualizing women: Patterns of spirituality.* Cleveland, OH: Pilgrim.

Olsen, M. (2000). Curriculum as a multistoried process. *Canadian Journal of Education 25*(3), 169 - 187.

Ostriker, A. (1985). The thieves of language: Women poets and revisionist mythmaking. In D. Wood-Middlebrook & M. Yalom (Eds.), *Coming to light: American women poets in the Twentieth Century.* Ann Arbor, MI: University Press.

O'Sullivan, E. (1999). *Transformative learning: Educational vision for the 21ˢᵗ century.* Toronto, ON: OISE/UT and University of Toronto Press.

Overton, W. F. (1997b). Beyond dichotomy: An embodied active agent for cultural psychology. *Culture and Psychology, 3*, 315–334.

Overton, W. F. (1994b). Contexts of meaning: The computational and the embodied mind. In W. F. Overton & D. S. Palermo (Eds.), *The nature and ontogenesis of meaning* (pp. 1–18). Hillsdale, NJ: Erlbaum.

Overton, W. F. (2003). Development across the life span. In R. M. Lerner & D. K. Freedheim (Eds.), *Handbook of psychology: Vol. 6. Theoretical models of human development* (pp. 13-42). New York: John Wiley and Sons.

Overton, W. F. (1998). Developmental psychology: Philosophy, concepts, and methodology. In W. Damon (Series Ed.) & R. M. Lerner (Vol. Ed.), *Handbook of child psychology: Vol. 1 (5th ed.,* pp. 107–188). New York: Wiley.

Overton, W. F. (1975). General system, structure and development. In K. F. Riegel & G. C. Rosenwald (Eds.), *Structure and transformation: Developmental and historical aspects* (pp. 61–81). New York: Wiley-Interscience.

Overton, W. F. (1994a). The arrow of time and cycles of time: Concepts of change, cognition, and embodiment. *Psychological Inquiry, 5,* 215–237.

Overton, W. F. (1997a). Relational-developmental theory: A psychology perspective. In D. Gorlitz, H. J. Harloff, J. Valsiner, & G. Mey (Eds.), *Children, cities and psychological theories: Developing relationships* (pp. 315–335). Berlin: de Gruyter.

Overton, W. F. (1984). World views and their influence on psychological theory and research: Kuhn-Lakatos-Laudan. In H.W. Reese (Ed.), *Advances in child development and behavior. 18.* (pp. 191-226). New York: Academic Press.

Overton, W. F. (2002). Understanding, explanation, and reductionism: Finding a cure for cartesian anxiety. In T. Brown & L. Smith (Eds.), *Reductionism and the development of knowledge* (pp. 29–51). Mahwah, NJ: Lawrence Erlbaum Associates.

Overton, W. F., & Jackson, J. (1973). The representation of imagined objects in action sequences: A developmental study. *Child Development, 44,* 309–314.

Overton, W. F. & Reese, H. W. (1972). On paradigm shifts. *American Psychologist, 27,* 1197-1199.

Overton, W. F. & Reese, H. W. (1981). Conceptual prerequisites for an understanding of stability-change and continuity-discontinuity. *International Journal of Behavioral Development, 4,* 99–123.

Pacienza, A. (2002, November 26). Aboriginal youth turning to hip hop, rap for same reason as black community. *Canada.com.* Retrieved January 18, 2003, from www.canada.com

Pelias, R. J. (2000). The critical life. *Communication Education,* 49, 220-228.

Pelias, R. J. (1999). *Writing performance: Poeticizing the researcher's body.* Carbondale, IL: Southern Illinois University Press.

Pepper, S. (1942). *World hypotheses: A study in evidence.* Berkeley: University of California Press.

Peters, M. & Lankshear, C. (1996). Critical literacy and digital texts. *Educational Theory.* 46(1), 51-70.

Pinar, W. F. (Ed.). (1975). *Curriculum theorizing.* Berkeley, CA: McCutchan.

Pinar, W. F. (2004). *What is curriculum theory?* Mahwah, NJ: Lawrence Erlbaum.

Pinar, W. F., & Irwin, R. L. (Eds.). (2005). *Curriculum in a new key: The collected works of Ted T. Aoki.* Mahwah, NJ: Lawrence Erlbaum.

Pink, S. (2004). Conversing anthropologically: Hypermedia as anthropological text. In S. Pink, L. Kurti, & A. I. Afonso. *Working images: Visual research and representation in ethnography* (pp. 166-184). London: Routledge.

Pink, S. (2001). *Doing visual ethnography: Images, media and repesentation in research.* London: Sage.

Pink, S. (2003, Fall). Representing the sensory home: Ethnographic experience and anthropological hypermedia. *Social Analysis, 47*(3), 46-63.

Pollock, D. (1998). Performative writing. In P. Phelan (Ed). *The ends of performance* (pp. 73-103). New York: New York University Press.

Prendergast, M. (2003). "I, me, mine": Soliloquizing as reflective practice. *International Journal of Education and the Arts. 4,* Article 1.Retrieved March 26, 2007, from http://ijea.asu.edu/articles.html

Probst, R. E. (1988). *Response and analysis: Teaching literature in junior and senior high school.* Portsmouth, NH: Heinemann.

Pryer, A. C. (2002). *Meditations on/in non/dualistic pedagogy.* Unpublished doctoral dissertation, University of British Columbia, Vancouver, Canada.

Pryer, A. (2004). Living with-in marginal spaces: Intellectual nomadism, and artist/researcher/teacher praxis. In R. L. Irwin & A. de Cosson (Eds.) *A/r/tography: Rendering self through arts-based living inquiry* (pp. 198-216). Vancouver, BC: Pacific Educational Press.

Quiroz Martinez, J. (1999, Winter). Poetry is a political act: An interview with June Jordan. *ColorLines. 1*(3). Retrieved April 4, 2007 from http://www.colorlines.com/article.php?ID=133

Readings B. (1996). *The university in ruins.* Cambridge, MA: Harvard University Press.

Reid, I. & Thornton, M. (2001). Primary school teaching as a career: The views of the successfully recruited. *Journal of Education for Teaching, 27*(1), 111-112.

Renold, E. (2004). 'Other' boys: Negotiating non-hegemonic masculinities in the primary school. *Gender and Education,* 16 (2), 247-267.

Richards, M. C. (1989). *Centering in pottery, poetry, and the person.* Middletown, CN: Wesleyan University Press. (Earlier work published in 1962)

Richardson, L. (2002). The metaphor is the message. In A. P. Bochner & C. Ellis, (Eds.), *Ethnographically speaking: Autoethnography, literature, and aesthetics,* (pp. 372-376). Walnut Creek, NY: AltaMira Press.

Richardson, L. (2000). Writing: A method of inquiry. In N. K. Denzin & Y. S. Lincoln (Eds.), *Handbook of qualitative research* 2nd ed., (pp. 923-946). Thousand Oaks, CA: Sage.

Richardson, L. (1994). Writing. A method of inquiry. In N. K. Denzin & Y. S. Lincoln (Eds.), *Handbook of qualitative research.* (pp. 516-529). Thousand Oaks, CA: Sage.

Richardson, L., & St. Pierre, E. (2005). Writing: A method of inquiry. In N. K. Denzin & Y. S. Lincoln (Eds.), *Handbook of qualitative research* 3rd ed., (pp. 959-978). Thousand Oaks, CA: Sage.

Riessman, C. (1993). *Narrative analysis.* Newbury Park, CA: Sage.

Rinaldi, C. (2001). Documentation and assessment: What is the relationship? In C. Giudici, C. Rinaldi & M. Krechevsky (Eds.), *Making learning visible: Children as individual and group learners.* Reggio Emilia, Italy: Reggio Children.

Roberts, H. (1981). *Doing feminist research.* London: Routledge.

Rockhill, K. (1987). The chaos of subjectivity in the ordered halls of academe. *Canadian Woman Studies/Les Cahiers de la Femme, (8)*4, 12-17.

Rogoff, I. (2000). *Terra infirma: Geography's visual culture.* New York: Routledge.

Rohd, M. (1998). *Theatre for community, conflict and dialogue: The hope is vital training manual.* Portsmouth, NH: Heinemann.

Sacks, G. (2002, June 9). The boy parent dilemma. *Los Angeles Daily News*, p.8.

Safran, W. (1991). Diasporas in modern societies: Myth of homeland and return. *Diaspora, 1*(1), 83-99.

Saldana, J. (Ed.). (2005). *Ethnodrama: An anthology of reality theatre.* Walnut Creek, CA: Altamira Press.

Saldana, J. (2006). This is not a performance text. *Qualitative Inquiry, 12* (6), 1091-1098.

Sameshima, P. (2007). *Seeing red: A pedagogy of parallax.* Youngstown, NY: Cambria Press.

Sameshima, P. (in press). A curriculum of embodied aesthetic awareness: Letters to a new teacher. *Teacher Education Quarterly.*

Sameshima, P., & Irwin, R. L. (2006). Rendering *dimensions of a liminal currere.* Paper presented at the Annual Meeting of the American Educational Research Association, San Francisco, CA.

Sameshima, P., & Leggo, C. (2006, April). *The poet's corpus: Seven letters for learning.* Paper presented at the American Association for the Advancement of Curriculum (AAACS), San Francisco, CA.

Sandelowski, (1994). Channel of desire: Fetal ultrasonography in two use-contexts. *Qualitative Health Research*, 4, 262-280.

Sanders-Bustle, L. (2003). Re-envisioning as a means for understanding literate worlds. In L. Sanders-Bustle (Ed.). *Image, inquiry and transformative practice: Engaging learners in creative and critical inquiry through visual representation.* New York: Peter Lang.

Sargent, P. (2000). Real men or real teachers? Contradictions in the lives of men elementary teachers. *Men and Masculinities, 2*(4), 410-433.

Sargent, P. (2001). *Real men or real teachers? Contradictions in the lives of elementary school teachers.* Harriman Tennessee: Men's Studies Press.

Sargent, P. (2005). The gendering of men in early childhood education. *Sex Roles*, 52(3-4), 251-259.

Sartre, J. P. (1984). *Being and nothingness.* NY: Washington Square Press.

Schonmann, S. (2005). 'Master' versus 'servant': Contradictions in drama and theatre Education. *Journal of Aesthetic Education,* 39 (4), 31-39.

Schrag, C. O. (1997). *The self after postmodernity.* New Haven, NH: Yale University Press.

Schwandt, T.A. (1997). *Qualitative inquiry: A dictionary of terms.* Thousand Oaks, CA: Sage.

Schwandt, T. A..(2000). Three epistemological stances for qualitative inquiry. In N. K. Denzin and Y. S. Lincoln (Eds.), *Handbook of qualitative research.* (pp. 189-213). Thousand Oaks, CA, Sage.

Searle, J. (1992). *The rediscovery of the mind.* Cambridge, MA: MIT Press.

Sebald, W. G. (2001). *Austerlitz* (A. Bell, Trans.). Toronto: Alfred A. Knopf.

Shaker, P., & Heilman, E.E. (2004). The new common sense of education: Advocacy research versus academic authority. *Teachers College Record, 106*(7), 1444-1470.

Shantz, S. (1999). (Dis) integration as theory and method in an artmaking practice. In D. Permutter & D. Koppmann (Eds.), *Reclaiming the spiritual in art: contemporary cross-cultural perspectives* (pp. 61-72). Albany, NY: SUNY Press.

Simon, R. I. (2000). The paradoxical practice of Zakhor: Memories of 'What has never been my fault or my deed'. In S. Rosenberg, R. I. Simon & C. Eppert (Eds.), *Between hope and despair: Pedagogy and the remembrance of historical trauma,* (pp. 9-26). Lanham, MD: Rowman and Littlefield.

Sinner, A. (2004). divining INTOXICATION. *Canadian Journal of Education, 27*(4).Retrieved January 1, 2006 at http://www.csse.ca/CJE/Articles/CJE27-4.htm

Skelton, C. (2002). Constructing dominant masculinity and negotiating the 'male gaze'. *International Journal of Inclusive Education,* 6(1), 17-31.

Slattery, P. (2001). The educational researcher as artist working within. *Qualitative Inquiry,* 7(3), 370-398.

Slattery, P. (2003). Troubling the contours of arts-based educational research. *Qualitative Inquiry, 9*(2), 192-197.

Smith, D. G. (1999). *Pedagon: Interdisciplinary essays in the human sciences, pedagogy and culture.* New York: Peter Lang.

Smith, J.B. (2004, December). Male primary teachers: Disadvantaged or advantaged? Paper presented to the *Australian Association for Research in Education Conference,* Melbourne, Australia.

Smith, L. T. (1999). *Decolonizing methodologies: Research and indigenous peoples.* Dunedin, NZ: University of Otago Press.

Smith, S. (1998). Performativity, autobiographical practice, resistance. In S. Smith & J. Watson (Eds.), *Women, autobiography, theory: A reader* (pp. 108-115). Madison, WI: University of Wisconsin Press.

Sontag, D., & Dugger, C. (1998, July 19). The new immigrant tide: A shuttle between worlds; here and there. *New York Times,* 1, 12-15.

REFERENCES

Spence, J. (1988). *Putting myself in the picture: A political, personal, and photographic autobiography.* London: Camden Press.

Spence, J. (1991). Soap, family album work...and hope. In J. Spence, & P. Holland (Eds.), *Family snaps: The meaning of domestic photography.* (pp. 200-207). London: Virago.

Spence, J. (1995). *Cultural sniping: The art of transgression.* New York: Routledge.

Spivak, G. (1999). *A critique of postcolonial reason: Toward a history of the vanishing present.* Cambridge MA: Harvard University Press.

Sparkes, A. C. (2002). *Telling tales in sport and physical activity: A qualitative journey.* Champaign, IL: Human Kinetics.

Springgay, S. (2003). Cloth as intercorporeality: Touch, fantasy, and performance and the construction of body knowledge. *International Journal of Education and the Arts, 4*(5). Retrieved January 1, 2006 from http://ijea.asu.edu/v4n5

Springgay, S. (2004a). Inside the visible: Arts-based educational research as excess. *Journal of Curriculum and Pedagogy, 1(1),* 8-18. *Image selected for cover of journal.*

Springgay, S. (2004b). *Inside the visible: Youth understandings of body knowledge through touch.* Unpublished doctoral dissertation, The University of British Columbia,Vancouver, Canada.

Springgay, S. (2005a). Thinking through bodies: Bodied encounters and the process of meaning making in an email generated art project, *Studies in Art Education, 47*(1), 34-50.

Springgay, S. (2005b). An intimate distance: Youth interrogations of intercorporeal cartography as visual narrative text. *Journal of the Canadian Association for the Curriculum Studies 3*(1). Retrieved January 1, 2006 from http://www.csse.ca/CACS/JCACS/V3N1/essays.html

Springgay, S. (2006). Dissertation award winner: Small gestures of the un/expected and the 'thingness' of things. *Arts and Learning Research Journal, 22* (1), 163-183.

Springgay, S. (2007). Intimacy in the curriculum of Janine Antoni. In S. Springgay & D. Freedman (Eds.), *Curriculum and the cultural body.* (pp. 191-202) NY: Peter Lang.

Springgay, S. & Freedman, D. (Eds.). (2007). *Curriculum and the cultural body.* NY: Peter Lang

Springgay, S. & Irwin, R. L. (2004). Women making art: Aesthetic inquiry as a political performance. In J.G. Knowles, L. Neilsen, A.Cole, & T. Luciani (Eds.). *Provoked by art: Theorizing arts-informed inquiry* (pp. 71-83). Halifax, NS: Backalong Books.

Springgay, S., Irwin, R. L. & de Cosson, A. (in press). Artist-researcher-teachers collaborating in the liminal (s)p(l)aces of writing and creating artful dissertations. In J. G. Knowles & A. Cole (Eds.). *Creating scholartistry: Imagining the arts-informed thesis or dissertation.* Halifax, NS: Backalong Books.

Springgay, S., Irwin, R. L., Wilson Kind, S. (2005). A/r/tography as living inquiry through art and text. *Qualitative Inquiry, 11,* (6), 897-912.

St. Pierre, E. A. (1997). Nomadic inquiry in the smooth spaces of the field: A preface. *Qualitative studies in education, 10*(3), 365-383.

St. Pierre, E. A.. (2000). Nomadic inquiry in the smooth spaces of the field: A preface. In E. A. St. Pierre & W. Pillows (Eds.), *Working the ruins: Feminist poststructural theory and methods in education* (pp. 258-283). NY: Routledge.

Steiner, R. (1964). *The arts and their mission.* Spring Valley, NY: The Anthroposophic Press.

Stevens, W. (1945) *Esthétique du mal,* Cummington, MA: Cummington Press.

Stewart, S. (1993). *Lovers and warriors: Aural/photographic collaborations.* Unpublished master's thesis. Simon Fraser University, Vancouver, British Columbia, Canada.

Stewart, R. (1999). *Theorizing praxis: Processes for visual research.* Unpublished manuscript, University of Southern Queensland, Australia.

Stout, C. (2006). A researcher's talk of ethics. *Studies in Art Education, 47*(2), 99-101.

Stout, C. (1999). The art of empathy: Teaching students to care. *Art Education, 52*(2), 21-27.

Strathern, M. (1987). Out of context. *Current Anthropology, 28* (3), 251-281.

Sullivan, G. (2000). *Aesthetic education at the Lincoln Center Institute: An historical and philosophical overview.* New York: Lincoln Center Institute.

Sullivan, G. (2005). *Art practice as research: Inquiry in the visual arts.* Thousand Oaks, CA: Sage.

Sullivan, N. (2003). Being, thinking, writing 'with'. *Cultural Studies Review, 9*(1), 51-59.

Sumara, D. J. (1996, Spring). Using commonplace books in curriculum studies. *Journal of Curriculum Theorizing, 12*(1), 45-48.

Suominen, A. (2003). *Writing with photographs, reconstructing self: An arts-based autoethnographic inquiry.* Doctoral thesis. Published online by Ohio Link Electronic Theses & Dissertations Service at [http://www.ohiolink.edu/etd] search by author.

Swanson, D.M. (2004). *Voices in the silence: Narratives of disadvantage, school mathematics and social context in post-apartheid South Africa.* Unpublished Ph.D. Dissertation: University of British Columbia, Vancouver, Canada.

Swanson, D. M. (2007). Silent Voices, Silent Bodies: Difference and Disadvantage in Schooling Contexts. In S. Springgay & D. Freedman (Eds.), *Curriculum and the Cultural Body.* (pp. 63-78) New York: Peter Lang.

Szewczyk, M. (2005). *chronocidal citizens.* Retrieved September, 2005 from http://www.germainekoh.com/pdf/szewczyk2005.html

Taylor, C. (1995). *Philosophical arguments.* Cambridge, MA: Harvard University Press.

Taylor, C. (2002). Understanding the other: A Gadamerian view on conceptual schemes. In J. Malpas, U. Arnswald, & J. Kertscher (Eds.), *Gadamer's century: Essays in honor of Hans-Georg Gadamer* (pp. 279-298). Cambridge, MA: MIT Press.

Thornton, M. (1999). Reducing wastage among men student teachers in primary courses: A male club approach. *Journal of Education for Teaching, 25*(1), 41-53.

Tierney, W. G. (1997). Lost in translation: Time and voice in qualitative research. In W. G. Tierney & Y. S. Lincoln (Eds.), *Representation and the text: Reframing the narrative voice* (pp. 23-36). Albany, NY: SUNY.

Tisdell, E. J. & Tolliver, D. E. (2003). Claiming a sacred face: The role of spirituality and cultural identity in transformative adult higher education. *Journal of Transformative Education, 1*(4), 368-392.

Todd, S. (2001). On not knowing the other, or learning from Levinas. *Philosophy of Education 2001*, 67-74. Retrieved on December 28, 2005 from http://www.ed.uiuc.edu/EPS/PESYearbook/2001/2001toc.htm

Todd, S. (2003a). *Learning from the other: Levinas, psychoanalysis, and ethical possibilities in education*. Albany, NY: SUNY Press.

Todd, S. (2003b). A fine risk to be run? The ambiguity of eros and teacher responsibility. *Studies in Philosophy and Education 22*, 31-44.

Torbert, W. (1981). Why educational research has been so uneducational: the case for a new model of social science based on collaborative inquiry. In P. Reason, & J. Rowan (Eds.), *Human inquiry: A sourcebook of new paradigm research* (pp. 141-151). Chichester, UK: John Wiley & Sons.

Towsend-Gault, C. (2002). Have we ever been good? *In the exhibition catalogue: The named and the unnamed*. The Morris & Helen Belkin Art Gallery, The University of British Columbia, Vancouver, Canada.

Treacher, A. (2000). Children: Memories, fantasies and narratives: From dilemma to complexity. In S. Radstone (Ed.) *Memory and methodology* (pp. 133- 153). New York: Berg.

Trezise, T. (2004). Editor's preface. In T. Trezise (Ed.), *Encounters with Levinas*, (pp. 1-3). New Haven: Yale University Press.

Tutu, D.M. (2000). *No future without forgiveness*. New York: Doubleday.

Ulmer, G. L. (1983). The object of post-criticism. In H. Foster (Ed.), *The anti-aesthetic: Essays on postmodern culture* (pp. 83-110). Port Townsend, WA: Bay Press

van Maanen, J. (1988). *Tales of the field*. Chicago: University of Chicago Press.

Varela, F., Thompson, E. T. & Rosch, E. (1991). *The embodied mind*. Cambridge, Mass: MIT Press.

Vella, J. (2000). A spirited epistemology: Honoring the adult learner as subject. In L. English & M. Gullen (Eds.), *Addressing the spiritual dimensions of adult learning: What educators can do* (pp. 7-16). San Francisco: Jossey-Bass.

Visweswaren, K. (1994). *Fictions of feminist ethnography*. Minneapolis, MN: University of Minnesota Press.

Voithofer, R. (2005). Designing new media education research: The materiality of data, representation, and dissemination. *Educational Researcher, 34*(9), 3-14.

Walkerdine, V. (1989). *Counting girls out.* London: Virago.

Warley, L. (2005). Reading the autobiographical in personal home pages. In M. Kadar, L. Warley, J. Perreault, & S. Egan (Eds.), *Tracing the autobiographical.* Waterloo: Wilfrid Laurier University Press.

Watson, S. (2002). Foreword: *In the exhibition catalogue: The named and the unnamed.* The Morris & Helen Belkin Art Gallery, The University of British Columbia, Vancouver, Canada.

Weaver, J. A., Morris, M., & Appelbaum, P. (2000). *(Post)modern science (education):Propositions and alternative paths.* New York, NY: Peter Lang.

Weber, S. J. & Mitchell, C. (1996). Drawing ourselves into teaching: Studying the images that shape and distort teacher education. *Teaching and Teacher Education: An International Journal of Research and Studies, 12*(3), 303-313.

Weil, S. (2004). *Gravity and grace.* London: Routledge Classics.

Weiss, Gail. (1999). *Body image: Embodiment as intercorporeality.* New York: Routledge.

Wenger, E. (1998). *Communities of practice: Learning, meaning and identity.* New York: Cambridge University Press.

Wenger, E. (2000). Communities of practice: The key to knowledge strategy. In E.L. Lesser, M. A. Fontaine, & J. A. Slusher. (Eds.). *Knowledge and communities* (pp. 3-20). Boston, MA: Butterworth Heinemann.

Wesch, M. (2006). *Nekalimin.net 3.0.* Retrieved July 23, 2006 from www.mediatedcultures.net/nekalimin

Wilber, Ken (1996). *A brief history of everything.* Boston: MA: Shambhala.

Wilson, B. (2003). Of diagrams and rhizomes: Visual culture, contemporary art, and the impossibility of mapping the content of art education. *Studies in Art Education, 44*(3), 214-299.

Wilson (Kind), S. (2004) Fragments: Life writing in image and text. In R.L.Irwin & A. de Cosson (Eds.) *A/r/tography: Rendering self through arts-based living inquiry.* Vancouver, BC: Pacific Educational Press.

Wisniewski, D. (1996). *Golem.* New York: Clarion Books.

Wolcott, H. F. (1994). *Transforming qualitative data: Description, analysis, and interpretation.* Thousand Oaks, CA: Sage.

Wolcott, H. F. (2002). *Sneaky kid and its aftermath: Ethics and intimacy in field work.* Walnut Creek, CA: AltaMira.

Woodlinger, M. (1989). Exploring metaphor and narrative as tools in assisting preservice teachers' development. Paper presented at the Annual Meeting of the Canadian Society for Studies in Education, Quebec City, Quebec, Canada.

REFERENCES

Woolf, V. (1932). *A letter to a young poet*. London: Hogarth Press.

Wong, H. (2005). "Falling leaves," wound, and curricular meanings. *Journal of Curriculum and Pedagogy, 2*(2), 139-156.

Wong, T. (2004). Further reflections on CBC TV's The National. In *Dec 3 Urban Road Stories Vancouver*. Retrieved April 2, 2007 from http://www.gunghaggisfatchoy.com/blog/_archives/2004/12/14/204794.html

Wright, S.P., S. P. Horn, & W.L. Sanders (1997). Teacher and classroom context effects on student achievement: Implications for teacher evaluation. *Journal of Personal Evaluation in Education*, 11, 57-67.

Yamauchi, R. (2005, January). Genes, romance, and the end of racism. *Shared Vision, 197*, 62.

Zuss, M. (1997). Strategies of representation: Autobiographical métissage and critical pragmatism. *Educational Theory, 47*(2), 163-180.

CONTRIBUTORS

David Beare is a PhD student in the Department of Language and Literacy Education at the University of British Columbia. His main research area is collective theatre for positive youth development. He has been teaching theatre for the past fifteen years, and he has co-created over a dozen original plays with youth. He currently teaches high school theatre in North Vancouver, Canada.

George Belliveau is an Assistant Professor in the Faculty of Education at the University of British Columbia where he teaches theatre education. His research interests include theatre education, drama across the curriculum, drama and social justice, and Canadian Theatre. His work has been published in journals such as the *International Journal of Arts Education, Arts and Learning Research Journal, Canadian Journal of Education, Canadian Theatre Review, and English Quarterly,* among others.

Ruth Beer is an artist and scholar who is interested in interdisciplinary approaches to artistic, collaborative, and pedagogical practices and community-engaged art. Her sculpture, installations, and photo-based work have been presented in solo exhibitions in museums and galleries both nationally and internationally. She is the recipient of several Canada Council Visual Art Grants and public art commissions and is a member of the Royal Canadian Academy of the Arts. She is actively involved in a Social Sciences and Humanities Research Council of Canada (SSHRC) Research/Creation Grant with colleagues at UBC. She is an Associate Professor and Coordinator of Visual Art at Emily Carr Institute of Art and Design, where her knowledge and expertise has influenced a new generation of Canada's most important artists. She also serves as a member of the Institute's Board of Directors. She is actively involved in the community as a member of the Board of Directors of Presentation House Gallery and as Vice-chair of the City of Vancouver Public Art Committee. She received the following degrees: a PhD (UBC), a MVA (University of Alberta) and BFA (Concordia).

Barbara Bickel is an artist, researcher, educator, and independent curator. She is currently working on a PhD in Art Education (Curriculum Studies) at the University of British Columbia where her arts-based research is focused on women, spiritual leadership, collaboration, and education. Barbara completed an MA in Education at the University of British Columbia in 2004. She holds a BFA in Painting from the University of Calgary and a BA in Sociology and Art History from the University of Alberta. Her art and performance rituals have been exhibited and performed in Canada since 1991. She is currently represented by the Fran Willis Gallery in Victoria, British Columbia, Kensington Fine Art Gallery in Calgary, Alberta, and School of Ideas Gallery in Welland, Ontario. She co-founded The Centre Gallery (1995-2001), a non-profit women's focused gallery in Calgary, Alberta. Her art and thesis can be viewed on-line at http://www.barbarabickel.ca.

Cynthia Chambers is Professor of Education at the University of Lethbridge, where she teaches curriculum studies with specializations in indigenous education and literacy. Her research focuses on Canadian curriculum studies, and what has been absent in those discourses. She is particularly interested in the costs associated with overlooking indigenous perspectives and relationship to place within mainstream scholarship. Her essays and stories perform a praxis of métissage—(re)tracing the biography of ideas through personal memoir/story/events as well as collective memory/history at particular places or sites of Canadian topography. Her work appears on-line in *Educational Insights* and *Journal of American Association for Curriculum Studies*, as well as in print in *JCT: An Interdisciplinary Journal of Curriculum Studies* and *Canadian Journal of Education*. She contributed an essay on curriculum research in Canada to W. Pinar's (Eds.), *International Handbook on Curriculum Research* (2003).

Dónal O Donoghue is an Assistant Professor and Curriculum Chair, Art Education at the University of British Columbia. His scholarship addresses issues of schooling and masculinities, art teaching and learning, and the intersections between art theory/practice and methodologies of educational research.

Veronica Gaylie is a teacher and researcher at The University of British Columbia Okanagan. She is currently directing a multi-year study that examines the role of poetry and oral language in low ranked urban and rural schools. Her writing is published in journals across the globe.

Kit Grauer is Chair of Art Education in the Department of Curriculum Studies at the University of British Columbia. Her interests include arts-based (a/r/tography) and image-based research, international issues in art education, teacher education, and art curriculum and instruction. Her current research includes the use of artistic pedagogical strategies in teacher education ("smART"—for secondary art specialists and "Teaching From the Heart", for beginning elementary generalist teachers which incorporates artists at UBC and in their practicum schools), graduate art education, and museum education. She is also part of the "Rich Gate" research creation group.

Anniina Suominen Guyas is an Assistant Professor at Kent State University. Her research interests include interdisciplinary research, critical theory, feminist theory, various forms of artistic inquiry, visual, silent and embodied knowledge, narrative as educational research/teaching/learning method, diversity education, and relational and contextual identities. She received her Ph.D. from Ohio State University, and her combined Master's and Bachelor's degree from the University of Arts and Design, Helsinki, Finland.

Sylvia Kind, Ph.D. is an artist and instructor in the Department of Curriculum Studies at the University of British Columbia. Her dissertation research, *Of stones and silences: Storying the trace of the other in the autobiographical and textile text of art/teaching*, highlights the silent and inarticulate spaces of curriculum. A pedagogy of listening and a desire to understand teaching and artistic practice as processes of inquiry shapes much of her work. Her current interests are in early childhood education and the role of the *atelier*, or studio workshop, in children's inquiries.

Erika Hasebe-Ludt is an associate professor of teacher education in the areas of language and literacy education (English Language and English as a Second/Other Language) and curriculum theory and practice in the Faculty of Education, University of Lethbridge, Alberta, Canada. Her background is in interdisciplinary studies in linguistics, literature, and cultural studies, with degrees from the Freie Universität Berlin (MA) and the University of British Columbia (PhD). Her teaching and research focus on local and global literacies and discourses of teaching. Collaboratively and individually, she investigates questions about the place of life writing and other auto/biographical texts in cosmopolitan educational settings. She uses interpretive hermeneutical frameworks to better understand the role of languages and cultures in education and the social sciences. She works with teachers to investigate their own practices and to advocate inclusive discourses for communicating across and between languages and cultures, genres and disciplines.

Rita L. Irwin is a Professor of Art Education and Curriculum Studies, and Associate Dean of Teacher Education, at the University of British Columbia, Vancouver, BC, Canada. Rita publishes widely, exhibits her artwork, and is well known for her work in teacher education, arts education, socio-cultural issues and especially a/r/tography. Her artistic pursuits are often autobiographical in nature and have recently been concerned with liminal identities. Her best known book on a/r/tography is entitled *A/r/tography: Rendering self through arts-based living inquiry* (co-edited with Alex de Cosson).

Carl Leggo is a poet and professor in the Department of Language and Literacy Education at the University of British Columbia where he teaches courses in English language arts education, creative writing, narrative research, and postmodern critical theory. In addition to degrees in English literature, education, and theology, he has a master's degree in Creative Writing. His poetry and fiction and scholarly essays have been published in many journals in North America and around the world. He is the author of three collections of poems: *Growing Up Perpendicular on the Side of a Hill, View from My Mother's House* (Killick Press, St. John's), and *Come-By-Chance* (Breakwater Books, St. John's), as well as a book about reading and teaching poetry: *Teaching to Wonder: Responding to Poetry in the Secondary Classroom* (Pacific Educational Press, Vancouver).

Marcia McKenzie is a Social Sciences and Humanities Research Council of Canada Postdoctoral Scholar. Her research interests include education as socio-cultural practice, teacher education, epistemological issues of educational research, digital ethnography, student agency and activism, globalization, social justice, and the ecological. Funded by a SSHRC Standard Grant (2005-2008), Marcia's current research centres on a collaborative web-based hypermedia project entitled,

Discursive Approaches to Teaching and Learning. Marcia has published in a range of journals and is co-editor of an in-progress book, *Fields of Green: Restorying Education* (Hampton Press). Marcia is also involved with a number of community-based non profit organizations. For more information, visit www.otherwise-ed.ca.

Renee Norman, PhD, is a poet, a writer, and a faculty member in the teacher education program at University College of the Fraser Valley. Her recent book of poetry, *True Confessions*, was published by Inanna Publications (Toronto) and received the Canadian Jewish Book Award for poetry in 2006. A second book of poetry, *Backhand Through the Mother*, is forthcoming. Renee is one of twelve Canadian woman poets whose poetry is featured in *The Missing Line*, published by Inanna Publications in 2004. Renee completed her doctorate at UBC in 1999 and received the outstanding dissertation award from the Canadian Association for Curriculum Studies. Her dissertation, *House of Mirrors: Performing Autobiograph(icall)y in Language/Education*, focuses on women's autobiographical writings, including her own, and was published as a book by Peter Lang Publishers, NY, in 2001. She lives in Coquitlam, BC, with her daughters and her husband.

Antoinette Oberg taught graduate courses in curriculum theory and interpretive inquiry at the University of Victoria (British Columbia) for three decades. An independent scholar since 2005, Dr. Oberg continues her research on imaginative, personal and reflective narrative writing and its value for both her own and students' inquiries. Dr. Oberg was awarded the University of Victoria's Alumni Teaching Award (1995) and the Canadian Association for Curriculum Studies Ted T. Aoki Award for Distinguished Service within the Field of Curriculum Studies (2005). Her articles and essays appear in periodicals such as *Educational Insights, Curriculum Inquiry, Journal of Curriculum Studies, Journal of Curriculum and Supervision, Phenomenology + Pedagogy, JCT: An Interdisciplinary Journal of Curriculum Studies, Peabody Journal of Education* and *Theory into Practice,* as well as in Wanda Hurren and Erika Hasebe-Ludt's *Curriculum Inter-text.*

Stephanie Springgay is an Assistant Professor of Art Education and Women's Studies at Penn State University. Her research and artistic explorations focus on issues of *relationality* and *an ethics of embodiment.* In addition, as a multidisciplinary artist working with installation and video-based art, she investigates the relationship between artistic practices and methodologies of educational research through a/r/tography.

Nora Timmerman is a Ph.D. student in the Institute for Resources, Environment and Sustainability at the University of British Columbia. Interested in environmental sociology, ecological justice education, arts informed research and poststructurally-informed theories, she aims to "walk the talk" of interdisciplinary graduate studies and research. Nora's current work focuses on developing theory to advocate for the incorporation of the arts, the body, and critical epistemological inquiry into education for ecological justice. Beyond this, Nora enjoys spending her time by practicing or choreographing modern dance, working on a variety of drawing/craft/sewing projects, or backpacking in the depths of desert canyons.

Pauline Sameshima's creative writing, research, and art-making centre on curriculum studies, teacher education, educational leadership, and system organization. She is particularly interested in life-history arts informed research, a/r/tography, artful scholastic inquiry, and alternate forms of knowledge production. Her novel, *Seeing Red—A Pedagogy of Parallax*, is described by Norman Denzin as "bold, innovative, a wild, transformative text, almost unruly, a new vision for critical, reflexive inquiry". When not asking questions, making art, living life indebted to earth, or bursting with the knowledge of touching the impossible, Pauline is still thinking about love and desire and how these words play out in living and learning. For more information on Pauline's projects, please visit her website at www.solspiré.org.

Dalene M. Swanson is a SSHRC post-doctoral scholar at the University of Alberta, and has lectured at The University of British Columbia. Her interests span curriculum studies; mathematics education; arts-based research, teaching and learning; narrative inquiry; interdisciplinarity; critical theory; cultural studies; indigeneity; global citizenship; and social justice. Dalene was born and educated in South Africa, and holds degrees in mathematics and education from the University of Cape Town. She has taught mathematics, dance, and drama in South African and Canadian schools and has taught education, global citizenship and qualitative research methods at university. Dalene's doctoral research was in South African schools with socio-economic, cultural, and historical differences. Her narrative-based dissertation at University of British Columbia addresses critical issues in mathematics education and contests hegemonic practices in schools and society. Dalene received four Canadian and international awards in Qualitative Research and Curriculum Studies for this research.

Sean Wiebe is principally a poet and a poet-principal at Heritage Christian Academy in Calgary. He is completing a doctoral degree in the Centre for Cross-Faculty Inquiry at the University of British Columbia. His dissertation explores how poets have influenced teaching practice and are insightful theorists in understanding life's complexities. His most recent poetry can be found in *Arabesques Press*, *All Rights Reserved*, and *Misunderstandings Magazine*. He has edited two collections of poetry, *The Last Red Smartie* (1996) and *A Nocturnal Reverie* (1994).

Gu Xiong, a multi-media artist from China now living in Canada, works with painting, drawing, printmaking, sculpture, photography, video, digital imagery, text, performance art, and installation. He has exhibited nationally and internationally including more than 35 solo exhibitions and three public art commissions. He has participated in over 70 prominent national and international group exhibitions, including: the Shanghai Biennale (2004), where he was one of four Canadian representatives; MultipleCity (Panama, 2003); Le Mois de la Photo

(Montréal, 2001); the Montréal Biennale (2000), the Kwangju Biennale (Korea, 1995); and the ground-breaking exhibition "China Avant-Garde" at the China National Museum of Fine Arts (Beijing, 1989). His work is represented in the collections of the National Gallery of Canada, the China National Museum of Fine Arts, and the Vancouver Art Gallery, among many other museums and private collections.

INDEX

Printed in the United States
101593LV00001B/19-36/A